# Media Praise for Kolbe Wisdom:

*Time Magazine* selected Kathy as...
"...one of seven Americans who exemplify the spirit that inspires this year's choice for Man of the Year.

"They are men and women who have seen a problem or public need and figured out a solution, who have successfully overcome all those familiar warnings that what they proposed to do what could not be done.

"...these new pioneers typify a spirit in the best American tradition: inventive, bold, resolute, eager to overcome the challenges that confront them.

"What all of them share is a certain quality of mind and character: imagination, boldness, energy and an iron determination."

"Kolbe provides a catalyst that can help you evaluate what you are doing, how you are doing it and whether you should be doing it at all."
*The Los Angeles Times*

"A number of organizations give the Kolbe test high marks. Psychologists say the Kolbe is an effective new tool. People who have taken the Kolbe say it has an uncanny knack for describing how they operate."
*The Wall Street Journal*

"Kathy Kolbe's instincts, insights, and intuitions have helped athletes spot their potential. Now she is doing the same for everyone."
*Dick Schaap, ABC Sports*

"Different from IQ or personality measures, the Kolbe index provides clues to a person's natural advantages in undertaking particular tasks." *The Washington Post*

"Kolbe is a new weapon against mismatch of jobs and personalities."
*Behavioral Sciences Newsletter*

"The Kolbe index has turned the old adage, trust your instincts, into cutting edge workplace strategy."
*Lou Dobbs, CNN*

"Kolbe is winning recognition from a slew of high-powered clients for her innovative approach to improving productivity and job satisfaction."
*Calgary Herald*

"Kathy Kolbe, you hit it right on the button every single time. The (Kolbe Index) works!"
*WGN-AM, Chicago*

"Kolbe ... has been swooped on by businesses in the U.S. Now 19 of Australia's top 50 businesses are following suit."
*The Sydney Morning Herald*

"...(*The Conative Connection*) is a landmark on the road to understanding what conditions and situations are necessary for people to do their best."
*The Dallas Morning News*

"Kathy Kolbe has developed a unique method of evaluating her fellow human beings and predicting how they will act."
*Chicago Tribune*

## Praise from professionals who have personally experienced the power of Kolbe Wisdom:

"A Kolbe validation can keep you level headed when authority figures try to convince you that their way is the only way."

*Jim Woodford*
GCI Solutions
jwoodford@gcisolutions.com

"I would not be exaggerating to say that seeing the results of my Kolbe index has changed my life and the lives of hundreds of our clients. We know what it does for people is nothing short of miraculous."

*Katherine Vessenes, esq.CFP*
Vestment Consulting
Katherine@vestment.net

"As an executive coach, Kolbe is my most powerful tool. Clients gain insights that make a huge difference in their success and enjoyment!"

*Susan Spritz Myers*
Kolbe@susanspritzmyers.com

"The Kolbe Wisdom is giving us the chance to really make a difference to personal productivity here in Europe, aiding our understanding of ourselves and each other, whatever our cultural diversity."

*Stephen Booy, Ph.D.*
MBF International Ltd
stephenbooy@mbf-international.com

"Painfully miscast by education and profession, it was Kolbe who validated my true talents and empowered me to excel through them."

*Maureen Grippa*
mgrippa@optonline.net

"Self-improvement books often tell us to become something we are not. Kathy Kolbe tells all of us to make the most of who we are... because we are perfect!"

*Tony Rose*
Rose, Snyder & Jacobs
trose@rsjcpa.com

"Kolbe gave me the courage to embrace my talents and begin being who I am, not the person others expect me to be."

*Jeff Brinkmann*
Satori
Jbrink8583@aol.com

"Kolbe Wisdom is for all ages. In one day a young person described it as 'really cool' and a senior said it affirmed his decision regarding a volunteer role. Its insights lead to greater satisfaction at all stages of life."

*Nancy M. Hall*
Outcomes Unlimited
NanCappy@msn.com

"Many assessment tools seem like fuzzy logic. The Kolbe System is surefire in its clarity. It is elegant and predictive."

*Pamela Armstrong, Ph.D., Psychologist*
Armstrong Coaching
drpam1945@aol.com

"The Kolbe concept is, without a doubt, the most useful and powerful system for improving decision making, team building, and leveraging instinctive abilities. It creates a more committed, motivated, and fulfilled atmosphere."

*Erik Schmikl, Ph.D.*
Synerlead International (Pty)
synlead@mweb.co.za

"The Kolbe assessment of our natural strengths was one of the most useful things my husband and I have done to better understand ourselves and each other. After seven years, we still have 'ah-has' as we use it in dealing with everyday situations, it's as valuable today as it was then."

*Barbara Galli*
Galli Associates
bgalli@earthlink.net

# Praise from professionals who have personally experienced the power of Kolbe Wisdom:

"Kolbe puts us in charge of our instinctive energies, giving us positive results and confidence. Passion abounds. Influence broadens. Trust and innovative environments are created. It's amazing. The knowledge gained is life-changing. What I know now moves me from judging to accepting, from confusion to clarity and from apprehension to trust."

*Tracey Morris*
Organizational Strategies
tmorris@dcr.net

"When my [Kolbe] results were interpreted, I realized I'd been given a profound gift: an opportunity to identify and celebrate my natural, instinctive talents. How validating! How useful!"

*Ellen Cole, Ph.D.*
Psychologist

"I am continually amazed by the impact Kolbe has had on my medical practice, volunteer work, parenting, and marriage. The effect has been electric and contagious! It's taught us to act with humor and compassion."

*Sherry Watts*

"If you want to discover your strengths and what gives you energy, take the Kolbe."

*Carmen Hannah*
Principal, Holland Public Schools

"Kolbe Wisdom is the catalyst for becoming an excellent leader and creating an environment in which people can succeed."

*Michael Pezel*
MAP Management Action Programs
mspezel@mapconsulting.com

"An MBA I coached, with 10 years in the business, had never made much money as a stockbroker. Every year since I introduced him to Kolbe, he has acted on his instincts - and made over six figures annually."

*Rev Fred Lybrand*
Pastor

"The most dramatic endorsement that I have experienced in my many years of offering Kolbe consulting services came from a recent workshop when one of the participants confessed: 'I was close to being fired, but made a 180-degree turn because I started acting on Kolbe's advice to trust my instincts.'"

*Hermann E. Eben*
TrimTab Solutions
heben@trimtabsolutions.com

"Over the years I have completed countless personality and other assessments. Kolbe's approach is very different and helped me to get more done - immediately."

*Dan Tepke*
Strategic Consultant
DanielT823@aol.com

"Conflict experienced by team members who have different instincts reduced. We now acknowledge and laugh at our differences rather than become annoyed and impatient with each other."

*Janet Avery, Ph.D.*
Vehicles, Inc.

"The 5 Rules creates a culture of acceptance in which people understand the diversity of their God-given gifts. Unity comes from our differences."

*John H. Barr*
Transformation Through Leadership
TTLJHBarr@aol.com

"Kathy Kolbe's penetrating insights into our instinctual inclinations are nothing less than revolutionary. Her passion for her remarkable system is clear on every page."

*Andrew Dornenburg*
James Beard Award-winning author of
*Becoming a Chef* and *The New American Chef*

Published by Monumentus Press

For information visit: www.poweredbyinstinct.com
Library of Congress Cataloging-in-Publication Data
Printed in the United States of America.

Library of Congress

1. Instinct
2. Conation
3. Mental Energy
4. Modus Operandi (MO)

*Powered by Instinct* may be purchased for educational, business, or sales promotional use. For information, please write to Kolbe Corp, Special Markets Department, 3421 N. 44th Street, Phoenix, AZ 85018.

FIRST EDITION

ISBN 0-9717999-1-1

# Powered by Instinct

## 5 Rules for Trusting Your Guts

### KATHY KOLBE

Published by
**Monumentus Press**

# Books by Kathy Kolbe:

*Pure Instinct*

*The Conative Connection*

Think-ercise Books
  Analyze
  Analyze Activity Center
  Bonkers Bingo
  Clever Combinations
  Do It Yourself Critical and Creative Thinking
  Enigmas
  Evaluate
  Fathom: Probe the Past - Plan the Future
  Interact: Character Building
  IQ Exercises
  Library Lingo
  Logi-sticks
  Nothing Doing
  Options and Observations
  Ouchless Curiosity
  Risk Taking
  Something Search
  Special Gifts
  Tip of the Iceberg
  TV- A Tool to Turn on Thinking
  Whoppers
  Why There?

# TABLE OF CONTENTS

# Kolbe Wisdom

*Kolbe Wisdom: Creating solutions through intelligence, integrity, and trusting your instincts.*

Kolbe Wisdom provides insight into the actions, reactions and interactions which allow individuals and groups of people to thrive and shape their own destinies.

Challenging individuals, as well as leaders in business, education, and government, Kolbe Wisdom defines both the opportunity and responsibility to fully develop all three dimensions of the mind in order to assure the birthright of every human being to find personal fulfillment.

Kolbe Wisdom embodies the following knowledge, developed exclusively by Kolbe, validated through independent research, case studies, and applications, and stated as benefits that apply to each individual:

- **You have a three-dimensional mind that does more than think and feel; it also drives instinct-based action.**

- **The intrinsic pattern of your conative actions determines your MO (modus operandi).**

- **You experience your Natural Advantage in life when you use four Kolbe Action Modes according to these innate strengths.**

**Fact Finder:** level of detail when gathering information
**Follow Thru:** method of organizing information
**Quick Start:** amount of risk a person takes when dealing with unknowns
**Implementor:** way of handling physical and mechanical tasks

- **Going against your instinctive grain leads to fear of mistakes, mental fatigue, and stressful frustrations.**

- **Commitment to acting on your MO will overcome these obstacles to your success. Compassion and appropriate expectations concerning differences in how other people need to take action will improve the quality of interactions.**

- **Creating solutions through intelligence, integrity, and trusting your instincts gives you the greatest freedom to be yourself. It is the difference between thriving and merely surviving.**

# Dedication

This book is dedicated to the memory of four people, each of whom overcame obstacles to exemplify the difference we can make when we trust our guts.

To Randy Tufts, the self-provoked explorer who used all the power of his instincts to protect his discoveries for future generations.

To Marcella Hunter, the help-mate labeled "disabled" by society, who was so wonderfully obstinate that she was a role model of strength for four generations.

To Jim Lincicome, the engineering executive, who lived by his great intellect until his seventh decade, then discovered the power of his instincts — and lived joyfully ever after.

And to Winifred Wonderlic, the homeless orphan who, with only her guts to help her survive an unimaginable childhood, became the mother who made me passionate about everyone's need for the freedom to be themselves.

# Acknowledgements

I love this book! That's largely because a team of terrifically talented people have contributed mightily to making it a joyful process. Embedded in it are the creativity of Mona Gambetta, who directed the final rounds of the project; John Walters, who playfully exchanged dialog with me in the early rounds; Bruce Wexler, who wouldn't let the dialog stop; David Kolbe, who kept the dialog challenging; Sheila Whalen, who made sure I used my authentic voice; and Will Rapp, who always spoke up for common sense, and who edited the Details section of the book.

Because I loved this book so much, I feared it spoke only to me. So I turned to friends and colleagues to voice their objections. Without exception, the following responded with the honesty of their gut reactions, coupled with well-thought-through advice that helped immensely: Sherry Lambly, Tony Rose, Cathy McKee, John Barr, Hon. Sarah Grant, Maureen Herron, Sheila Kern, Ed Sweet, Holly Lorant, and Kerry Graham. Kevin Stock carried out my design peculiarities, and Wayne Rapp worked wonders doing the comprehensive indexing.

This book could well have been lost in the hundreds of emails and Word documents that became its bits and pieces – were it not for the commitment of Susie Bernard to keep everything in its proper place, and James Trujillo to retrieve it from technology traumas. The entire team at Kolbe Corp supported the effort and contributed in a thousand ways.

The first several books I wrote, Think-ercises for kids and adults were also filled with joy in the development process. Then, what seems like long ago and far away, I suffered brain damage and severe physical injuries in a car accident that cost me my ability to read and write for more than a year. I knew I had overcome most of that trauma when I could finally write *The Conative Connection*.

Far worse trauma came with the creative trauma and physical suffering inflicted upon me by a major publisher when I tried to write another book, *Pure Instinct*. I called the book "Pure Hell." In the Acknowledgements for that book – which was edited without my permission and hidden in the back of the book – were these comments which the publisher dared not remove: "I feel as if I've spent the last two years of writing this book in a constant battle to preserve my creative integrity. It's difficult enough to write a book...it's even more difficult to do it within a system that betrays the very principles about which you are writing."

While I never compromised the integrity of the concepts in that book – and the publisher would undoubtedly say I was very obstinate – I was not obstinate enough. Therefore, I refused to write another book until I figured out how to do it according to the principles I advocate. People who never touched this manuscript nevertheless greatly influenced my ability to figure out this riddle. Their unquestioning support, coupled with questioning about my ideas, led to an essential realization: I needed to write the way I taught, with the give-and-take of discussion and activity allowing others to discover truths in their own ways.

Thanks to the following for the many discussions we've had that clarified both the purpose and process for this book: Elizabeth Berry, PhD, John Kelly, Karen Kolbe, Corrine Larson, Laurel McKiernan, Ryan Thomas, PhD, Anne and Bill Tobey, and Jim Woodford.

As an always boot-strapping entrepreneur and intrinsic Theorist, the grandmother of five little ones with whom I choose to have lots of play dates, and a gardener who cannot stop planting new gardens, my plate overflows. Despite all the available help and encouragement, this book would have stayed on the back burner, had it not been for David Kolbe, President of Kolbe Corp, and Amy Bruske, its EVP. They came to me with a deal they thought I would refuse, one that began the book writing process in earnest. Each being a parent of those grandkids, they knew I would not give up my time with my family, my gardens, or my theories. So they offered to manage the business so I could take a sabbatical "to do whatever you want to do – but we hope you'll write a book – whatever book you want to write."

I began that sabbatical within about three minutes. Within three weeks, I knew it was a permanent arrangement. Their excellent leadership within the company gave me a very great gift, the freedom to spend the time and energy I needed to write this book and the program that is evolving from it. And to do it in my garden.

# GETTING ON BOARD

Maybe it was a blind date you sensed you shouldn't have gone on, or your hunch about the stock market that you should have acted upon.

How many times have you wished you had trusted your guts, but didn't?

Your instincts are an amazing early warning system designed to protect you from danger, lead you to opportunity, and help you do your best work. We often call them our guts, but they're really our natural abilities. Most of us aren't aware that we can tap into this power every day, instead of waiting for it to suddenly appear in extreme or unusual situations.

Acting on your instincts is especially important today, when there's so much turmoil and uncertainty in our lives. The one thing we can count on is this intrinsic drive. Yet, we don't. It's time you discover how you can direct this personal asset, using it to help you achieve your highest purposes.

When you have the freedom to be your yourself, acting according to your gut reactions, you'll naturally exude:

· Joy in being who you are

· Confidence in your choices

· Pride in your accomplishments

My life's work includes researching why each of us, while equally endowed with natural talents, doesn't do everything well. With more than 500,000 case studies, I've gathered overwhelming evidence to support the theory that you will operate most effectively – and with greater satisfaction – when you trust your particular form of instinctive energy. You ignore it at your own peril.

I've seen it happen thousands of times. Athletes, business execs, entertainers, students, and parents who discover their natural ways of tackling problems make dramatic strides in careers, relationships, and self-esteem. You can, too.

The *5 Rules for Trusting Your Guts* are practical guidelines for engaging your instincts. Straightforward and results-oriented, these rules deal directly with how you can thrive under any circumstances – even incredibly stressful ones. Follow them and you will:

- **Make better decisions in a crisis.**

- **Never have to worry about someone else controlling your mind.**

- **Reduce conflicts and improve communication in relationships.**

- **Increase your effectiveness at work and make better career choices.**

- **Improve awareness of your personal needs and health considerations.**

- **Focus on your own and others' natural strengths so you can build on the positive potential in all your actions, reactions, and interactions.**

- **Discover how to harness the power of your instincts to get more done, and still have time for a fulfilling personal life.**

Why has no one ever shown you how to take charge of this innate ability? Why has no one ever shown you how to practice using it so you can maximize its benefits? Why does society teach us ways to do things that go against our grain? Why do we continue to deny our natural talents?

It's not that the great philosophers didn't understand the power of instincts. From Plato and Aristotle to Freud and Jung, instincts have been recognized and celebrated as top contributors to human achievement.

But once modern psychologists got caught up in the excitement of being able to measure IQ in the early 1900s, they conjured up cognitive explanations for most of our decisions. They totally lost sight of human instincts in explaining why some of us are "all thumbs," for example, and why others can fix just about anything.

My father played a pivotal role in measuring cognitive powers through his development of an IQ-based test that became widely used by American businesses in personnel selection. There was a time when it was difficult to get a job in this country without scoring well on his Wonderlic Personnel Test.

When I was a kid, sitting at the kitchen table doing research on that very test, I was already aware of how unfair this single standard was to people without equal educational opportunities and anyone (like me, a dyslexic) with a unique approach to decision making.

Dad didn't squelch my instinctive drive, but those who misused his work certainly limited job opportunities for anyone who didn't fit the mold. And even for those who did. Doing well on the test could get you slotted into a job that you could handle, but that didn't necessarily maximize your innate potential.

**In all areas of life, an unending litany of problems emerges when the power of instincts is ignored.**

In education, it has led to abusive approaches toward those who can't learn through standardized methods. We not only dole out horrifically negative labels (Attention Deficit Disorder), but force youngsters into treatment regimens that reinforce so-called weaknesses and ignore strengths.

Workers are often treated as cogs in mechanized machines, trained to act how they're "supposed to act" – not how they're best suited to contribute. The havoc this plays with productivity is then blamed on bad attitudes, and organizations resort to such band-aid solutions as anger management programs – instead of removing obstacles and freeing workers to perform in optimum ways.

At home, the misunderstanding of instinct-based energy interferes with the relaxation and rejuvenation we all need. An extremely organized and tidy mother, who tries to impose her instincts on a daughter who thrives on what looks like chaos, will only set up a no-win situation that creates tension and leaves both drained of mental energy.

Other relationships suffer when we jump to the conclusion that people who act differently than we do are trying to be difficult or don't care about our feelings.

**Instead of trying to change each other, we would all benefit from nurturing the best each of us has to offer.**

Few will thrive under the dictates of those who would make us conform to standard operating practices or a single path to success. Giving the "right" answers on IQ tests or SATs cannot foretell your ability to innovate, construct, or design solutions. The instinctive underpinnings of creative talents are not measured by what we've learned.

It's time to right the wrongs that intellectual biases have caused in education, health, safety, productivity, parenting, and personal development. If you've dodged these problems and found the joy, peace, and freedom to be yourself that is your birthright, you're among only 20% of the population that reports a sense of personal satisfaction.

If you're not in this group, then you have quite an adventure in store for you. Discovering how to trust your guts will unleash an awesome power within you. You'll discover an energy and drive that is ready, willing, and able to propel you toward the success that comes when you're *Powered by Instinct.*

**The instinctive ability to excel is within each of us. As I'll explain, instinctive talents are universal, individualized, and equal.**

I can guarantee that through your own free will and self-determination, you can convert your natural, instinctive abilities into the foundation of future wise decisions.

You don't have to be one of those parents, students, patients, or employees desperate to change who he or she innately is – in a vain quest for self-improvement – when there's already something absolutely perfect within you. You don't have to wait several more decades for the professional world to decide that it just might have been wrong – and then take a few more decades to try and fix things. You can liberate your natural abilities right now, right here.

Each of the *5 Rules for Trusting Your Guts* is presented in a chapter on WHAT the rule will do to eliminate fear, frustration, and fatigue – what I call the *Failure Factors*.

You'll then learn HOW to use each rule to achieve positive results in your life, using specially designed Think-ercises to help you practice.

The final chapter of *Powered by Instinct* focuses on WHY instinctive power is critical to your future and to the major issues confronting society today.

*Powered by Instinct* is a self-directed discovery process. I've chosen to write it as if you're overhearing a conversation between me and another person. Imagine that we're on an airplane, and that my companion's name is Ev – short for Everyone, or Evan, or Evelyn, as you please.

Ev's part of the dialog is a composite of the many reactions I've gotten to my theories about instincts over the years. Ev is a bit of a skeptic, but he/she is definitely looking for a way to improve things in his/her life.

It's my job to convince Ev – and you – that what I'm talking about is real, not just another self-help gimmick. And believe me, I pull out all the stops. I share stories, research data, and interesting visuals from my briefcase. It's all there for you to consider as you follow the conversation.

I occasionally refer to Details, which includes information I often send to curious people like Ev. It's added background that you have immediately available in the back of the book.

The Index for this book is a Think-ercise of sorts. Think: idea mapping, not just word-matching. It often takes you to discussions of ideas, rather than to particular words – so  you can trust your instincts to choose applications that suit your situation.

If you wish Ev had asked me a particularly burning question, you can e-mail it directly to me. I'll be pleased to respond, and perhaps even have a side conversation with you. Just send your message to **info@poweredbyinstinct.com**. I'll post some of the more interesting questions and answers on the website, so you can visit us and check out what other people are asking.

Now the only thing left to do is dive in! **Act – before You Think**, and see if you can provoke yourself into fighting for the freedom to be who you really are. Commit only to getting started, and see where it takes you. **Be Obstinate** and argue along with Ev! And stop and **Do Nothing** for a while so you can hear your instincts loudly and clearly.

Most of all: trust your guts, and help the other people in your life trust theirs.

**Powered by Instinct brings out the best in whoever you are. That, in turn, offers the following essential benefits:**

- Increased awareness of natural abilities

- Greater joy in what you do

- Improved performance with less effort

- Increased resistance to stress

- Enhanced creativity

- More effective problem solving in less time

- Improved ability to communicate why you need what you need

- Humility because you know your natural ability is no greater or less than that of any other human being

CHAPTER ONE

# TAKING OFF

**Ev:** I can't believe we're taking off so late. Just what I need.

**Kathy:** Yeah, travel can be such a hassle. You headed home?

**Ev:** I wish. I'm on the road for five more days.

**Kathy:** You can join the crowd suffering from the *Failure Factor* of fatigue. There seems to be a lot of it going around.

**Ev:** Fatigue Factor? Yeah. That's in there with the Fear Factor, right? There's too much of both.

**Kathy:** People I watch in airports sometimes seem like zombies, whether it's from fatigue, fear, or the frustration of being stuck in so many lines.

**Ev:** I like to think that I'm pretty aware. If anything strange happens on this flight, I think I'd be able to take action.

**Kathy:** As the person sitting next to you, I sure hope you would. I'd be shouting at you to trust your guts!

**Ev:** Why on earth would *you* trust *my* guts?

**Kathy:** I'd trust your guts – as long as *you* trusted them.

**Three *Failure Factors*:**
- Fatigue
- Fear
- Frustration

**Instincts are:**
- Universal
- Equal
- Intrinsic
- Ingrained
- Natural
- Authentic
- Innate
- Drives
- Patterns of Action
- Modes of Operation
- Unlearned

**Ev:** I'm not sure I know how to trust my guts. Ever since 9-11, I've wondered how I'd handle a crisis. There's so much uncertainty around us, and I'm certainly not certain of my own reactions anymore.

I used to turn on music when I got up in the morning. Now I turn on the news.

You obviously aren't traveling for pleasure. What do you do?

**Kathy:** My expertise is in those human instincts we're talking about. My life's work is helping people improve their decisions by trusting their instincts. [Details: p. 203]

**Ev:** Well, I guess it's your guts we should trust, not mine.

**Kathy:** It goes farther than that. We better hope the pilots trust their instincts and react immediately in a dangerous situation. We better hope the mechanics trusted their instincts if they noticed something unusual. And we better hope that the air traffic controllers are acting on their instincts if they sense a problem. We need everyone around us contributing to the cause.

**Ev:** Maybe all those people just need to do what they were trained to do. What do instincts have to do with their decisions?

**Kathy:** Your guts sense when action is required. They're your personal early warning system.

Your instincts provide the power, or mental energy that causes you to take action. Your instincts are the urges behind decisions you have to make instantly.

**Ev:** How would I know the difference between an instinctive urge to act and an emotional desire to just bash some terrorist?

**Kathy:** Your emotions are attitudes, values, hopes, and preferences that determine how you feel about the things you do. Your instincts drive what you actually *will* and *won't* do.

Ev: There are plenty of things I want to do that I never get around to, but I figure it's because I don't care enough.

Kathy: Actually, heightened emotional states – like fear, or even joy – can dull your senses and cause you to delay acting on instinct. This is when situations become dire – or "DIRe," an acronym for Delayed Instinctive Response.

To give a truly gruesome example, look what happened in the Rhode Island nightclub fire that killed nearly 100 people. If you saw the amazing video taken inside the club as the fire broke out, you saw a party atmosphere in which people didn't react immediately to the obvious danger. Most of them kept cheering and singing for several seconds, then seemed too stunned to run toward the exits.

Ev: That might have been because they were drinking and their reactions times were slowed.

Kathy: Possibly. Your instincts aren't on full alert when you're under the influence of alcohol or drugs.

Ev: Great. So now I won't be fully prepared to respond with urgency when I've been drinking – which I do, of course, to relieve the stress of worrying about such crises.

What else could interfere with my instincts doing their job?

Kathy: The number one cause of the DIRe syndrome is overthinking what you should do. That wastes precious time in an emergency – when every second counts.

Ev: Isn't it important to analyze before acting?

Kathy: In most emergencies, you have little knowledge of what's really going on. Unless your instincts urge you to do otherwise, immediately following planned procedures is your best bet. The worst thing you can do is second-guess yourself rather than get moving.

Ev: So I shouldn't worry too much and I shouldn't think too hard if I'm

---

DIRe Syndrome can be caused by:
- Over-thinking
- Heightened Emotions
- Mind-altering Substances

---

"People were standing there sort of like, 'Wow, this is cool. I've never seen anything like this!' I triaged almost every one of those people, and alcohol was definitely a factor in slowing their reactions."
Rescue Captain Warwick, Rhode Island Fire Department

---

Definition of Dire:
1. exhibiting horror
2. dismal, oppressive
3. warning of disaster
4. desperately urgent, extreme

New York, NY – May 14, 2001 – A new Court TV/ABC News poll reveals that while 57% of Americans let their concerns about crime influence their actions, only 29% feel that they know a great deal about how to protect themselves and their families.

going to save myself from danger. How often do instincts actually save people from disaster?

**Kathy:** Most of the time. Those who survive catastrophies do so by trusting their guts. That's why so many law enforcement, medical, and public safety experts recommend trusting your instincts.

Your chances of successfully achieving any goal – including survival – are reduced by heightened emotions.

**Ev:** So my obvious shock at what's going on during a disaster could kill me?

**Kathy:** As silly as the warnings to "stay calm" may sound, it's very wise advice. Your instincts are your best weapon against any danger. Keeping your instincts active, alert, and able to achieve results is essential to your mental preparedness.

You can become frozen with fear, which means your instincts can't get through to you. You can't afford that in daily life, let alone in a life-threatening circumstance.

**Ev:** Now that you're saying these things, it makes sense. But why isn't anyone else saying them?

**Kathy:** Beats me. I've spent years telling people that instincts power the actions you take to solve problems and create opportunities.

You can count on their ever-present pattern of energy in any situation.

**Ev:** How on earth do you tap into that energy?

**Kathy:** You have to trust your guts. Most people work against their own instinctive grain. If you free your instincts to take action, they'll drive you toward a natural pattern of action, or your best way of getting things done. You'll accomplish your goals with less effort – and suffer less fatigue, fear, and frustration.

**Ev:** Is there any evidence that instincts really exist?

**Kathy**: Yes. I've gathered convincing proof that everything you thought might depend on trusting your instincts really does. Now there's indisputable evidence that instincts are definable, measurable, and manageable.

We can identify the natural ways you take action. And we can quantify the degree of stress you'll suffer if you operate contrary to those instincts. [Details: p. 204]

You may have false self-expectations of how you should perform, other people may place unrealistic requirements on how you should act, or you may be in conflict with someone whose actions you don't understand.

**Ev**: I think I'm suffering from all those problems. I'm expected to be a neatnik at home – which I'm not. In order to succeed at work, I have to follow frustrating procedures, spending hours filling in forms when I ought to be on the phone making sales calls. And I suspect I have a lot of conflict with the way my oldest kid does things. I've always looked up answers and he just guesses or makes them up. We're always arguing over that kind of thing.

**Three _Failure Factors_:**
- Fatigue
- Fear
- Frustration

**Action Advantages:**
- Ambition
- Alertness
- Achievement

**Kathy**: All of this leads to the _Failure Factors_. You're fatigued, or mentally burnt out. You live with fear of the unknown. You're frustrated because you can't get things done in a timely manner.

Unrelentingly high levels of the _Failure Factors_ in your life lead to despair. Your instincts can overcome this pain.

**Success is the freedom to act on your instinctive power. It's achieving your goals without suffering from the _Failure Factors_.**

**Ev**: I want some common-sense, practical help for getting things done. But I'm skeptical if you're telling me there's a shortcut or quick fix.

**Kathy**: There's a readily available solution, but you've been unaware of it your entire life. So it'll take some dedicated practice to get used to using it. You need to learn how to recognize and use your mental energy – the power of your instincts.

**Ev:** What do you mean my problems are "mental?"

**Kathy:** Certainly nothing bad. I wouldn't bring up my work if I thought your issues were abnormal. I deal with positive approaches for healthy people who are struggling with the challenging and stressful realities of today's world.

**Ev:** If instincts are a *natural* energy, why should I have to do anything to get them working?

**Kathy:** You don't have to get them working. They're trying to do their job every minute of every day but they have trouble getting through to you when you don't pay attention to them. Sometimes you actually work contrary to the impulses they try to send you. When you overlook your instinct-based energy, you operate like a dim light bulb.

And you have a finite amount of instinctive energy – so you can (and it sounds as if you do) run out of it temporarily. Fortunately, you can reenergize or recharge your instinctive batteries, but you have to learn how.

**Ev:** I can't believe I'm sitting here talking about this as if it could be true. Excuse me for saying so, but it just sounds goofy.

**Kathy:** The goofiest part is that people are struggling so hard when the solution is already within themselves.

**Ev:** Have any universities paid attention to what you're talking about?

**Kathy:** More than a dozen have conducted research related to my work. And, interestingly, some of those major universities – including Stanford, Northwestern, University of Chicago, Texas A&M, UCLA, and BYU – used my work to help teach management, engineering, and leadership. [Details: p. 205]

**Ev:** I didn't mean to be rude. Actually, I'm sufficiently intrigued and I'd like to pick your brain. I just didn't want to waste your time or mine getting into something, only to find out later that it had no substance.

**Kathy:** I usually ask skeptics, "What have you got to lose?" Our instincts could help us design affordable health programs, improve interpersonal communications, and protect the environment – things our logical minds have great difficulty figuring out.

**Ev:** Some of what you're saying sounds New Age to me.

**Kathy: More like age-old!** I'd bet that we humans have survived through the ages in large part because many of us used our instincts, along with intelligence and desire, to solve some pretty major challenges. [Details: p. 208]

**Ev:** But this talk about instincts still has a certain hocus-pocus ring to it.

**Kathy:** There's nothing tricky about it. Everything springboards from these basic ideas:

  · **Your instincts are the indelible, reliable part of you.**

  · **Your instincts are your natural advantage.**

  · **If you understand this incredible asset, you'll realize that you don't have to alter it – you just have to use it well.**

**Ev:** I guess I'm afraid not to believe in instincts. I marvel at those people in the Twin Towers who seemed to just trust their guts and get out of there, even when the guy on the bullhorn was telling them to go back to their desks.

**Kathy:** And you wonder what you would have done?

**Ev:** I like to think I would have trusted my guts. But I really don't know if that's true.

I believe there's something inside me that will tell me what to do in a crisis if only I can hear and interpret it. I don't know if I'm supposed to feel it in my stomach, or if it's supposed to make my heart race, or if it actually speaks in my brain. How can I trust it when I don't even know what "it" is?

**Delay Meant Death On 9-11**
by Martha T. Moore and Dennis Cauchon
USA Today
September 3, 2002
"To survive the terrorist attacks on the World Trade Center, the right thing to do was to follow instinct, not procedure."

**Kathy:** You've asked the types of questions that have fueled the controversy surrounding instincts for centuries.

**Ev:** I don't know if this will work for me. I've always been leery about self-help advice.

**Kathy:** Oh, it'll work for you.

**Ev:** What I really need right now is help with the tough decisions I'm facing. I need to weigh the pros and cons of career changes, research financial decisions, and set daily priorities. But I can't afford to get sidetracked by a whole study of how the mind works.

**Kathy:** Do you at least agree that trusting your guts could help you accomplish those goals?

**Ev:** That's really interesting. I guess that's what I'm saying. I'm afraid *not* to believe it.

**Kathy:** Just checking. If you wanted a self-improvement discussion, I'd opt to watch the in-flight movie. Remember, your instincts will never need improving. They're perfect. And I'll help you take charge of using this natural advantage at will – when you decide you need it – not just when your instincts can't stand it any more and kick in on their own.

There's a lot to cover in the *Powered by Instinct* program, but we're going to be on this plane together for a few hours…

**Ev:** It's actually a program, not just a theory?

**Kathy:** Yes, and it includes five rules for trusting your guts. Each rule is very specific, has been proven effective with all types of people, and is immediately doable.

**Ev:** So you really do believe people can control their instincts?

**Kathy:** You can't mess with your MO, your *modus operandi*, your natural way of doing things. You are who you are. One great philosopher said, "I am what I am, and that's all that I am." Do you know who that was?

**Ev:** Sounds like Popeye to me!

**Kathy:** Right! And what makes him a great philosopher is that he stated a universal truth. In every country in which I've done seminars (about 20), people recognize Popeye and those words.

**Ev:** If I am who I am and that's all that I am, how does that put me in charge of my instincts? Sounds like I'm just stuck with my old, boring self.

**Kathy:** You're gifted – not "stuck" – with a pattern of abilities. Your natural advantage is a set of talents you need to put to good use.

**Ev:** I think of "talent" as being things like singing or painting.

**Kathy:** Actually, your talents are your innate or instinctive natural advantages no matter what form they take. Because they're ingrained, they don't go away even if you don't use them. These attributes are always ready, willing, and able to give you an assist. They'll give you the greatest help if you call on them when you need them the most. That's what the Powered by Instinct program will help you do.

It's a guide that fits into any lifestyle, with a realistic promise of results. The minimal requirement for trusting your *guts* is a willingness to try it and see what happens.

**Ev:** So my natural advantages are just waiting in the wings and can take center stage when I want them to perform?

**Kathy:** Yes, as long as you don't abuse this energy or waste it frivolously so it's worn out when you need it most. You have as much mental energy as Leonardo da Vinci, Benjamin Franklin, Agatha Christie, and Tom Hanks.

**Ev:** I just don't buy that everyone has the same amount of energy. I see lots of people who don't get anything done, and others who seem to have 32 hours in a day they do so much!

You know, this is getting very complex. I thought understanding my instincts was supposed to save me time, not be something else I have to study.

Instinct:
term used generally to indicate an innate tendency to action, or pattern of behavior, elicited by specific stimuli and fulfilling vital needs of an organism.

David Hume (1711-1776) in his "Treatise on Human Nature" Book II, Part III, Section II, argued that intellectual awareness or "reason" cannot move us to do anything.

**Kathy:** Before this flight is over, you'll be able to make better decisions. It's that immediate because you'll be using a resource that's been with you since birth. [Details: p. 210]

Operating on instinct is actually more natural for you than the way you're probably acting most of the time. The authentic you – as with any truth – is far easier to handle than a bunch of trumped-up personas you have to pull out at just the right moment.

That doesn't mean that everyone around you will be thrilled with your way of getting things done. Everyone on this airplane has an instinctive nature. Some travelers pack their bags with everything in an exact place, and others just stuff things in any old way.

**Ev:** Do instincts determine our social style?

**Kathy:** No. Your social style, or personality, is a different dimension of the mind. Emotions, values, and personality come from the affective preferences – how you *want* things to happen. Your instincts deal with what you will and will not *do*, regardless of what you *wish* you would do. [Details: p. 215]

You may hate wrinkled clothes and wish you had folded yours more neatly, but you just won't do it.

**Ev:** What types of things do I have to do to be better at using my instincts?

**Kathy:** Here are the rules that will get you *Powered by Instinct.*

- Rule #1: Act – before You Think

- Rule #2: Self-Provoke

- Rule #3: Commit – but to Very Little

- Rule #4: Be Obstinate – in Overcoming Obstacles

- Rule #5: Do Nothing – when Nothing Works

**Ev:** I don't see how following rules can help you trust your guts.

**Kathy:** I know it seems strange. I personally resist most rules because they usually focus on what you have to do – whether it suits you or not. Rules that limit the options for how you act are restrictions, not instructive guides. People naturally rebel against anything or anyone who inhibits their freedom.

**Ev:** How are your rules any different?

**Kathy:** The *5 Rules for Trusting Your Guts* tell you how to break the rules – if and when that's necessary.

If you make a commitment to act on them for just a few weeks, you'll be amazed at the change they make in your life and in the relationships that matter most to you.

**Ev:** If I act before I think, for example, will I get out of dangerous situations faster?

**Kathy:** Yes. This rule helps you sense danger before it's physically apparent. The implications of that in terms of your health and safety are dramatic. It means that you're more likely to sense a tumor before it shows up in medical exams, or perhaps have a sensation of dizziness before you fall...

**Ev:** You say *sensing* things. Is that the same as intuiting?

**Kathy:** It is an intuition of sorts, but intuition is only a part of the instinctive process. Having a sense of something is the result of your instincts reacting to a message that can't yet be defined in objective reality. Intuition alerts you to get involved.

**Ev:** I'll bet a lot of people don't get it, when it comes to instincts driving our actions. Doesn't that frustrate you?

**Kathy:** Serious thinkers about the mind have been too caught up in thinking about how we think. The irony is that their instincts have told them that something is missing in their two-dimensional (right brain/left brain) model. They've searched for answers by staying within the

The human mind is Three-Dimensional. It has three equal parts.
- **Cognitive:** thoughts, intelligence, learned behaviors, knowledge, recall, skills
- **Affective:** feelings, emotions, personality, preferences, desires, attitudes, values
- **Conative:** purposeful actions, drives, urges, natural abilities, innate talents, MO, instincts

intellectual box, seeking forms of multiple intelligence. They're ignoring what every parent knows: we come into this world with our own way of getting things done - with multiple instincts.

Ev: And I can just imagine your saying to them: It's not intelligence, stupid. It's instinct.

Kathy: I consider those who join me in a field that's now being called Positive Psychology, to be kindred spirits. We're all striving to bring out the best in everyone. I just hope they'll try trusting their guts – along with their academic research.

Ev: How do you get them to change directions?

Kathy: The same way I suggest you bring out your best efforts. Start by Acting - before You Think.

# CHAPTER TWO

RULE #1

# ACT – BEFORE YOU THINK

## Do what you never thought you could.

**Kathy**: When you Act – before You Think, it keeps you from rationalizing your way out of making a decision. Don't stop and consider what you should do, instead trust your instincts. Too often people fear looking foolish and, as a result, end up being victims. They don't run out of the church when their guts tell them not to say "I do," or run for cover before disaster strikes.

This rule does not remove thinking from the process. Thinking comes later.

**Ev**: But if I don't think *before* I speak, I might say something stupid.

**Kathy**: Or you might say something profound – that you hadn't thought of before. Or you might express a gut-wrenching truth that would otherwise be edited from a conversation.

I'll bet you cheer for athletes whose performance is energized by acting on instinct rather than waiting to think through every maneuver.

I remember Tiger Woods said his approach to problem solving in major

"I don't think about things that much," Tiger Woods said, analyzing his success. "I watch, I absorb and then I follow instinct."

Tiger Woods
Sports Illustrated, 2000

golf tournaments is that he follows his instincts. And champion cyclist, Lance Armstrong, who won a battle with cancer, said about the same thing when he was asked how he came up with the energy to win exhausting races.

**Ev**: He's one of my heroes, and I can give you the exact quote: "I didn't plan those attacks. It is just instinct."

Do most professional athletes get their drive from trusting their instincts?

**Kathy**: Those who succeed certainly do. It's especially sad when a hardworking, intelligent athlete doesn't follow Rule #1 for trusting his or her guts. Watch for the result. They don't play in the zone, their swing or movement isn't natural, or their timing is off. An athlete who overthinks will underperform.

**Ev**: Do you think that's what happened to the former Arizona Cardinals quarterback, Jake Plummer, who seemed to lose his touch?

**Kathy**: One sportswriter actually commented that Plummer had his instincts "coached out of him."

**Ev**: I wonder if that explains Phil Mickelson's failure to win major golf tournaments, what some people have interpreted as fatigue on the final rounds. Maybe he starts to overthink when the stakes get that high.

Why aren't you concentrating on athletes? It seems they'd be a better market for this than the rest of us who live more ordinary lives?

**Kathy**: I'm a sports nut, and I love working with athletes. Competitive sports are a great way to see instincts in action. The energy they generate is much more visible – and accountable – than in most other situations.

Life, however, has higher stakes than winning athletic contests. Act – before You Think – and the other four Rules for being *Powered by Instinct* – are just as important for you and for every other person walking the face of the Earth.

Consider the benefits we all derived from the way the leader of the free world handled the crisis immediately following the destruction of the

"And somewhere along the line, the men in headsets have managed to coach the instincts out of a promising young quarterback, Jake Plummer."

Dan Bickley,
sports writer,
Arizona Republic
12/02/02 on
Jake Plummer,
Quarterback,
Arizona Cardinals

World Trade Center. George W. Bush has spoken often about how he gets his energy from his instincts. Specifically relating to Rule #1, he said:

"When I have a tough decision to make, I don't think about it that much, I go with my gut."

**Ev:** This isn't exactly the advice most professionals give you.

**Kathy:** Today's psychologists consider the word for acting on instincts – conation – archaic. The conative part of the mind doesn't even have a topic card in the Library of Congress. (One of my life's goals is to change that!) Microsoft's Spell Check automatically "corrects" the word *conative* to *cognitive* (ironic, but oh so typical).

Yet the power of Act – before You Think was advocated by the eminent psychologist Carl Jung, whose work led to today's personality test scales of introvert to extrovert. Jung said, *"The creation of something new is not accomplished by the intellect but by the play instinct acting from inner necessity."*

His phrase "creation of something new" is the same thing as:

· **Problem solving**

· **Decision making**

· **Productivity**

Jung said those are *not* accomplished by the intellect.

**Ev:** I knew there was a reason that people with MBAs aren't necessarily any better at problem solving or any more productive than others in the workplace.

**Kathy:** We don't have to be neuroscientists to be smart about using our minds. Each part of the mind – cognitive, affective, and conative – gets its chance to move your effort toward a goal or to stop the process. It works best when each part waits for its turn. [Details: p.218]

---

"I have always thought the actions of men the best interpreters of their thoughts."

John Locke

**Definition of Conation:**
action derived from instinct; purposeful mode of striving, volition
**Pronunciation:**
ko-'nA-shun meaning to strive, adjective – co·na·tive

The Latin "conatus," from which conation is derived, is defined as "any natural tendency, impulse, or directed effort."

Stanford University's Richard E. Snow says, "Historically, the concept of 'conation' was coordinated with cognition and affect, the three comprising the main domains of mental life. There has been recent interest in the interaction of cognition and affect…
But the conative seems to have dropped out of modern psychology's consciousness. It deserves reinstatement and research."

**Ev:** Then why is Rule #1 Act – before You Think, instead of something like Just Be Yourself?

**Kathy:** Funny you should ask. I actually toyed around with that idea.

**Ev:** Glad you didn't say you thought about that first!

**Kathy:** I try not to get hoisted on my own petard…which makes me a big stickler for the accurate use of the language in *Powered by Instinct*. We could argue all day about the *5 Rules* and not get anywhere if we didn't stick with a careful definition of terms. I think the "garbaging up" of psychological language is one of the main reasons for the confusion about what's really going on in our minds.

Note that I refer to the mind, not the brain. I am not a neuroscientist, but I know what happens in the mind – wherever you choose to locate it. I don't even care if, concerning physiology, you follow the thinking of at least one author who says the mind is in every single piece of our DNA – and, therefore, in our guts (literally), hearts, eyes, ears, and brains. Sounds pretty good to me. But that's not my area of expertise.

**Ev:** How could thinking before you act slow you down if you "think smart?"

**Kathy:** When you think before you act, it kills your momentum. Your mental hard drive stalls. You freeze the creative flow that otherwise moves toward solutions. You've figured out a brilliant way to make more money, but you don't get off the dime and make it happen.

Kurt Goldstein (1963) included conation in his concept of "Coming to Terms with the World." He called conation "self-actual-ization," the matrix of all motivation of "basic drive" which accounts for all human activity.

Thinking about things before you say them can keep you from saying what most needs to be said. **This, by the way, is not a license to be rude or hurtful to others.**

When you are driven to take action, something quite amazing takes place: Your whole mind clicks in. You become Powered by Instinct. Here's the process that automatically falls into place when you make such a concerted effort:

1. You feel strongly about something.

2. That triggers your instincts into action.

3. Then you think about what you're doing and improve upon it – or discontinue the process.

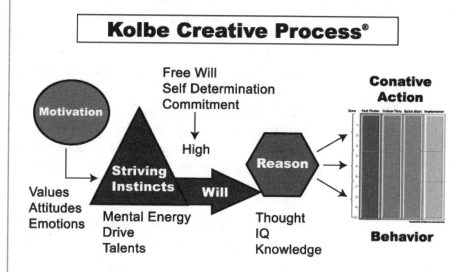

**Kolbe Creative Process®**

"Imagination is the beginning of creation. You imagine what you desire, you will what you imagine and at last you create what you will. "

George Bernard Shaw

I am *not* suggesting that you should act *without* thinking. Remember: It's all a matter of timing. [Details: p. 219]

**Ev:** What would happen if a surgeon just took a knife to someone without thinking it through ahead of time?

**Kathy:** That's what the good ones do all the time. A highly regarded obstetrician describes the decision to do an emergency Caesarean section as an instinctive moment of truth when he just senses the urgent need to operate. "The doctor who doesn't trust that instinct," Dr. John Swagert says, "and hesitates for even a moment, will never be a good surgeon." It would be wise for med schools to help future doctors experience the value of trusting their instincts.

"I make more mistakes than anyone else I know. And, sooner or later, I patent most of them."

Thomas Edison

**Ev:** We've learned that there's an intellectually correct reason for just about everything – and that if we don't follow that logic, we'll fail. I'm serious about being concerned that I'll just look stupid if I act on instinct before I've thought things through. And I could harm myself or others, too.

**Kathy:** Give me an example of something that your instincts might cause you to do that would be harmful.

**Ev:** Before I even have time to wonder why that child is standing in the path of the oncoming train, I dive toward him and push him out of the way. I'm acting before I'm thinking, but I may get killed in the process.

**Kathy:** Great example. We would have no heroes if everyone thought before they took action. True, you might get killed in the process. But **your own chances for survival are best if you leap without a moment's hesitation.** It's amazing how many people do survive heroic acts. Too bad it's impossible to interview those who save others but lose their own lives – to find out if their split second thoughts cost them their lives.
[Details: p. 219]

We do know that many heroes have been sued by people who determined they should have thought of every outcome before they acted.

**Ev:** The Good Samaritan laws that protect people from such litigation are a start in the right direction.

**Kathy:** Yet they are quite limited in whom they protect. I personally think that almost anyone who sues someone who acted for the purpose of saving another person's life commits a crime against society.

**Ev:** See? This gets confusing. **Aren't we responsible for being thinking human beings? Isn't that what makes us different from the rest of the animal kingdom? It seems to me that we can't learn to do anything without thinking about it, or be responsible for what we do if we don't think about it before we act.**

**Kathy:** *Strange as it seems in our culture of the intellect, we cannot learn just by thinking. We have to learn by doing. It's interesting to see how learning to do something can actually interfere with doing your best.*

**Ev:** I need an example.

"I never came upon any of my discoveries through the process of rational thinking."
Albert Einstein

Definition of Instinct: Natural inward impulse; unconscious, involuntary, or unreasoned prompting to any mode of action, whether bodily or mental, without a distinct apprehension of the end or object to be accomplished.

"Don't fight forces.
Use them."
R. Buckminster Fuller

**Kathy:** When have you experienced "beginner's luck?"

When I was an undergraduate at Northwestern University, I signed up for a bowling class as a fun way to fulfill a physical education requirement. I'd only bowled a few times as a kid, and just winged it during the initial sessions when we bowled competitively for a ranking within the class. Much to my surprise, I did well, so well I was invited to join the women's intercollegiate bowling team!

At the team's first practice, I was taught (that's a clue to why this story is worth telling) the proper way to release the ball, and coached on several matters of style. After that, my scores dropped dramatically – the ball ceased to roll right into the pocket and my ability to pick up spares diminished. I quickly became a bowling has-been. I couldn't think and bowl well at the same time.

"It was through conation that one persevered in one's own being."
Benedict Baruch Spinoza
1632-1677

**Ev:** Was that because you started overthinking what you were doing, or because you were trying to do it in a way that went against your natural grain?

**Kathy:** Both. Beginner's luck happens because you act with gusto before you concentrate on how you're "supposed to" do something. People think of it as "dumb luck" because they haven't realized the impact of instincts.

Your results drop off even more spectacularly if the way you're taught to do something goes counter to your instinctive strengths.

**Ev:** That happened to me in sales training. When they tried to get me to follow the script, I was dead. I don't think it would be possible for me to have gone from a top performer to a dunce any quicker than I did in that situation.

Could be that's why I also blew it when I read about "dressing for success," and started wearing clothes that just weren't me. I knew I was wearing the right stuff, but it sure didn't come off as suitable – so to speak.

"Nobody can think and hit at the same time."
Yogi Berra

**Kathy:** You may have had a high school English teacher who encouraged you to write in your natural voice. That was probably your favorite teacher because he or she believed in your instincts rather than teaching you that there's a correct way to write an essay.

**Ev:** You're right. I never understood how I was supposed to outline before I'd written a paper.

**Kathy:** Your papers eventually had to be structured into a logical order, but your particular creative process may not have begun there. You might do best when you get it all down, then refine it, and then outline what's there.

**Ev:** I can't tell you how much time I wasted writing outlines after my papers were done. I kept being told I had to learn to write the "right" way before I could go off in my own direction.

"Creativity is a characteristic given to all human beings at birth."
Abraham Maslow

**Kathy: Creativity taps into your instincts before getting edited by your conscious thoughts.** When I could go off in my own direction the words would flow. When I had to follow "the rules for writing" it was pure torture.

When teachers who naturally organize consider what would happen to them *if they were told to write without being allowed to outline first*, they empathize with how it feels to go against your guts. That would be like trying to tell a bird it had to fly according to an airplane pilot's flight-training manual. The only right way for anyone to write or fly or do anything else is by trusting his or her native abilities – then adding necessary information.

**Ev:** What if the instincts of the pilots of this airplane *were not* to complete the take-off checklist? Would that mean that in a crisis they wouldn't naturally go to the procedures they've learned?

**Kathy:** I wish I knew the MO of the pilot (or maybe it's best that I don't!) because that's exactly the point. **We can learn how we're supposed to do something, and can improve our performance by adding the cognitive lessons once we've acted on our instincts. In split-second decision making, we'll always go right to our instincts. We will lose critical moments having to recall what we're supposed to do.**

**Ev:** It's like driving. Most of us have learned how to drive a car. I know that if I don't pay attention to what I'm doing, I could have an accident.

**Kathy: Actually, if you thought about everything you were doing while you were driving a car, your mind would go into overdrive.** You just couldn't cope with all the details of the sights, sounds, smells, and other sensory input your instincts cope with as you maneuver through even the most normal traffic. Imagine trying to think your way through an accident in process.

I've developed some unique Think-ercises that will help you experience the benefits of acting before you think. Why don't you try them now, so you get practice trusting your guts. You'll be amazed at the difference it will make in your life.

# CHAPTER THREE

# HOW TO ACT – BEFORE YOU THINK

**Kathy**: I've come up with some Think-ercise activities that give you practice in trusting your guts. Each Rule has a practical set of activities designed to make it easier to follow it. These are ideas that are useful in everyday situations.

As you get involved with the Think-ercises, the benefits of trusting your guts will become quite obvious. It'll no longer be just a slogan or advertising phrase; it'll mean the difference between struggling with the *Failure Factors* of fatigue, fear, and frustration, and actually using the Action Advantages – being able to control this third dimension of your mind.

**Ev**: You mean I'll actually be able to control the use of my instincts? It would be great if I could take charge of this energy, so I could use it when I need it.

**Kathy**: That's the idea. The exercises are designed to engage your instincts in the process of learning how to use them most effectively. That'll happen only if you commit to getting conative about the following activities – doing some or all of them rather than passively hearing or reading them.

The first exercise involves "beginner's luck." Earlier I asked you to think about an example of such luck in your own life. Did you come up with anything?

**Ev:** Yes, I tried to learn to dance before I went to my first school prom. I got my aunt to teach me some steps, which turned out to be a nightmare. Everyone told me she was a really good dancer, and I'd always been pretty close to her, so I thought it was a safe bet that it would work.

Well, she had me counting out the rhythms, and concentrating on the pattern my feet were supposed to make on the floor. What a joke. I turned into a total klutz.

**Kathy:** How did that lead to your acting before you thought?

**Ev:** When I got to the party, the music was nothing like what my aunt had been playing. It was stuff I liked. I got up and just kinda moved to the music. I didn't even think of it as dancing until we got into it more and I looked around and realized I was doing pretty much what others around me were doing – dancing! I'm not sure my aunt would have approved. But my date did; that was all that mattered at the time.

I know people who drink at parties so they can "loosen up," or turn off the cognitive part of their minds. Maybe they think that will help them act more naturally.

**Kathy:** The "real you" doesn't need that kind of help. Mind-numbing substances actually lessen your creativity. Being at your creative edge requires all three parts of the mind, so you never want to shut out the cognitive – you just want it to wait its turn. When you stay in charge, you're far more effective than when you shut down your mind so you never think about the consequences of your actions.

## THINK-ERCISE #1

# Beginner's Luck

A. Think of some examples from your adult life when you have experienced beginner's luck, and jot them down.

1. _____

2. _____

3. _____

4. _____

5. _____

Ev: Do I have to write them down?

Kathy: No. But it may help to do more than talk or read about this phenomenon. Writing it down forces a little more discipline, so you move from ad-libbing your response (which is acting before you think) into the thinking-about-it part of the creative process. Until you go all the way through the three parts of your mind – the desire to do something, instinctively acting upon that desire, and thinking about your action – you haven't fully engaged your mind on a project.

Ev: I'm counting on this becoming clearer if I go along with your suggestion.

**Kathy**: Your *hope* is just the kind of affective attitude that helps get you into the activity. That's good news.

Now go back to the Beginner's Luck Think-ercise.

B. **Circle the examples in which you started an activity on a high note, but became less energized as it evolved.**

C. **Compare the examples you circled with those you didn't. Identify patterns such as types of activities you do better just by trusting your guts.**

D. **Describe for someone else (in writing or aloud) a guideline that makes sense for you, personally, regarding when you should trust something to beginner's luck – and when and why you'd make an exception to this rule.**

Keep adding examples. As you give yourself permission to act before you think, you'll find that the examples become more varied and the results reduce your *Failure Factors* more significantly. You'll also gain greater trust in your instincts.

**Ev**: Before I complete this, I have a question. You've given me the rule to Act – before You Think as if it's essential to always follow it. What's an example of when you've been glad you haven't followed it?

**Kathy**: I'll give you an example with roots in another out-of-classroom situation. It goes back to junior high school, when I was giving the graduation speech. In front of a couple hundred people, I lost my place on the page I was reading. Maybe it was my dyslexia coupled with my nervousness, but I couldn't find where I had left off.

I simply set the paper down and ad-libbed the remaining two-thirds of my speech. At the end, I received a standing ovation. **While part of that applause may have been a sympathy vote, I knew I had done a far better job just winging it than if I had read the practiced words from the paper.**

I remember thinking, "It's much easier and it works, too. Why didn't someone tell me about the beauty of being spontaneous?" I did not elect to write out or practice a speech for decades after that.

Then I was forced to break the rule as the first female keynote speaker for the Million Dollar Round Table. It's an organization for top performers in the insurance industry and is filled with people who succeed by ad-libbing. But they don't trust their speakers to do the same.

That may be fine in some cases (it's an elaborately produced performance for several thousand people), but the procedure of submitting written text and having to practice it in front of a committee took lots of speakers out of their game. It cost many speakers their instinctive edge. Mine included.

**Ev:** But still that proves the rule – not the exception.

**Kathy:** That's right. Which is why the exception was an even more interesting lesson for me. The one time since that junior high speech that I've *chosen* to read my comments was in giving a eulogy for a dear friend. My daughter, a psychotherapist, advised me that reading my remarks would be my best hope of not becoming so emotional that I'd have difficulty getting through it. She was absolutely right.

I wrote it in a way that was as true to my form as possible – in the wee hours of the morning, before the cognitive mind kicked in and I had overthought what I would say. We might call that writing from the heart, but just as we refer to "gut" instincts or "guts" as instincts, these phrases refer more to it not being a cognitive process than to there being a physiology for the place from which instincts appear.

**Ev:** Did it work?

**Kathy:** Those in attendance – especially my friend's widow – would be the better judges of that. I *felt* good about it afterwards. I figured out ways to make it work (reading it out loud several times, marking the text where the "natural" inflections would go, using giant, bold text with color reference marks), so it flowed smoothly. But I could never make that work on a regular basis without adding to my fatigue and frustration big time. It ate away my time and energy. **I normally "prepare" for a speech in a few minutes – and only by focusing on the benefits I'm committed to**

providing. **Going against my natural method of delivery took 10 times that long.**

Ev: Would you break the rule again, under similar circumstances?

**Kathy:** Yes. The longer I personally live by the *Rules*, the clearer I am that *rare* exceptions help make them work as well as they do.

Ev: I hate a diet program that doesn't tell me how I can cheat occasionally.

**Kathy: You have to trust the magic inside you – your instincts – more than any outside lesson or rule, including a rule about using these instincts.**

Ev: Do you often have beginner's luck but decide not to go any further with an activity?

**Kathy:** That might happen because you weed out the less important activities (bowling, in my case), or the ones you realize would eventually force you to work against your instinctive grain, or the ones that just don't make sense to carry out (financially, time-wise, or for any other reason). I often refer to this weeding out as "saving me from myself."

This leads us into the next Think-ercise.

## THINK-ERCISE #2

# Things You Were Driven To Do – But Didn't Get Done

Make a quick list of the things you really wanted to do but didn't because someone told you to "Stop and Think before you..."

Some examples might be "major in art," "invest in that business," or "marry that person."

1. _____

2. _____

3. _____

4. _____

5. _____

Circle anything on this list that you convinced yourself not to do that you still wish you had done. Consider how long you've held on to such desires that you never converted into realities.

What would happen if you now acted upon those desires before you thought about all the reasons not to do them?

**Ev:** What do you mean?

**Kathy:** Some people have wanted to play a musical instrument all their lives, but thought better of taking the time or money to learn how to do it. Others have wanted to travel to an exotic place, start their own businesses, dump a particular part of their lifestyle, or connect with a special person; however they couldn't bring themselves to do it because it seemed stupid to think it would work out.

Is this true of anything on your list?

You could think of these as your unrequited loves. What is not acted upon will never become a reality. Those things you desire to do, but think about and decide against doing – prior to taking action – often become your unfulfilled hopes and dreams.

**Ev:** What came immediately to my mind were things I've thought about saying before I said them, which kept me from saying what most needed to be said. You mentioned that before. Movies in the genre of romantic comedies would be over in minutes if the central characters would just profess their love up front.

**Kathy:** The angst keeps us in our seats – for a while – and we want to call out for them to "just say it." As the tension mounts, we know what they should do and fear the lost love if the words go unspoken. As every TV series producer knows, this contrivance can go on just so long before we lose respect for the characters. Why the heck don't they trust their guts?

**Ev:** If they don't have enough oomph to be who they are, the false pretenses cause me to lose interest.

**Kathy:** Let's deal with your oomph.

Try this next Think-ercise.

**THINK-ERCISE #3**

# "Just Doing" What You're Driven To Do

How often have you just trusted your guts? List actions you took because you were driven to do them – things you "just did" without thinking.

1. _____

2. _____

3. _____

4. _____

5. _____

6. _____

7. _____

Put a check next to those that turned out to be good decisions, and a zero next to the ones that didn't work out. Which happened most?

**Ev:** It's what you expected. Most of them worked out quite well.

**Kathy:** What was the worst result from any of these actions?

**Ev:** I had to start over with things a couple of times.

**Kathy:** It could have been much worse if you hadn't thought about the consequences of your actions. Clearly, you have to inject an evaluation process before you get too deeply involved in any dangerous activity.

Do you regret taking any of the actions you used as examples?

**Ev: Not really. I think what I did was modify my action because of what I learned from my initial mistakes. I guess, in a way, that meant trusting my guts got me off the dime – and it worked out better than if I hadn't launched the attempt.**

**Kathy:** Compare the things you were driven to do – and actually did – with the things you were driven to do – but stopped yourself from doing. Which list has the most regrettable examples?

**Ev:** Oh, for sure my greatest regrets are from the paths not taken. It reminds me of Robert Frost's poem, "The Road Not Taken."

**Kathy:** The mischievous Frost's apparent intent was to tease the reader into questioning whether that path was taken on purpose or not. At least some scholars have attributed the choice to "impulse." Frost, I believe, was encouraging us to trust our instincts.

The less poetic, more mundane approach is to measure the mistaken paths you took because they're often more apparent – even glaring. Unfortunately, most people dwell on the things they wish they didn't do or did wrong, rather than on their strengths and opportunities. **There's an insidious need in our culture to dwell on weaknesses. It's a significant factor in self-esteem problems.**

Low self-esteem – which can lead to high dropout rates from high school, substance abuse, bad marital choices, and scores of other problems – comes in part from not valuing your innate abilities. When wonderfully instinctive talents are unappreciated by their owners, these resources are lost to those individuals and the world around them.

I don't teach people how to be sure they're right. Being right is rarely the most significant issue. *Powered by Instinct* is a program that will free you

> "I shall be telling this with a sigh. Somewhere ages and ages hence: Two roads diverged in a wood, and I took the one less traveled by, And that has made all the difference."
> The Road Not Taken
> By Robert Frost
> [Ending]

to fail – *without regrets* – so you can live without rue.

**Ev:** "Rue?" What's "rue?"

**Kathy:** You know...It's what you feel when you "rue the day."

**Ev:** And trusting my guts to act before I think will give me a life without rue?

**Kathy:** It'll go a long way toward that.

If you had trouble coming up with even seven examples for the act-before-you-thought list, you may soon be changing the way you think about thinking. If you could easily list many such examples, this program will validate that you're not crazy or lucky, but that you truly are on a path that will help you replicate your successes.

· **Problem solving starts with the drive "to do," then moves to the necessity of doing it your own way.**

· **If you think about how you were taught to do things, you will only replicate known solutions.**

· **Your instinctive drive is the source of your mental energy, the force behind your actions.**

· **The forms your instincts take are your gut reactions, which determine your MO (modus operandi). They are the necessities for action, the parents of your inventions or creativity.**

For instance, your best way of making more money won't be the same as everyone else's. This part of the process is all about trusting your guts to do what works for you.

Years of doing what you think you should be doing can erode confidence in your ability to read your instincts. A guy who was laid off from a job he had worked in for over a dozen years came to me for help because he wanted to be sure his new career allowed him the freedom to be himself. He didn't have the foggiest idea how to make that happen. I gave him the following Think-ercise to find out.

## THINK-ERCISE #4

# Gut-o-Meter

Using the Gut-o-Meter Exercise, log every decision you make for a week according to how much of it is made by acting before you think about it.

Using a thermometer-style chart, give yourself:

· 1 point every time you play a hunch

· 2 points for choosing instinct over the other means of problem solving

· 3 points for going with your guts from the get-go.

Your goal is to get 50 points in one week.

Here are some examples:

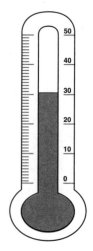

## 1 Point Actions:

· Tried a new brand of olives just because I liked the color.

· Found a mall parking space by idling near a coffee shop.

· Wore a suit and tie to a luncheon because the guy I was meeting sounded a bit formal over the phone.

· Didn't take the marked detour because I could probably find a less traveled alternative.

## 2 Point Actions:

· Knew mom loves perfume as birthday gifts, but decided to give her a sweater that just "looked" like her.

· Was fearful about scheduling meetings so close together, but decided I'd just make it work so I didn't have to miss either one.

· Knew how to answer the question the way an interviewer thought was correct, but decided to respond with a more genuine example of how I really do things.

· Wanted approval from my girlfriend but launched into a description of the mistakes I'd made that cost me my job, with no sugar coating.

## 3 Point Actions

· Took a day off of "looking for work," without scheduling anything in particular.

· Stopped in to see a guy I'd met at a seminar a year ago, although I had no reason to think he would even remember me.

· Rewrote my resume because I woke up with it on my mind.

· Turned down a second interview when nothing "felt right" about the place.

Ev: Are those examples from the guy who got laid off?

Kathy: Yes.

Ev: Some of the things he listed are pretty ridiculous.

Kathy: That's in the eye of the beholder! What's important is that they mattered to him.

Ev: I don't understand how he came up with the number of points he gave things.

Kathy: It's okay that the assignment of points is arbitrary because it's the process that's important. He was forced to think about just how much he had trusted his instincts in each situation. Sometimes he used more thought than instinct, as with his strategy for finding a parking place. However, he was beginning to get the idea.

Ev: His chart came nowhere near 50 points.

Kathy: That's to be expected in the early stages of the exercise.

Ev: So I should try this for myself?

Kathy: Of course. If you put the *5 Rules* to work in your life, you'll probably be getting about 100 points per week.

## THINK-ERCISE #5

# Do a Gut Check:

Do a Gut Check by rating how often you trust your guts without immediate hesitation.

On a scale of 1-5, with 5 being Very Often, and 1 being Rarely, circle how often you:

Rarely...Very Often

| | | |
|---|---|---|
| 1. Wait until you're sure. | 1 2 3 4 5 | |
| 2. Just do it. | 1 2 3 4 5 | |
| 3. See what others think. | 1 2 3 4 5 | Even Numbers: _____ |
| 4. See what happens. | 1 2 3 4 5 | Odd Numbers: _____ |
| 5. Consider the consequences. | 1 2 3 4 5 | = |
| 6. Go out on a limb. | 1 2 3 4 5 | Total Number: _____ |
| 7. Recall how it has worked best. | 1 2 3 4 5 | Are you trusting your guts? |
| 8. Do it off the top of your head. | 1 2 3 4 5 | |
| 9. Make sure you are right. | 1 2 3 4 5 | |
| 10. Play a hunch. | 1 2 3 4 5 | |

Add up the circled numbers for the even-numbered questions. Then add up the circled numbers for the odd-numbered ones. Deduct the odd number total from the even number total. If you don't end up with a positive number, you are not trusting your guts.

As you probably guessed, the odd-numbered questions are about how you perform when you think before you act. The even-numbered ones are about acting before you think.

Repeat this exercise again every few weeks. The timing is up to you. You'll see the positive number take off as you put effort into trusting your guts.

**Kathy**: A TV anchor I worked with thought he had to say only what was scripted – until he ended up with negative numbers on this exercise and negative numbers in his viewer ratings at the same time. When he was convinced that the two low ratings might have something to do with each other, he decided he didn't have a lot to lose by experimenting with acting before he thought. The very thought of doing this before a live audience made him queasy, however. He imagined getting fired as he walked off the set, but he decided that would be less painful than continuing a professional persona that gave him little freedom to be his true self. And he might get fired anyway if the ratings kept tanking.

**Ev**: I'll bet there are a lot of "talking head" newscasters just like that.

**Kathy**: This guy took a risk and started being more true to himself, which let his natural energy shine through. As his Gut Check numbers went up, he began ad-libbing some hilarious lines rather than canned chatter. His audience approval rate soared. People wondered where he had gone for the makeover. He was not made over; he simply trusted his guts and acted before he thought.

## THINK-ERCISE #6

# Instinct Igniters

Jump-starting your natural energy is required when you have stalled it by putting your mind into thinking gear too soon. Following are some techniques for solving the problem.

1. Put yourself in situations that force you to act, without any notion of what you'll do once you're there.

For instance:

· Make an appointment with a prospect. Then think through how you'll handle the meeting.

· Sign up for a class, test, or some project. Then rate how well you'll do.

· Make a difficult phone call. Then figure out what to say.

· Ask for a date. Then figure out where to go.

· Buy the materials. Then figure out how you'll put them together.

· Start writing. Then discover how your story will turn out.

Ev: Some of these sound like I'd be setting myself up for failure, but I suppose you'd see it as setting myself up for taking advantage of my natural inclinations.

Kathy: Now you're even writing my script. Of course you're right. The indomitable spirit within you will come to the fore under such circumstances.

Try it. If you're not doing these things now, you'll be amazed at your terrific ability to bail yourself out. You'll do just fine. In fact, better than that, you'll discover how creative you are. It'll be inspiring to watch yourself succeed when you didn't know you could do it.

2. Stop doing what you're doing if you have serious qualms about it. Don't try to understand or rationalize your feelings.

**For instance:**

· **End a discussion that you believe is going nowhere.**

· **Quit climbing the mountain if you sense that the weather has turned against you.**

· **Get out if you sense the building is unsafe.**

· **Turn around if the direction you're going doesn't seem to be leading where you want to go.**

· **Don't finish filling out the form when the questions seem suspicious.**

· **Don't walk down the aisle if everything inside you is screaming, "Stop!"**

· **Don't finish a book your friend gave you if you aren't enjoying it.**

Actions you take to avoid problems are just as important to your creative contributions and self-protection as are those you initiate.

And remember to check back later. It's very likely that you'll see the wisdom of what you didn't do. Don't wait to act until you know for sure that your instincts are telling you to do the right thing. You may be very sorry.

☐ Angela Young
Cal State N.

**TEMPE MISSION PALMS**
HOTEL & CONFERENCE CENTER

☐ podcasts -
explain process
- exp. of terms.

Oct - Professional Growth Seminar -

Can/can't vs. will/won't.
No conative weaknesses.
Building Self Esteem.
Ethics an action not an emotion
        ↳ always come back to conation
You must not strive to re-energize.
Intuition vs. Instinct ⟹ PhD.
- working against mo - ultimately ⟹ health
☐ Slide that talks abt. Motivation Instinct ⟹ Behavior
Strain  A to B
Tension  A to C
Conflict  A to A

Charisma = is being authentic.
No body listens - when no one is themselves.
☐ chart - ↑
Team ≠ together (physically).
- Synergy - Horse example.
- I can't create perfect world to you - but I
  can help you in your people problems &
  it starts w/ you - How can we help you be you.

60 East Fifth Street       Tempe, Arizona 85281       480.894.1400       Fax 480.968.7677
www.missionpalms.com

DESTINATION
HOTELS & RESORTS
DESTINATIONHOTELS.COM

**Member**
**International Association**
**of Conference Centers**

Printed on Recycled Paper

write — Conation — write down — to start a conversation.

5-10 double spaced,
outline Conation & our
position.

~~Amanda etc......~~

- fit (Amanda)
- person/role
- disposition/trait measure. ~~KABe~~ A&B.
  (context of role/fit fit).

\# leadership (Ty, pierre, David) ~~...~~          (A)
(1st) OB disposition/traits. — indiv fit into orgs.

Early Fall → paper by Christmas.

\# Transformational Leadership &
related theories.
- How add something other variables out
  there (personality, EI, values, motivation

HD add something new |

**Ev:** I'm not going to *try* doing these things. I'm *committed* to doing them.

**Kathy:** Then here's what I predict will begin happening.

**You will:**

- Do what you didn't think was possible.

- Say what you're feeling before you self-edit.

- Run from unknown dangers.

- Trust without proof.

- Get out before the price falls.

- Lead the way to new trends.

- Dance without knowing the steps as you did when you were young.

# CHAPTER FOUR

# RULE #2

# SELF-PROVOKE

## Get where you want to go.

Provoke:
- goad
- inspire
- push
- direct
- trigger action
- make happen
- cause

**Ev**: Does this mean that I'm supposed to make my own trouble? *Provoke* sounds as if you're being rude or annoying.

**Kathy**: Here's how I mean it. **You often have to goad yourself to initiate the action you desire.** Let's say you're tired, listless, and have trouble getting going in the morning. If you don't give in to that and provoke yourself into action, you'll be off and running. You will:

· **Inspire your own achievements.**

· **Direct your energies.**

· **Push yourself into action.**

· **Make what you want to happen, happen.**

· **Ignite your own instincts.**

· **Create your own opportunities.**

"Hide not your talents, they for use were made; what's a sundial in the shade?"
Benjamin Franklin

**Ev:** Let me guess – this is an excuse for doing more of what I want to do. If so, I like it. I'd really like to know how to do what I want when I don't have any time, and when I'm too tired to even think it's possible any more.

**Kathy:** You don't always get to do what you *want* to do. But you won't accomplish anything if you don't ignite your own instincts. Don't wait to respond to others. Create your own opportunities. Then you can fight for the freedom to do what you do in your own way.

**Ev:** Why should I have to *fight* for that? Aren't I *entitled* to be free to be me?

**Kathy:** Having the right to personal liberty – which I believe includes acting according to our instincts – doesn't ensure that the freedom will always be there. Just as our nation has to do battle to keep our liberty a reality, so you have to take action to ensure that you're free to be your authentic self.

You may want something very badly, but that's not going to get the job done. You have to direct your own energy – push yourself in the right direction.

**Ev:** I'm not going in any direction. I'm at a crossroads between exhaustion and despair. I'd say the situation is pretty "dire" – to use your term.

**Kathy:** You can push right past that fatigue, not by changing who you are. BE who you are by challenging yourself to act according to your natural abilities. Go with the flow, as they say.

**Ev:** How am I going to provoke myself to do anything when I'm already so exhausted?

**Kathy:** Actually, going against your instincts can be what's causing your fatigue. *Powered by Instinct* includes techniques to help you trigger your own response, no matter how much you've drained your energy. Remember, **your instinctive energy is rechargeable.**

**Ev:** Give me some examples.

---

**Definition of Dire**
1. exhibiting horror
2. dismal, oppressive
3. warning of disaster
4. desperately urgent, extreme

**DIRe Syndrome can be caused by:**
• Over-thinking
• Heightened Emotions
• Mind-altering Substances

The goal is to have the energy to take actions that give you the freedom to be yourself.

**Kathy:** Even better, I'll show you how to climb what I call the **Dynamynd decision ladder. It's a simple model of the dynamic process your mind goes through when you make decisions.**

**Ev:** It seems more like a staircase than a ladder. And it looks like there are three different paths you can take.

**Kathy:** It's actually a set of three ladders, each with a series of stages or steps. There's a ladder for each of the three parts of your mind, but don't make the mistake of looking at them independently. Each ladder would be dangerous to climb without the support of the others. So as your mind climbs to higher levels of achievement, it draws benefits from each of the mind's three dimensions. [Details: p. 220]

The Dynamynd is a model of the emotions, thoughts, and actions involved when making different levels of decisions.

It clarifies the need to go beyond simply having these amazing attributes, and will coach you on maximizing your use of them.

Your self-fulfillment and contribution to society can be tracked by assessing the levels you achieve in each of these aspects of your mental makeup.

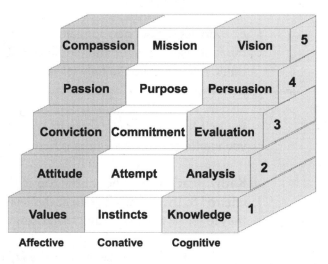

**Dynamynd®: Kolbe Decision Ladder**

# Individual

| | | | |
|---|---|---|---|
| Compassion | Mission | Vision | 5 |
| Passion | Purpose | Persuasion | 4 |
| Conviction | Commitment | Evaluation | 3 |
| Attitude | Attempt | Analysis | 2 |
| Values | Instincts | Knowledge | 1 |
| Affective | Conative | Cognitive | |

**Ev:** I thought you might tell me that the instinct ladder was the most important one.

**Kathy:** You need instinct to take action, but it has to be supported by your intellect and emotions. Let's say you want to help a homeless person, but you know that most handouts don't get used for food. If you give the person five dollars, you're really just letting your emotions rule your actions.

**Ev:** So I shouldn't do anything unless I know for sure it'll be done the way I think it should be done?

**Kathy:** You need to match your conviction to make a difference with a commitment to do something that will make that difference. You need to be on the same step emotionally, conatively, and intellectually.

**Ev:** So in this example, I need to intellectually evaluate the effectiveness of different actions to see which ones will truly help the homeless person?

**Kathy:** Exactly. As you can see, the higher you go up the Dynamynd, the tougher the issues. But we can't just start at the top, especially if we've been ignoring our instinctive side! First we have to be self-aware to know what our values are and what makes us tick in terms of our natural MO, and to be sure of what we know vs. what we believe.

At every level, your decisions are authentic because they're enriched by the inner voice of your instincts, in addition to how you feel and what you think. And when you're fully self-actualized, your decisions become persuasive.

**Ev:** Isn't that pretty self-centered? Wouldn't deciding from this level make you indifferent to advice from others or even the needs of others?

**Kathy:** That's why it's not at the top of the Dynamynd. Some people have referred to those who operate at this level as narcissistic leaders because they're self-actualizing rather than doing what is best for all of humanity.

Social responsibility is Level 5 of the Dynamynd because it goes beyond having a passion to having compassion, from having a personal purpose to having a mission to help others, and from being persuasive about what needs to be done to having a vision that makes sense for the greater good.

**Ev:** I don't know many people who hang out in that stratosphere.

# Dynamynd®: Kolbe Decision Ladder

## Culture

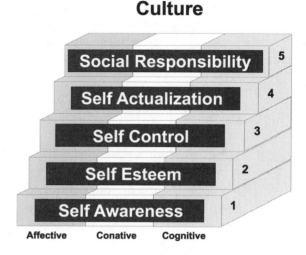

| | | |
|---|---|---|
| Social Responsibility | | 5 |
| Self Actualization | | 4 |
| Self Control | | 3 |
| Self Esteem | | 2 |
| Self Awareness | | 1 |

Affective    Conative    Cognitive

"What the superior man seeks is in himself; what the small man seeks is in others."

Confucius

**Kathy:** I've searched for examples and found a few. It's exciting to watch a Level 5 person in action. And horrifying to watch people in positions of leadership who operate at the lower levels.

**Ev:** Do some people get to the top of the Dynamynd and then succumb to false rewards and drop down some steps?

**Kathy:** No one can sustain all their decisions even at Level 3. You may just hand the homeless guy money while you're on your way to improve the educational system.

Sometimes you operate at a high level emotionally, but can't commit the time conatively to do much more than write a check, or maybe a letter to your Congressperson. You might regret later that your emotions were way out in front of (or higher on the Dynamynd than) the actions from which you could have learned more about the situation.

**Ev:** Should I feel guilty that this all makes a lot of sense to me, but that I don't think I have the energy to learn much more about it right now?

**Kathy:** Of course not. You're trusting your guts when you set some things aside, even when you know you will want to get back to them later. That puts you at the self-control level on the Dynamynd.

Ev: Oh, good. I was afraid I'd be condemned to being a low-level person.

Kathy: We all go up and down the Dynamynd many times a day. For now, just realize that if you goad yourself to go up the ladder, it'll help you get out of mental ruts. The more steps you take up the Dynamynd on all three paths, the more you'll do things that give you a greater sense of purpose.

Ev: I'm supposed to make myself work harder? Wouldn't that just add to my *Failure Factors?*

**Provoke Work =**
Action Advantages

**Provoke False Effort =**
Failure Factors

Kathy: Quite the contrary. Provoking yourself to move up the ladder will improve the way you make decisions. It's the best way I know to inspire the use of your natural advantage. There's no way you can step up to the next level without being more Active, staying more Alert, and Achieving higher standards.

The beauty of the Dynamynd is that it puts your decision making into the context of results. It shows you how your decisions impact your *self*, your influence on others (leadership), and your work group (team).

You can aspire to higher standards in the areas that matter most to you. The language of the Dynamynd helps you define and explain your reasons for setting specific goals for different situations.

Ev: Yeah, but it sounds as if I'd be considered a bad person if I didn't always challenge myself to climb another damn ladder. Talk about the self-improvement world!

Kathy: Sometimes your best decision is to lie low on the ladder in a particular area.

Don't provoke yourself to make foolish efforts. Those are efforts that force you to work against your grain.

Ev: Why would I intentionally do that?

Kathy: Because you care a great deal about the result.

**Efforts**: Conative actions you take to solve problems.

**Best efforts**: Actions that use your four Impact Factors or instinctive abilities.

**Foolish efforts**: Actions you take that you know are not your best efforts.

**Wasted efforts**: Energy you use to take action that goes against your grain, or is contrary to your best efforts.

"No work is ever done unless its force succeeds in producing motion in the body on which it acts. A pillar supporting a building does no work; a man tugging at a stone, but failing to move it, does no work."

*Practical Physics*
Millikan and Gale
Copyright 1920

In physics, work is defined in a way that explains why some work is more tedious than other work.

· Work is what happens when you accomplish something. It is seemingly effortless.

· Effort is energy expended whether or not it moves you toward your goal.

That is what I call foolish or wasted effort. **You will do your best work when your efforts fit your MO.**

The *Failure Factors* intrude into your life because of the foolish efforts you make.

**When you work according to your natural advantage, you provoke Ambition, Alertness, and Achievement – the good old Action Advantages.**

**Ev**: I remember this from physics. I just never saw it as applying to *my* life.

**Kathy**: The authors of the 97-year-old book, *Practical Physics*, say (as do modern physics books – but *Practical Physics* really lives up to its title) that **no work is ever done unless its force succeeds in producing motion in the body on which it acts. A pillar supporting a building does no work; a man tugging at a stone, but failing to move it, does no work.**

**Ev**: That's absolutely astounding in the context of what I'm going through right now. I'm tugging at a whole lot of stones. I've been trying to support way too many pillars. I thought that I was working hard. But I get it: It's just a heck of a lot of foolish, wasted effort.

**Kathy**: Don't beat yourself up over it. None of those courses we've taken has helped us with the most critical of our decisions – where to put our best essential resource, the power of our instincts.

Now you know. **Climbing the Dynamynd takes work, but provoking yourself to do it through your instinctive, natural advantage will make the climb seem almost effortless.**

**Ev:** Don't you find out that you run out of energy as you get nearer the top, even doing it through your instincts?

**Kathy:** The best fuel for your mental energy is achieving a goal. Success does breed success. Or you can think of it in these terms: the **Action Advantages** are your best defense against the *Failure Factors*.

**Ev:** On the one hand, I'm very excited about how this model could cut through my thick head and get me to reform my foolish efforts. On the other hand, it seems too cute – almost sloganeering on your part. I don't like all the F to A stuff – not if it's just another formula that adds up to my having to do more work.

**Kathy:** You can find plenty of authors who tell people their books contain a magic formula for losing weight, gaining popularity, making money, or assuming power. The *Powered by Instinct* program is designed to help you achieve worthwhile results by provoking your own action. It doesn't duck the fact that this takes work.

**Ev:** Too bad. I hoped the next step was handing me the magic wand!

**Kathy:** I have one on the bookshelf right in front of me when I'm working on my laptop. It always makes me smile. There's magic in that.

Working according to your natural talents is very liberating. It'll feel like magic.

With the help of all the *5 Rules for Trusting Your Guts*, you'll be able to preserve and protect your mental energy. You'll learn when not to force action from yourself when we talk about Do Nothing – and Recharge.

**Ev:** I wish I could take you home to talk with my spouse. It'd be a lot easier to do this together. I'm going to sound like an idiot when I say I'm committed to reining in some efforts – so I can achieve more.

**Kathy:** Don't just say it, do it. The proof, as they say, is in the pudding.

You need to Self-Provoke and get to work. Being *Powered by Instinct* doesn't take you off the hook for getting things done.

**Ev:** Let me try to get into this provoking stuff. I think what I hear you saying is that:

- **I have to challenge myself to get into mental gear.**

- **I have to work according to my instincts.**

- **I'll get more done without wasting effort.**

- **I'll even have energy in reserve to do what I want to do.**

Right?

**Kathy:** I think you've got it!

Just one thing is missing. You don't have to wait until your "work" is done before you do what you want to do. **Your "work" ought to be purposeful, so that it *is* what you want to do.**

**Ev:** Yeah, right. Like we all get to do what we want. Hey, most of us are earning a paycheck so we can go home and do what we want. Maybe your work is a mission for you, but for most of us work is just a means to an end.

**Kathy:** Everyone needs a purpose. Otherwise our God-given talents – our instinctive energy – will be frittered away with nothing to show for it.

**Purpose is:**

- **Ambition**

- **Resolve**

- **Decision**

- **Self-determination**

It is what you aspire to do.

"There is a vitality, a life force, an energy, a quickening, that is translated through you into action, and because there is only one of you in all time, this expression is unique. And if you block it, it will never exist through any other medium and will be lost."
Martha Graham

"Even if you're on the right track, you'll get run over if you just sit there."
Will Rogers

**Purpose in action is:**

- **A pursuit**

- **A quest**

- **An intended adventure**

**Fulfilling a purpose requires being:**

- **Resolute**

- **Decisive**

- **Persevering**

Purpose takes tenacity and perseverance. It is your strength of mind. You can't always wait for a coach or boss to motivate you, so you need to learn how to provoke your own action.

Ev: The ever-growing list of things I have to get done at work and at home doesn't leave any room for adding other things, even if I did want to do them.

Kathy: A good deal of your life is spent either working against your grain or doing stuff that is downright annoying but has to get done. We do these things because we're not willing to suffer the consequences of "forgetting" to take out the garbage or not brushing our teeth.

You may have to provoke yourself to do regular chores such as filing papers or balancing the checkbook. You don't have to let such routine efforts drain you of your instinctive power, however. This is where habit takes over.

I'll show you some ways to convert energy drainers into habits that don't consume instinctive energy.

Ev: I've seen habits that can get in the way of good results. They can make people operate in a mental dead-zone, just going through the paces, not having a work ethic.

**Kathy**: Work doesn't need to be exhausting to be of value. Acting with a greater sense of purpose is easier when you go with your guts – not against your grain.

**Ev**: You keep mentioning the importance of not working against my grain. How do I know what that is?

**Kathy**: You can identify your MO or Natural Advantage by completing the Kolbe A index. Your Kolbe result explains your best methods of problem solving or making decisions. It's what you need to focus on doing when striving or provoking yourself toward any goal. [Details: p. 222]

**Ev**: If self-provoking is a learned process, why do we need this assessment? Why can't we just do what we need to do?

**Kathy**: We can. But you'll be far better off when you provoke yourself to use the four talents through which you do your best work. Provoking yourself to use them is how you get more done in less time, with less fatigue, fear, and frustration.

A thought-provoking situation just makes you think. Self provoking makes you use your instincts to act on those thoughts.

It shows **my modus operandi or Mode of Operation – my MO – which is determined by where I naturally operate in each of the four Action Modes. The Action Modes tie to the four instincts I've found which are the universal ways humans try to achieve.**

**Ev**: Wait. You've lost me.

**Kathy**: It's really quite simple. We each have four instincts for creative problem solving. Our particular way of using each of them defines our MO.

# Kolbe A™ Index Result

## Kathy Kolbe

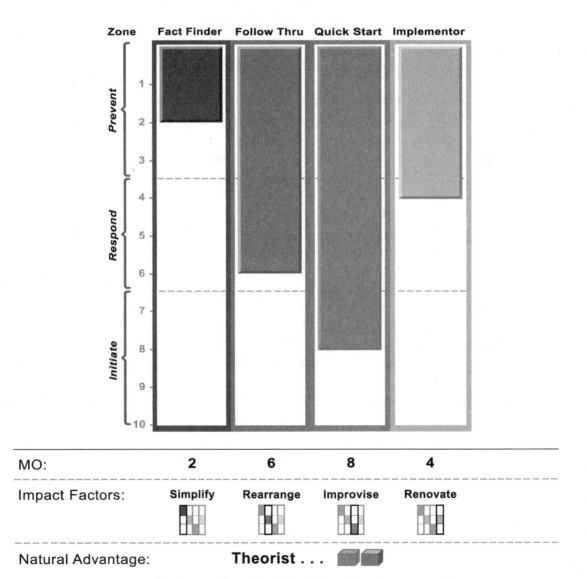

| MO: | 2 | 6 | 8 | 4 |
|---|---|---|---|---|
| Impact Factors: | Simplify | Rearrange | Improvise | Renovate |

Natural Advantage: **Theorist . . .**

*Your conative creativity is in originating concepts,
innovating systems, and initiating trends.*

Kolbe Action Modes

**Fact Finder:**
The instinctive need to gather information

**Follow Thru:**
The instinctive need to organize information

**Quick Start:**
The instinctive need to deal with unknowns

**Implementor:**
The instinctive need to deal with tangibles

We all:

· gather information – the **Fact Finder** mode

· store and retrieve information – the **Follow Thru** mode

· tackle the unknowns – the **Quick Start** mode

· deal with space and physical elements – the **Implementor** mode

**Ev:** Everybody does all of these things?

**Kathy:** Yes, but in different ways. I have created a scale of 1-10 and divided it into three Zones of Operation for each mode. If your MO is in the 7-10 zone (on a scale of 1-10), you will initiate solutions through that mode. I initiate in Quick Start, which makes me a big risk taker.

You will respond to a problem or need through a mode in which you are in the mid-zone. That's when you act in an accommodating way. I accommodate systems and follow procedures because of my six in Follow Thru.

Any mode in which your Kolbe index shows a 1-3 indicates a talent for preventing problems through its use. I get right to the bottom line – and put the details of my research in the back of my books because of my two in Fact Finder. [Details: p. 223]

**Ev:** So it's best when you have Action Modes in which you initiate solutions, right?

**Kathy:** No. Everyone has an equal amount of instinctive energy, or the natural ability to solve problems. Thank goodness we have the diversity of doing it differently. If everyone initiated action when there was a problem, the world would be in a mess. The energy that goes toward preventing problems creates many unsung heroes.

One of the ways I've simplified this is by putting it into a model of Kolbe Impact Factors – a chart of the 12 possible ways to solve any problem. They cover the three Zones of Operation in the four Action Modes.

"We can't all and some of us don't. That's all there is to it."
Eeyore in Winnie the Pooh

61

While you can use all 12 of these methods of problem solving, four of them are your natural ways of working and give your solutions the highest impact.

The particular four Impact Factors in your instinctive makeup define your MO.

Each Action Mode is displayed across three zones of operation, determining how we initiate action, respond to opportunities, or prevent problems.

Zones of Operation

Initiate/Insist:
How you will act.

Respond/Accommodate:
How you are willing to act.

Prevent/Resist:
How you won't act.

# Kolbe Impact Factors[tm]

| Fact Finder | Follow Thru | Quick Start | Implementor |
|---|---|---|---|
| Simplify | Adapt | Stabilize | Imagine |
| Refine | Rearrange | Revise | Renovate |
| Justify | Organize | Improvise | Construct |

**Ev:** So are the people with modes in the mid-zone the wimps of the world?

**Kathy:** Hardly. An MO with a mode in the mid-range indicates a terrific talent for facilitating the differences between those who <u>insist</u> on a

**Kolbe A index question**

If I was working on a
project, I would:
1. build the prototype
2. plan the workflow
3. start from scratch
4. examine the details

Select one Most and one
Least answer.

method and those who <u>resist</u> it. We'd live in a constant state of conflict (even more than we do now), if there wasn't a natural inclination within some people to contribute energy to bridge such gaps.

It would help if we paid more attention to those people who are natural Facilitators, those who accommodate in three or four modes – without having to initiate or prevent.

**Ev:** Can't you figure out your MO intuitively? I mean, I'll bet I could make some good guesses because I know myself pretty well.

**Kathy:** It's not as easy as you think. I'm pretty perceptive about people's MOs, but I don't always get it right. I could make an educated guess about your insistences by the way you ask questions. But I haven't seen you in a wide enough variety of problem-solving situations. Even then, I might misjudge a resistance or preventative talent because you may have learned how to behave against your grain.

We're often wrong in guessing our own innate abilities because we've tried so hard to do things the way we were taught to do them, or we've tried to mimic a strong role model.

**Ev:** But I might have learned to actually "be" what gets me the best grades, for example.

**Kathy:** You don't change who you are, you just frustrate yourself when you work contrary to your authentic nature. The reason some teachers – or bosses, or scout leaders – were your favorites was because they nurtured your natural abilities. As you'd expect, most teachers are Fact Finder and Follow Thru insistent and are most likely to reward the kids who follow their pattern of teaching. The good news is that we're now finding ways to encourage everyone's strengths.

**Ev:** I got good grades in school. How can I check out my MO and see how much Fact Finder I have?

**Kathy:** The easiest way is to go to www.kolbe.com, but since you can't get on the Internet from this airplane, I'll power up my laptop, which has it preprogrammed. It should take you only about 15 minutes to answer the

36 questions on the Kolbe A index. I'll write down my guesses as you're completing the index. It's always fun to see how close you can come to figuring out someone's MO. Your spouse would be most likely to guess wrong, by the way.

Ev: Sometimes I don't think mine has a clue. This will be interesting to share.

Kathy: You're used to figuring out a "right" answer. There really aren't any here. Act – before You Think! Let your instincts make the choices.

Provoke yourself to pick one of the choices. When you're stuck in a real-life situation in which none of the options seem "good," you still have to do something.

Ev: The instructions reinforce the need to Act – before You Think and Self-Provoke, even though they don't use those terms.

Kathy: The results actually pick up the small percent of people who haven't followed their instincts – for whatever reason. Sometimes they're living with so many of the *Failure Factors* in their lives that they can't seem to focus on how they'd act if they were free to be themselves. Sometimes people intentionally mess with the index. Either way, they need to retake it when they can or will provoke themselves to trust their instincts.

Ev: Don't tell me I'm in that category.

Kathy: I doubt it. When you click for your result you get it in a second. So, here's your Kolbe A index result.

**Ev's Kolbe A index result includes:**

Ev's Kolbe
Natural Advantage–
"Manager"

Your instinctive creativity is in developing strategies, assessing options, and allocating resources.

Ev, you have a special talent for:

- setting flexible agendas
- assessing options
- weighing alternatives
- switching priorities to take advantage of opportunities
- intuiting the relative merit of probable outcomes

When you target your efforts, you come up with practical solutions that have bottom-line impact.

Ev, your instincts are to cut through complexities so they become manageable options.

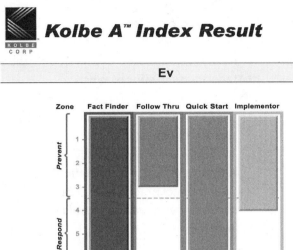

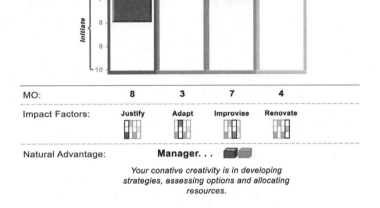

*Your conative creativity is in developing strategies, assessing options and allocating resources.*

**Ev:** Wow! That's my MO? Can I print out my eight page test result?

**Kathy:** Yes, as often as you like. You can even email it to others.

**Ev:** I may know exactly who I am, but I never thought of these words to describe myself. It's how I act when I'm in my groove, but it's interesting that I'm not actually a Manager. I mean that's not my job.

**Kathy:** Your Natural Advantage is not meant to be a job title. It's how you proceed when you Self-Provoke action. It's what will get you where you're trying to go.

Ev's Kolbe index result highlights that an

**Initiating Fact Finder will:**
• Collect Data
• Research
• Define Terms

**Preventative Follow Thru won't:**
• Be rigid with plans
• Stay boxed in
• Get stuck in routines
• Follow a schedule

**Initiating Quick Start will:**
• Take risks
• Originate options
• Seek challenges

**Accommodating Implementor will:**
• Work with tangible goods
• Use models
• Incorporate tactile clues

"The people who get on in this world are the people who get up and look for the circumstances they want, and, if they can't find them, make them."
George Bernard Shaw
Mrs. Warren's Profession
Act II, 1893

**Ev:** So, if I manage a situation by doing the things listed on my result, I'll be more successful?

**Kathy:** Yes, if success is measured by the amount of freedom you have to take action in your own way.

**Ev:** Aren't some instincts more effective at solving particular types of problems?

**Kathy:** Sure. There are situations in which you need a Follow Thru insistent person to cover for your resistance to organizing things sequentially. You multi-task very well, but could sure use someone to arrange all the loose ends in your life.

**Ev:** I never met a plan I didn't change. I mess up all the systems in our house, from electronics to the alphabetical spices. I need a keeper – to organize my files and my travel receipts at work, to remember to pick up my laundry. It isn't fair that some people do these things naturally.

**Kathy:** Provoke yourself to cut a deal with those folks. Find the insistent Follow Thrus in your life and offer your innate ability to do the research if they'll create a structure for storing it so you can find it when you need it. *Trust your guts* to do what you need to do, and trust *their* guts to cover for you in the other areas.

**Ev:** How much of this do I have to learn in order to use the *5 Rules?*

**Kathy:** It always helps to know the particular ways you'll act when you're free to be yourself. The *5 Rules* help you gain that freedom. So even if you didn't know your MO, you could use the *Powered by Instinct* guidelines to reduce your fatigue, fear, and frustration.

**Ev:** I'd like my spouse and kids to take the Kolbe index. How do they do that?

**Kathy:** Go to www.kolbe.com and click on Take the Kolbe Index. Your spouse would pick the Kolbe A, and kids who are at a fifth grade reading level or above would take the Kolbe Y (for Youth) version.

**Ev**: And it's free of course?

**Kathy**: Free assessment tools on the Internet can be fun – but they're not validated instruments with the years of research behind them like the Kolbe index.

There's always a great deal of free information on kolbe.com, but the index itself is far too significant to think of as a freebie game.

**Ev**: How can I tell my kids how to use the *5 Rules* if they don't want to complete the Kolbe index?

**Kathy**: We can't afford to wait until we convince every human being that he or she needs to know his or her MO before we help them learn how to benefit from the power of their instincts. People who practice using the *5 Rules* will have less fear, fatigue, and frustration than they're suffering from right now. They won't reduce the *Failure Factors* as much as those who have greater awareness of their best paths for achievement – but it'll be a big step in the right direction.

**Ev**: My index result shows me how I'll act and the *5 Rules* are guidelines for *when and why* I should take action. Don't I also have to try to improve things like my short line in Follow Thru?

**Kathy: Your short line in Follow Thru is a strength**; you have the ability to *adapt*. That's a way you prevent problems – by resisting getting bogged down in too many procedures.

Your mid-zone result in Implementor indicates that you accommodate tangible problem-solving. You'll make repairs or fix equipment, when sufficiently provoked.

The faucet will drip for a while before you'll get the tools out, however. You're most easily provoked to use your Implementor talent when others need your help or the situation requires it. Others may fight for the chance to get their hands (literally) on a problem. That could be digging in the dirt, taking a computer apart, sawing the boards, or kneading the dough.

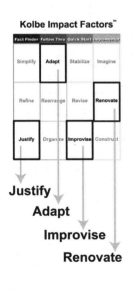

**Kolbe Impact Factors™**

| Fact Finder | Follow Thru | Quick Start | Implementor |
|---|---|---|---|
| Simplify | **Adapt** | Stabilize | Imagine |
| Refine | Rearrange | Revise | **Renovate** |
| **Justify** | Organize | **Improvise** | Construct |

**Justify**
**Adapt**
**Improvise**
**Renovate**

"To find out what one is fitted to do, and to secure an opportunity to do it, is the key to happiness."
John Dewey

You're frustrated when you don't have time to weigh the pros and cons, or can't get the information you need. With your long Fact Finder line, you initiate action or insist on using that approach to *justify* your solutions. I'll bet you get very annoyed with what you consider superficial information.

**Ev:** I always thought it was because my parents are sticklers for detail and taught me to get all the facts before I made decisions.

**Kathy:** If your natural tendency wasn't to load up on specifics, you'd have rebelled against their approach.

**Ev:** But aren't most kids' instincts pretty much like their parents'? Isn't that part of being born with these traits?

**Kathy:** I find no genetic link in the many families we've studied. Even identical twins can have different MO's.

**Ev:** That's so odd. I've sure never heard anything quite like this before. Maybe it's the Quick Start in me that's quite curious about all this.

My result feels like me, all right. But isn't it like a horoscope? What's said about me could be just as true for everyone else. **Everything the Kolbe index result says about me is positive. That makes me suspicious.**

**Kathy:** Spoken like a true Fact Finder! Of course you'll need to check it out. **You're not used to a "test" result that doesn't find some fault with you.**

Cognitive tests (IQ, skills, and academic tests) always tell you what you "missed" and still need to learn. Affective tests tell you how you could improve your personality even if they say there are no right or wrong answers.

The only part of you that has always been and always will be perfect is your instincts. And don't ever let anyone tell you otherwise!

**Ev:** If I naturally do these things, why would I need to know all this in order to push myself into gear?

**Kathy**: Great question. Young children act according to their MOs. That's why they're so unpretentious and delightful to watch tackling problems and discovering solutions. As soon as they hit school – and sometimes even before that if their parents want them to conform to their MOs – they're taught the "right" way to solve problems. This only works for the 20% of kids who naturally initiate in Fact Finder. Other kids can get all sorts of negative labels, from "A.D.D." to "uncooperative."

The more your culture – school, home, and work – teaches you that your natural inclinations are wrong, the more you have to Self-Provoke and take charge of activating your own best efforts.

**Ev: Then the trick is to provoke myself to find the freedom to do things my own, instinctive way.**

**Kathy**: That's the bottom line for Rule #2. Now, let's get involved with the Think-ercises that will help you learn what it feels like to Self-Provoke.

# CHAPTER FIVE

# HOW TO SELF-PROVOKE

**Kathy:** This is the get-a-life rule because it drives you toward finding and staying with a purpose.

Wouldn't it be a daunting task to persist in your purposes without your instincts to guide you? They give you a major assist in carrying out your personal mission. Exercising your innate abilities as you work toward your goals helps you learn to control this power for your desired purposes. The process is an upward spiral toward self actualization.

**Ev:** Do you find many people actually have a purpose they can articulate?

**Kathy:** It no longer surprises me when people say they wish they could *find* a sense of purpose, but it always saddens me. I remember Daphne, a brilliant professional woman who used to think that making it to partner in a law firm was her most important purpose. She has a good marriage, many friends, and a terrific reputation. Everyone loves her wit and her caring attitude. She's an extrovert who gladly goes to every social and community function that comes up for her firm or her husband.

**Ev:** Sounds like she has the good life.

**Kathy:** Except that she was feeling "empty."

Dynamynd®: Kolbe Decision Ladder

**Individual**

**Purpose**

71

"I'm trying to make a difference," she said, "I used to think that law was a way of doing that. I truly believed that I would be helping society when I became a lawyer. But my days are spent arguing points of law that are not relevant to quality of life. It all has so little meaning to the big picture."

She was moving up in her *levels* of purpose, not moving away from *having* a purpose.

**Ev**: As exhausted as I am just keeping up with life, I wonder how people like Daphne and me find those higher purposes – the ones that go beyond remembering to put gas in the car or return the rented video.

**Kathy**: No one truly wants to live without a purpose. Yet the most help anyone's likely to get in figuring out a purpose comes from role models. This is such a bonus, if it does happen, that it's important for the *Powered by Instinct* program to provide a format for developing your personal sense of purpose, even in the absence of someone to inspire you.

Seriously consider all of your responses in the following Think-ercise.

This is especially important for people to use when they've recently gone through or are about to go through a significant life change, such as:

- Loss of a job

- Move to a new community

- An empty nest

- Loss of a loved one

- Retirement

- Divorce

- Graduation

- Physical trauma

## THINK-ERCISE #7

# Finding your Purpose

## Provoke yourself to answer this question:

Is something missing?

This can be as immediate as a sense that you've just been robbed or it can be a long-term yearning for a companion. Your purpose is to figure out what's missing, find it, and keep it.

Write down your answers without judging them.

1. _____

2. _____

3. _____

4. _____

5. _____

Ev: What if nothing comes to mind?

Kathy: You might actually be thinking about it too much, which keeps the question from tapping into your instincts. Wait until there's a time when you're not preoccupied with activities, and ask yourself again if something is missing.

**Ev**: Exactly when do you think that I'm not overburdened with activity? The one thing I'm definitely missing is time to do these exercises!

**Kathy**: I appreciate your dilemma. One of the best times to do this is just before falling asleep at night. Don't think of it as doing anything. Just ask yourself the question. Often, you'll wake up with an answer.

## Ask your instincts to tell you:

## Do improvements need to be made in your environment?

It could be as simple as fixing a rickety stair rail, or as complex as pursuing more education, changing careers, or generating better communication with loved ones.

Your purpose is to figure out what's wrong and decide how to fix it.

Start by affirming that your instincts are perfect, and that you do not need to change the natural way you do things.

## Ask your instincts to tell you:

## Is there something in your environment that you could improve?

**Give your answers here.**

1. _____

2. _____

3. _____

4. _____

5. _____

Ev: So I can't just keep saying I need more time and energy? It's a problem in my environment? That broadens the scope.

Kathy: This will provoke you even further.

# Ask your instincts to tell you:

## What feels wrong?

· Is there something wrong with the way you're approaching a task?

· Do you feel you've done something wrong?

· Do you feel sick or run-down?

· Does the way another person responds to you make you uncomfortable?

· Is there something physically unsafe about your situation?

· Are you ill at ease with the way things are happening?

"What feels wrong?" That is the question to ask whenever you feel lethargic or upset, or are suffering from the *Failure Factors* of fear, fatigue, or frustration.

Get to the heart of it and you'll become more resolute in fixing it.

# Ask your instincts to tell you:

## Do you have the right amount?

It could be that you have <u>too much</u>:

· To do

· Stress

· Space

· Noise

· Downtime

**It could be that you have <u>too little</u>:**

· To do

· Adventure

· Space

· Time

· Money

· Love

## Your purpose is to change the formula.

### At the moment when you're feeling totally frustrated, <u>ask your instincts to tell you</u>:

### "Why is there too much or too little...?"

1. _____

2. _____

3. _____

4. _____

5. _____

**Ev:** What popped into my head surprised me. At first I thought, there's too much yard work, and too much furniture we still need to buy. Then I realized that the reason there's too much space might tie in to the reason there's too little time and money.

We never have enough time or money to take care of the house and our rather large lot. My purposes in life are greater than the short-term project of putting in storage shelves and mowing the grass every weekend. This is actually making me think that we should talk about moving into a smaller, less energy-consuming place.

**Kathy:** Every purpose comes with a challenge or problem that you need to prevent or a solution you need to concoct. It's an opportunity to provoke action. If you're in a relationship that's going along very comfortably, you don't have to target your instinctive energy to make it work better. You can enjoy relaxation together. **You don't always have to be provoked or be provocative in a truly comfortable setting with another person. That's when you get true mental downtime.**

**Ev:** And the opposite is also true: that I can provoke too much because I want something so badly?

**Kathy:** In sports this is often referred to as "choking." It may be the cause of the kicker shanking what could have been the last-second, game-winning field goal. It's similar to what happens to lots of good students who "freeze" on tests.

**Fear of failure, like fear of success, is an emotion that can paralyze the creative process. You can push yourself or be pushed too far or too fast.**

Extreme emotions can shut down your instincts, whether the emotion is sadness, anxiety, silliness, love, hate, or some ambiguous mix of emotions.

Some marketers push you too far. They over-stimulate your affective responses, so that you love the ad or the show or the gizmo, but you just can't see yourself buying it. This can be very beneficial for your budget. They've entertained you or captured your emotions for the moment, but **your instincts haven't been engaged to convert that desire into the action to buy.**

You get the thrilling sensation without the shock when the credit card bill arrives!

> "The true test of character is not how much we know how to do, but how we behave when we don't know what to do."
> John Holt

Provoking yourself does require some affect. Crying is an active demonstration of affect. You can provoke yourself to tears. **When you're terribly sad but don't act on your emotions, holding them in keeps you from creating solutions.**

That's why it is so helpful when you're feeling negative emotions to ask yourself what you're going to DO about it.

It also helps others who are caught up in the feelings to ask what you can DO to help them. Good customer service reps use that line to defuse the pent up energy of an angry customer.

Simply being sympathetic is very helpful when there's nothing you can do, as with the death of a loved one. But even then bringing in food or making necessary phone calls **shows "do-fullness," in addition to thoughtfulness.**

**Ev:** Okay. I'm provoking myself here – and maybe you as well. This last exercise has me committed to a bigger purpose. Why doesn't that feel like more effort than the smaller stuff like mowing the grass?

**Kathy:** Some people imagine solutions. That's one of their Impact Factors. With that forte, they don't have to kick the tires to make a decision on which car to buy, so their preventative Implementor nature has its advantages – as do all of the Impact Factors.

**The moment you try to work against your instinctive grain, you cause a resistance that might make the effort not worth it. That's what happens when you have to use Implementor in the *Construct* zone.** When work becomes foolish effort, you lose the benefit of your instinctive abilities.

**Ev:** So the strategizing that goes into selling my house works well for me, the Implementor *effort* I've had to put into maintaining the house has been counter-instinctive.

Implementor
Impact Factors
Prevent = Imagine
Initiate = Construct

**Efforts**: Conative actions you take to solve problems.

**Best efforts**: Actions that use your four Impact Factors or instinctive abilities.

**Foolish efforts**: Actions you take that you know are not your best efforts.

**Wasted efforts**: Energy you use to take action that goes against your grain, or is contrary to your best efforts.

**Kathy**: You've actually avoided a lot of those efforts, and, by your description, have let your house "go," as they say. Obstacles that cause you to resist taking action can be of your own doing or come from an external force, but both equally negate the positive instinctive forces within you.

**Ev**: If I made more of an effort, perhaps we could stay where we are. If the budget weren't so tight, we could hire people to cut the grass and help around the house. Maybe both of us could figure out how to moonlight to make that happen.

**Kathy**: It's interesting that we give so much praise for "making an effort," and consider work to be onerous. What we need to do is provoke our best efforts – those that tie to our Impact Factors.

Try evaluating the return you get on your efforts. That's a good measure of whether you're provoking yourself to do things the right way – for you.

## THINK-ERCISE #8

# Postcard Provoker

The following Think-ercise clarifies the difference between

· actions you provoke that result in productive work

· efforts you make that lead to fatigue and frustration

## Postcard Provokers

| | |
|---|---|
| Postcard Provoker<br><br>Today I worked to... | Postcard Provoker<br><br>Today I wasted my efforts by... |

Look at the two types of postcards shown on this page. Each type of card begins with a message to complete. Create a stack of each type of postcard. Starting tomorrow, select one card from each stack to write on every day. It doesn't matter who you imagine will receive it.

On the set of cards that begins with "Today I worked to..." write about work you did that day that moved you toward accomplishing a goal.

On the set that begins with "Today I wasted my effort by..." describe what you did that took effort but did not move you closer to a goal.

**Ev:** What you're doing here seems so obvious that I doubt most people will even bother writing anything on the postcards.

**Kathy:** Meaning you aren't going to do it? I think you should reconsider if that's the case. Writing these messages provoked a strong response in a grocery store manager. He found that everything he did after the store opened in the morning could go on a wasted effort card, and that he accomplished things only before and after the workday.

**Ev**: And actually doing the exercise made it clear to him what the problem was?

**Kathy**: It made him stop and realize that the way he was managing people and handling customers was not working well for him. The actions this exercise provoked led to his changing the way he did his job.

Over the next few weeks he tried various solutions until he found those that made the job more effortless. His most effective solutions were:

- **carving out a couple of hours during each day to work at his desk**

- **categorizing problems that recurred frequently**

- **establishing effective policies and procedures for handling problems**

- **creating an employee incentive program related to customer satisfaction**

He was completely energized as he worked at sending out more positive messages.

Here's another example. The director of a non-profit agency thought that she really earned her paycheck when she struggled through budget meetings and scheduled shifts for over a hundred staff and volunteers.

"Public speaking comes so easily for me, I would do it just because I love talking about what we do," she said. She didn't count it as work because – for her – it was so effortless. The **Postcard exercise** provoked her to get out and give more speeches that brought in more money – which allowed her to hire someone to do the scheduling.

**Ev**: So I guess some people are led by this activity to find more positive messages to convey. But others may have completely bought into a culture, so they find it quite satisfying to brag about how much effort they're making. They'd paper their living room with postcards (lets call them "boastcards") about all the hours they put in struggling against all the odds. I get sick of hearing it from a couple of my friends who seem to be martyrs to their jobs and families.

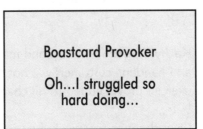

Boastcard Provoker

Oh...I struggled so
hard doing...

**Kathy:** Boastcards are a wonderful idea. Maybe you could use those to remind people that you'll be more impressed when they can share stories of how they provoked themselves to work with less effort.

That reminds me of a technology team member who told me, "My boss rates me high because I get in so early in the morning and stay so late most nights. He doesn't check on whether I'm accomplishing more than the people who are here shorter – or longer – hours."

**Ev:** What action did that provoke on his part?

**Kathy:** He decided that having to work against his grain was not a productive environment for him and put his resume on-line.

---

**Have you received more praise for making foolish efforts than for doing work that easily achieved results? If so, what action has that provoked on your part?**

1. _____

2. _____

3. _____

**If you sent these postcards to a boss or co-worker, what kind of response would you provoke from them?**

1. _____

2. _____

3. _____

**Would it help to write out the postcards, but – rather than send them – discuss them with people in your personal and work life who could help you reduce the wasted efforts you think you have to make?**

**Ev:** I don't think I can expect much help at work, or that I'd even ask. My spouse is suffering from the fatigue factor as much as I am. So if anything is going to change, I'm going to have to provoke myself, without much help. How can I get myself geared up to do that?

**Kathy:** Nothing I've given you so far is very time consuming, but I sense that's not the real problem. My take is that you aren't motivated to expend your already stressed energy on provoking yourself. I have a few suggestions to induce Self-Provoking.

Working according to your natural abilities often requires that you become your own agent, and the first person you have to sell on employing your talents is you. You need to get excited about the possibilities inherent in who you are.

Even if you love your job, your family, and your friends, it can become difficult to do the work they require. You'll find it helps under any circumstance to keep your mind focused on the goal.

## THINK-ERCISE #9

# Instinct Igniters

You can provoke your own actions with inducements that target your instinctive energy. There's a certain amount of bribery involved any time you reward yourself. That's one way to tempt yourself to get to work.

· Bet yourself regarding an outcome, and make it worth your while. You either get or give what you agree upon, depending on the results of your actions.

· Offer yourself a reward based on your results. This needs to be something that only you can give, whether it's buying yourself a gift or giving yourself some downtime.

· Set up a test. Make the standard high enough that there's a thrill of accomplishment. Decide in advance how you'll measure the way you use your natural talents.

· Give praise. Leave yourself a congratulatory voice mail. Send an email that you'll open when you succeed. Post some positive words on your bulletin board or refrigerator door.

· Tell others your goal. That gives you the fun of telling them when you've reached it. Make lack of commitment to success unacceptable.

Ev: These aren't all new ideas for me. I've tried some of them. I think that I'll approach them differently though, because now I see them in context. Now I see how they could work if I used them the right way.

Kathy: They also work for provoking responses from others. Be sure that you involve them in setting up their own evaluation criteria. Goals need to be clearly defined and mutually agreed upon.

Ev: If I'm going to provoke myself, it's certainly going to be so I get a result that's important for everyone involved. Doing anything just for the sake of doing it would be an incredible waste of energy. I want to be a winner – which I see as a person who operates at high levels on your

Dynamynd, but I'm not sure I'm competitive enough to pull that off.

**Kathy:** Stories abound in most competitive situations – whether among musicians, astronauts, bull riders or chili cook-off contestants – about the incredible lengths winners go to in order to get what they want.

**Ev:** How do they keep themselves pumped up for one more practice session? For the pain and agony of success?

**Kathy:** People with their eye on the goal become magnets for those who share their missions. Others feed off the reflected energy. They take essential action that may be unpleasant at first, but is focused on the larger goal.

Their success requires endurance. Endurance takes stamina. They have to coax their foolish efforts over and over again. They have to discover how to keep cajoling themselves and others to stay the course.

That requires being sure the action they spawn is worthy of their energy. Everyone I've ever worked with who falls into this category has had to continually ask himself or herself if what's required to get something done is worth the price. It's all too possible to get caught up in the thrill of the chase and forget the potential downsides – especially once you've accomplished your quest.

**Ev:** Are you alluding to people in high places who don't find much pleasure in being where they are?

**Kathy:** I've known too many people who've found that the goal wasn't worth the effort.

**Ev:** So that's why you bring up the importance of constantly reevaluating whether you're provoking yourself in the right directions.

**Kathy:** I can't emphasize that enough.

**Ev:** Which makes me think of the opposite issue, of putting too much energy into the little things, of getting all tired out doing things that really don't matter much.

**Kathy:** Not all actions need to come from high levels of emotion – or use up your instinctive energy. Many actions, ones that you repeat daily such as dealing with junk mail or turning off the lights, should require none of your instinctive resources. Such actions should be taken on autopilot – not even a Level 1 on the Dynamynd.

A receptionist in a very active, 50-person office was going nuts with all she was supposed to do. Interruptions upon interruptions caused her to lose track of half her agenda. With her job in jeopardy, she decided to take a few minutes to list the tasks that were repetitious enough to be done in "mental neutral."

**Fran's list for conversion to habit included:**

· **Set out daily sign-out sheets**
· **Take telephone off night ring**
· **Turn up the heat**
· **Open the blinds**
· **Check voice mail**
· **Check e-mail**
· **Circulate lunch list**

Well, you get the point. Her list went on and on, with over 30 things she did in the course of her workday that she could do without wasting a bit of her precious creativity. Making the list provoked Fran to transfer many of these responsibilities from action items to routine duties. After consciously doing them at the same time in the same way for a month, she got most of them solidly ensconced in her habit category.

Fran stopped being so fragmented, and targeted her talents on the more essential problems. Within four months, she had convinced her bosses that she could handle greater responsibilities.

She's been promoted three times in the last two years. Fran also signed up for college night school classes after she provoked herself into preventing her own brain drain. Her potential has become unlimited.

"Beyond the mountains there are mountains again."
Haitian Proverb

**To self-provoke effectively, figure out how many tasks you can move into the no-brainer list. Take every routine task that doesn't require**

creative effort and convert it into a habit. Don't even think about which detergent gets clothes whitest, just dump in what's on the shelf. If the brand is important to you, it'll *be* on your shelf.

**Ev:** I need to get a better handle on how to provoke myself in the right direction. The things I want are in a tug-of-war. My desire to sleep in conflicts with my desire to get to work on time. My desire to spend time with my kids conflicts with my desire to socialize with friends.

When wants pull you in opposite directions, which actions do you provoke?

**Kathy:** The answer is found in what you're willing to act upon. Your instincts send you a message every time you find yourself acting on one option and not another. Pay attention to what they're telling you.

# CHAPTER SIX

# RULE #3
# COMMIT – BUT TO VERY LITTLE

## Target your top priorities.

**Ev:** Isn't one of our problems with young people today that they don't make commitments? Why on earth would you endorse this lack of commitment?

**Kathy:** This rule for trusting your guts doesn't say that you shouldn't make commitments. **It's essential that we all commit our instinctive power – our conative talent – to the most critical matters in our lives. That's the only way that we're going to reduce the *Failure Factors* of fear, fatigue, and frustration.**

Yes, you need to make commitments, but if you commit to too many things at one time, your instincts will get whiplash. They'll be thrust back and forth among so many priorities that you'll find it difficult to concentrate on what matters most.

**You'll be at your best when your instinctive power is targeted on your top priority needs.**

"Never put off until tomorrow what you can do the day after tomorrow."
Mark Twain

Commit – but to Very Little is good self-management. It's your way of controlling a limited personal resource.

Committing to very little will make it easier to decide whether (or not) to:

· Take the job

· Change careers

· Have a baby now

· Sell the house

· Finish your education

· Get married (or divorced)

· File the lawsuit

· Have surgery

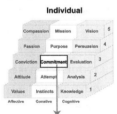

Dynamynd®: Kolbe Decision Ladder

**Individual**

**Commitment**

**If you're putting off decisions because you're overloaded with critical issues, you have a particular need for this rule.** If your instincts are telling you not to make the decisions because the time isn't right, then you're following this guideline already.

**Ev:** I don't always have a choice. I have to deal with a multitude of issues whether I want to or not.

**Kathy:** Just because you have to get something done doesn't mean you have to do it with all your mental might. Some responsibilities can be fulfilled without having to give the full amount of mental energy that it takes to make a commitment.

**Ev:** Don't you believe that if it's worth doing, it's worth doing well?

**Kathy:** Winston Churchill said, "Anything worth doing is worth doing badly." That means – if it's important – **do it.**

I wouldn't suggest doing things haphazardly, but lots of things that are worth doing don't have to take a huge amount of time and energy. **There are some things you should commit to doing – but getting them done may be more important than doing them through the best efforts. That's when "close enough is good enough"** – especially for a person like me whose MO is to generalize rather than delve into the specifics.

Ev: That sounds like a cop-out. Doesn't your approach give people an excuse not to do what they don't want to do?

Kathy: *Powered by Instinct* gives everyone the same "excuse to be themselves" – or to have the freedom to be who they are. That's not a cop-out. We all have to fulfill our responsibilities.

We have to be realistic about the amount of time and energy we have available before we make commitments, which are guarantees that we'll allocate the necessary instinctive power to accomplish a goal.

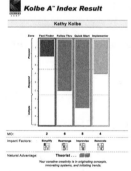

If I know I have either the wrong stuff (conatively) to do something well, or that I don't have *enough* of the right stuff available, I shouldn't make the commitment.

That doesn't mean I won't ever clean up my piles of papers. I'll probably wait until there isn't a surface available for anything else. It would be foolish for me to commit to straightening up the piles every day.

Ev: What *if* it bugged your husband to have stacks of papers everywhere?

Kathy: I could commit to keeping certain places off-limits for my papers, and I could commit to moving the stacks out of the way when I'm not actively working on projects during holidays, for instance. If I committed to much more than that, I'd be disingenuous. That doesn't mean that I refuse to *try* to condense the piles of papers.

Ev: My spouse is always trying to get me to "get to the point, dear." I guess my Fact Finder goes on and on some times, giving all the details about a book or conversation. I try to condense the story, but I can't ever seem to make it brief.

**Kathy:** You can commit to being brief some of the time, but if you had to change your natural way of communicating to satisfy your spouse, I think you'd turn to other people to meet your need for communication. Your marriage would suffer.

**Relationships involve commitment of time and energy, and the only way they'll last is if these commitments are freely given, and therefore not oppressive.** Instincts can feel as if they're quivering if you have to make one commitment too many. They become taut as your mental energy is stretched too far. You sense the strain and tension. You're out of kilter with stress that robs you of your natural advantage.

**There's a breaking point at which your instincts tell you to run as fast as you can in the other direction. It comes when you've made too many commitments that you can't fulfill, or that you made against your will, or that you made and feel guilty about not being able to fulfill.**

**Committing to work against your grain can make you dread your job so much that you take more sick days or leave altogether. [Details: p. 226]**

**You're wise to Commit to Very Little in the first place so you don't get to this level of stress. It not only destroys relationships and job performance, it cuts deeply into your self-confidence.**

A Yahoo! Career search found that more than 25% of the site's users rate "doing work that makes a difference" as the most critical factor in job happiness.

**Ev:** I know a guy whose job was extremely demanding, and who was in a graduate program at night. He was stretched to the gills with commitments, but his wife didn't get it. She would demand that he take her out to dinner on weeknights, and that they party on weekends. Poor guy looked exhausted all the time. But he kept making the commitments, promising her that he'd take her out. He would, but he'd practically fall asleep in the restaurant.

She decided that he wasn't committed to the marriage and ditched him. I wonder what would have happened if he had mapped out for both of them what he thought had to be his commitments and what he would *attempt* to do.

**Kathy:** I often recommend commitment contracts between people, both at work and at home. It's a process that lays out the use of time and mental energy so both parties can see the logic of how they're allocated. It brings reality into conversations that can become strictly emotional and accusatory.

We all have the same amount of mental energy, or equal instinctive power. I think of it in terms of ergs, or units of mental energy. An erg, in physics, is a unit of work.

I consider 100 individual ergs as representing your full amount of instinctive power or capacity to work. It accounts for 100% of your mental energy. Your Kolbe index result shows these ergs in a pyramid, with the ergs divided according to the percent of your conative talent that resides in each Action Mode.

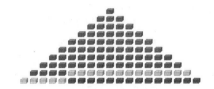

**Ev's erg pyramid**
FactFinder: 36%
QuickStart: 32%
Implementor: 18%
FollowThru: 14%

**Ev:** That's obviously why I have more Fact Finder and Quick Start squares than the other modes. Is Fact Finder always on the top of the pyramid?

**Kathy:** Only for those of you who lead off with Fact Finder when you're fulfilling a commitment. My pyramid has Fact Finder on the bottom, because that's my last resort as a method of problem solving.

Even though you're an insistent Fact Finder who naturally justifies your actions, if those Fact Finder ergs are already allocated, you won't be able to effectively fulfill any more commitments that involve having to justify conclusions or explain things in detail.

---

**Dynamynd®: Kolbe Decision Ladder**

**Individual**

| | | | |
|---|---|---|---|
| Compassion | Mission | Vision | 5 |
| Passion | Purpose | Persuasion | 4 |
| Conviction | Commitment | Evaluation | 3 |
| Attitude | Attempt | Analysis | 2 |
| Values | Instincts | Knowledge | 1 |
| Affective | Conative | Cognitive | |

↓

**Commitment**

**Definition of Erg:**
a centimeter/gram/ second/unit of work equal to the work done by a force of one dyne acting through a distance of one centimeter

**Kolbe Definition of mental Erg:**
unit of instinctive power

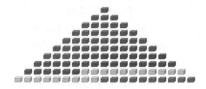

Kathy's erg pyramid
QuickStart: 40%
FollowThru: 30%
Implementor: 20%
FactFinder: 10%

**Ev:** So even I run out of the capacity to give any more details?

**Kathy:** Yes, but fortunately, you can reenergize.

It's a whole lot easier to Commit to Very Little – and keep those commitments – by using your instinct to power your way through them.

I have some Think-ercises that can help you control your energy, by identifying the things you have to get done and the things you hope to get done.

**Ev:** Isn't this just good time management?

**Kathy:** It's a new form of time management. Deciding how to use your instinctive energy requires asking yourself two key questions:

*Do I want to take the time to do this?*

and

*Do I have the resources I need to do this?*

The other two dimensions of the mind – thinking and feeling – can't be measured in time.

**Ev:** How can time relate only to instincts? It takes time to learn something.

**Kathy:** How long does it take to learn to use a new power tool?

**Ev**: That depends on how handy a person is with tools. Some people just pick them up and use them right away. Others have to read the instructions.

**Kathy**: And then may get frustrated and wait for someone to show them how it's done. Which means that the time it takes to learn to use a power tool is related to the instinctive MO or talent of the individual. An Implementor insistent person would catch on without reading anything.

Every person has his or her own sense of time through his or her MO. That makes the use of time very personal, and anyone's intrusion into your taking the time you need is a direct cause of the limiting factors of fatigue, fear, and frustration. [Details: p. 227]

I recall when Dan, a guy from the East Coast, called me to ask for help. His voice sounded strained and flat. Even though I didn't know Dan well, I sensed that this was not his "normal" tone. If you've ever been the recipient of a cold call from a telemarketer or heard business associates make a request that you know they didn't want to make, you've experienced this inauthentic voice.

Dan talked about all the projects and programs he was involved in. He clearly was enthusiastic about some of his commitments, but he referred to other things as "tasks I can't get out of" or "jobs that if I don't do, no one will." In order to accomplish even half of the projects Dan described, he would need every ounce of instinctive power he possessed, no matter what his MO. He'd be forced to rely on either or both of the other parts of his mind (emotions and intellect), without being able to also trust his guts.

After describing all his commitments, Dan talked about an opportunity he was offered and wanted my advice. He said he was tremendously excited about the opportunity because it would offer him the chance to contribute to his community in a meaningful way and be involved in a project he was passionate about. Yet it was clear from his tone of voice that he was overwhelmed at the prospect of taking on one more thing. He talked about how he'd analyzed the time commitment the new project would require and that he was nervous about being able to fulfill this commitment. Finally, Dan said it probably wouldn't be fair to take on

"We have our own inner clock, and it ticks at a certain rate and you're going to get to certain places at a time different than everyone else."
Itzhak Perlman

"The persistence of the distinction between the three components of the mind and the tendency to favor the cognitive component over the other two is all the more surprising since there are countless examples in the literature that show the need of adopting an integrated, synthetic approach to mental functioning."
Klaus R. Scherer
University of Geneva

this new responsibility and that as much as he wanted to do it, it would be wiser to take a pass.

Dan had cornered himself into making a decision based strictly on his rationalizations and belief about what he should do. **Of course his voice sounded drained!** What would you say to him?

**Ev:** Wouldn't I have to know his MO?

**Kathy:** The first steps involve his learning how to trust his guts. That includes helping him assess whether he's overcommitted, and if so, what to do about it. His MO comes later.

Dan was used to being a highly committed person who acted on everything he believed was important – and he received much praise (and some cynicism) for being a "Do Gooder." But it was doing him little good, personally.

You can't improve your life by filling it so full that you drown out your own internal calls for help.

In our culture, we walk the line between living life to the fullest and overdoing it. We celebrate someone who appears to be successfully keeping all the plates spinning, yet once those plates come crashing down we tsk-tsk and whisper that perhaps the person was taking on more than he could handle. Perhaps he was so busy manipulating the plates that he couldn't hear his instincts warning that his timing was off.

**Ev:** But how did Dan get out of the responsibilities he had loaded on himself?

**Kathy:** He lowered his own and others' expectations of the time and energy he would devote to some activities. He had to **stop promising unrealistic achievement levels.**

He moved several commitments down to the attempt level of action, renegotiating his involvement in non-critical activities.

Overcommitment is a problem that occurs when you're doing many things that matter a great deal to you. It's sad to see people who care so

Dynamynd®: Kolbe Decision Ladder

**Individual**

**Commitment**

Dynamynd®: Kolbe Decision Ladder

**Individual**

**Attempt**

much, and who've proven to be outstanding performers, have trouble staying at the top or become unable to repeat their best efforts.

**Ev:** What made Dan call? How did he know this was happening to him?

**Kathy:** Dan knew he had become indecisive, but didn't know why.

**An important indicator of conative stress is taking much longer to accomplish goals than would be typical, or becoming indecisive and not as persuasive as usual. You just don't seem to have the mental stamina to carry out actions about which you have strong feelings.**

Causes of conative stress:
- false self-expectations
- impossible requirements from others
- conflicting MOs of interdependent people

**Conative stress results when there's interference with the natural flow of your instinctive power. It's triggered by:**

- **the strain of working against your grain**

- **the tension of efforts to fulfill another's requirement that you operate contrary to your MO**

- **the natural conflict of working with someone whose instincts go counter to yours**

[Details: p. 227]

One way to get back on track when you suffer from any of these forms of stress is to take the things you've committed to and lower the intensity of your involvement. Make them something you will attempt to do.

Strain is self-induced conative stress caused by trying to act outside your natural talents.

You'd need to review such "attempts" periodically – making sure that the projects or tasks you truly want to accomplish (or are required to do) are reinstated to the commitment level as soon as possible.

Unchecked strain can lead to burnout. Kolbe indexes indicate where you have gaps between your reality and self-expectations.

The problem with piling up attempts – or even making them mere intentions – is that they can become a dumping ground or black hole where you hide from responsibility. You need to set priorities within this lowest category, so when you do have some extra energy you can elevate them.

**Ev:** What if I really, really *want* to do something and it requires operating against my grain? It's not a requirement. It's a desire.

**Kathy:** Desire has been confused with conative action. Desire is an *affective* want or strong preference. You can want something to happen all day long. It will only happen if you get *conative* about it – and make a commitment to action that achieves the desire.

**Definition of Conation:**
One of the three modes, together with cognition and affection, of mental function; a conscious effort to carry out seemingly volitional acts.

One of the few dictionaries that even includes the word conation makes this mistake, which I think stems from a bad translation from a hundred years ago. [Details: p. 229]

**Ev:** You make it sound as if desire is one of the main reasons people become overcommitted. I think it has a lot to do with the greater responsibilities people have today. Those aren't choices.

**Kathy:** We can decide on the level of energy we'll give to various responsibilities. Single parents who work have to manage an amazing number of responsibilities, as do parents of handicapped or specially-challenged kids.

These people recognize "the look" when someone isn't sympathetic to their saying they'll *try* to participate in an *extra-conative* activity, but their instincts tell them to ignore those people and not to make any promises. When others go into the song-and-dance about a need for "balance" in life, the wise working parent listens to his or her guts instead.

Life can "balance" over the long haul, but short-term most people don't have the luxury of doing everything they know would be good for them to do.

When the need to Commit to Very Little stems from having no spare ergs to allocate, acting responsibly to fulfill a long-term commitment to a child you brought into the world trumps any other commitment, at least in my value system. People in this situation need our support when they say their guts tell them to stay home. They don't need pressure to make them show up at the club's annual meeting or drive hundreds of miles to the family reunion.

**Ev:** I understand the responsibility of the single parent. But don't some other people become too single-purposed or narrowly-focused?

**Kathy**: Yes. No instinct I know of would ever lead a kid to think that her life would be over if she didn't make the cheerleading squad or get into Harvard.

Those are emotional values, not innate needs. It's often when we don't get that one thing we think is so important that we finally turn to our instincts for help.

**Ev**: Isn't that call for help more a prayerful desire for guidance from a higher power?

**Kathy:** Trusting your instincts does take faith – and a belief that you've been endowed with a gift that will never let you down. People in despair need faith in their instincts to move on more than they need a lesson in logic or a motivational pep talk (which is usually what they get).

We've made role models out of people who've committed to very little and made a very large impact – without becoming too narrowly focused. Think about:

> Mother Teresa
> Martin Luther King, Jr.
> Lewis and Clark
> Henry Ford
> Madame Curie

All of them must have trusted their guts, committed a significant amount of their instinctive power to their primary missions, and avoided being distracted from their causes.

When you have many things that you're passionate about, you have trouble converting everything you want to do into viable action. If you have more passion than energy to act on your desires, it may lead to feelings of guilt and regret, rather than to positive results. It's like the person who talks a lot about wanting to read for the blind, but goes home after work each evening and collapses, feeling brain dead. He can't make the time to help others until he has fewer commitments.

"Lord, grant that I might always aspire to more than I can accomplish."
Michelangelo

99

Ev: Many people I know would never need this rule. **Most people I work with don't seem to commit to much of anything in the first place.**

Kathy: You might be surprised if you knew the full picture of each person. It can be pretty annoying when a coworker doesn't commit to a team effort – and causes others on the team to suffer. One person on the team who isn't putting forth any mental energy can cause big problems. You can tell when people aren't committing their best efforts. It makes them seem to lack the courage of their convictions.

Dynamynd®: **Kolbe Decision Ladder**

**Team**

**Courage**

"A problem is a chance for you to do your best."
Duke Ellington

What you may not know is that the person may be going through marital problems, has an elderly parent who's disoriented and calls for help in the middle of the night, or is struggling financially – to the point of fearing that her car is going to be repossessed. She's stretched to the max and comes to work to mentally hide out. She, too, is suffering from all the *Failure Factors* – but not from work-related commitments.

Ev: Well, it won't help her much if she loses her job.

Kathy: Which is why she needs to commit to very little right now and get her instincts involved in solving her personal dilemmas, so she can get back to being productive at work. How can you help her?

**Ev:** I'd suggest taking some time off to sort out her personal problems.

**Kathy:** Do you think she can afford time off?

**Ev:** If this were happening to me, I'd figure I couldn't afford not to take the time off. I'd quit worrying about everything and get down to doing what has to be done, like getting my parent into some kind of care facility, repairing the situation with my spouse or getting out of the marriage, or talking with my lender about refinancing my car. I'd plead for patience at work so I could do these things, then I'd prove that I could come back full-steam-ahead.

**Kathy:** You've just done an excellent job of describing what it takes to Commit – but to Very Little. It's often a matter of making serial commitments – devoting your energy to a series of commitments and ticking off the objectives one-by-one.

**Ev:** I can see how that could work for many people. But I'm a multi-tasker. I'm at my best when I have a lot on my plate. So I don't think I could just let work wait until my personal life was put back into some semblance of order – even though I know it could work for some people.

**Kathy:** That fits with your MO. Your natural inclination is to *adapt* and have many projects going at one time. That doesn't mean they all have to be at the commitment level on the Dynamynd. In the start-up stage, maybe, but you're likely to lose interest and delegate project maintenance to others.

**Kolbe Impact Factors**

| Fact Finder | Follow Thru | Quick Start | Implementor |
|---|---|---|---|
| Simplify | Adapt | Stabilize | Imagine |
| Refine | Rearrange | Revise | Renovate |
| Justify | Organize | Improvise | Construct |

**Adapt**

Some of your projects may hover as intentions for quite a while. Even if you intellectually evaluate their importance and have an emotional conviction that they should be put into action, nothing happens until you take control of your instinctive power and make them commitments. You have to allocate a greater amount of your limited instinctive power – thus making a commitment.

This is the point when people bail out of many projects, at least mentally. Therein lies the problem with many teams. **When team members don't work at a commitment level, the team doesn't get the benefit of their innate abilities.**

Even if a team member is convinced of the importance of the project, not having the mental energy available or not targeting it on team goals can bring the whole project down to the lower levels.

**Ev:** I can't stand working with people who don't give a damn. I'd rather work alone than wait for them to show up mentally.

Does that mean that I should trust my guts and get off a project team that has people like that on board?

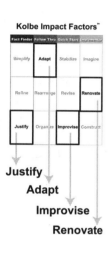

**Justify**
**Adapt**
**Improvise**
**Renovate**

**Kathy:** Be careful with the phrase "people like that." We all refuse to make commitments to things others wish we would. I'm not suggesting that you leave people or projects stranded. You may have to pass your responsibility on to others or call a halt to a project, especially one where few people are committed.

You ought not do anything that doesn't allow you to use your natural talents. That causes you to lower your self-expectations and others to lose respect for your abilities.

**Ev:** Sometimes, though, you have to juggle a lot of balls.

**Kathy:** Here's a technique that illustrates how to manage multiple projects using your talents to govern the levels. Create a Commitment Game with deadlines.

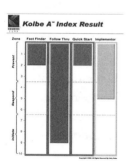

You could slant the first activity so that the participant who organizes would win. Requiring players to sort out a lot of stuff by categories and draw charts showing the relative quantity in each category. Give scores based upon completeness and neatness of the charts.

Insistent Follow Thrus will finish while those without this knack will be struggling to redraw neater lines.

**Ev:** I wouldn't play that type of game.

**Kathy:** You could go through the paces, just to be a good sport, but it would be foolish of you to commit much energy to this part of the game because you'd lose anyway.

It's interesting to watch the reality TV games where people tend to waste lots of energy on contests they're unlikely to win. If they conserved their instinctive power for the types of challenges that give them their best shot, they'd be far better off.

For you, as a person who naturally researches, there's a better chance of winning a game that requires using library or online references to find obscure information. Your time is better spent when the scoring is based upon accuracy and detail. Since you also *improvise*, you'd have the winning combination if the game also requires giving original or unique answers.

**Ev:** Couldn't I also be set up for failure?

**Kathy:** Yes. Especially if you take the bait, and make a commitment to every challenge put in front of you. The best way to assure that you win the grand prize is to work on a team that covers all the forms of instinctive power – all of the Impact Factors.

Since each of us covers only four of the 12 ways of impacting results, we need to barter our talents, cover for each other, and know when to pass the baton.

Sometimes you have little choice. Schools, jobs, and life circumstances often require us to work individually, against our grain. The best way for you to dodge those bullets is to commit to actions that give you the highest probability of success – and let go of the rest.

**Ev:** Now it's sounding simplistic. I have to do the work that's assigned to me.

**Kathy:** The theory *is* pretty simple. Acting on it is not. It requires "unlearning" a lot of the ways you've been taught to do things – so that you truly are free to be yourself.

Commitments take so much less time and effort to carry out when you do them according to your natural strengths that it makes no sense to ignore them. Yet we've all been taught to do things the way that worked best for a parent, or is some self-help guru's idea of a quick fix.

"There are three things that are extremely hard: steel, a diamond, and to know one's self."
Benjamin Franklin

If you Commit – but to Very Little, and accomplish those commitments through your natural, instinctive strengths, you will be able to move on to other commitments – and actually be more productive. You'll get more done, not less.

I'm not suggesting that you become a quitter every time a task doesn't fit your MO. I'm suggesting that you figure out how to do it with your greatest instinctive impact, and know when to make it a more intellectual exercise.

Ev: You're giving new meaning to the term "work smart."

Kathy: And I'm adding to my own definition of success. Success is the freedom to act on your instinctive power, so you can achieve your goals without suffering from the *Failure Factors* of fatigue, fear, and frustration.

If you commit to doing the Think-ercises, Ev, you'll begin learning to trust your guts. You'll make more effective decisions – without using so much energy.

Ev: Promise?

Kathy: Promise.

Kathy Kolbe's definition of success:

Success is the freedom to act on your instinctive power.

# CHAPTER SEVEN

# HOW TO COMMIT – BUT TO VERY LITTLE

**Ev**: It's a good feeling to be reminded that I make the choices in my life. I have an almost desperate need to find ways to sort through all the demands on my time and energy and choose the most important ones. I'd like to think that you really can help me do that.

**Kathy**: I'm not saying that it's easy, but, yes, people have been able to make that happen. I should add, though, that if you don't start trusting your guts to help you get your commitments under control, the consequences can be catastrophic. Not only will it cause serious problems in relationships because people will consider you undependable – even irresponsible – but being out of control in this arena can cost you your job and even your health.

**Ev**: OK, but start with the easy part. I'm feeling overwhelmed by the very thought of tackling this rule.

**Kathy:** The first step is to sort out what you really want or need to commit to over the next month. Consider a commitment a task which you guarantee you'll complete within that time frame. Remember, you haven't made a commitment unless you have set a time frame in which the task will be accomplished.

**Ev:** Is the task something that takes a lot of time, or is it a very little thing I'm responsible for doing?

**Kathy:** Start out by considering a commitment to be a task with a measurable goal that will take at least four hours over the course of the month. For instance, planning a party could take that long, even though you may not devote all that time in one sitting.

**Ev:** What about promising to straighten up the family room? I create such a mess it would take me either a few minutes every couple of days or a major cleanup once in a while.

**Kathy:** That could count.

**Ev:** What if I have no idea how long something will take? Reducing our insurance costs could take every waking hour, or I might find an amazing deal pretty quickly.

**Kathy:** I'm not going to ask you to predetermine a specific amount of time each commitment will take. This is one of the areas in which you'll need to trust your guts. If your instincts tell you a task will be very simple and not take much time, you may choose not to list it. If you sense a commitment is going to take a tremendous amount of time and energy, make a mental note of that.

## THINK-ERCISE #10

# Commitment Contract

1. Draw a triangle. Separate it into thirds with two horizontal lines. In the upper third, write every commitment you have for the coming month, either at home or at work.

2. In the middle third, write everything that you'll attempt to accomplish in the coming month, if you can find the time.

3. In the bottom third, list your intentions, the things you hope to do and might do, if you happen to get a chance, during the month.

4. Cross out any commitment that would require you to work against your instinctive grain, or that causes you fear, fatigue, or frustration.

Example Triangle:

**Commitment Triangle**
- **Commitment** (the top of your triangle) is the highest level of effort, causing you to focus energy on assigned tasks.
- **Attempt** (in the middle) is the second level, where you try to accomplish a goal, but don't use your full mental energy.
- **Intention** (at the bottom) is the third level, which implies no current allocation of effort.

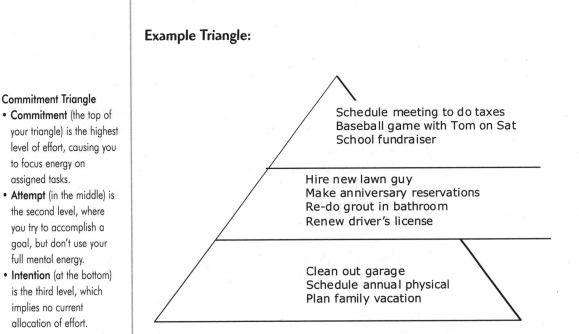

Schedule meeting to do taxes
Baseball game with Tom on Sat
School fundraiser

Hire new lawn guy
Make anniversary reservations
Re-do grout in bathroom
Renew driver's license

Clean out garage
Schedule annual physical
Plan family vacation

According to a Gallup Poll, 6 in 10 American workers would continue to work even if they won $10 million. Though only 35% overall would stay at the same job.

**Ev:** How can I just cross out something that has to be done?

**Kathy:** That's what you do every day of your life. If you don't have the "right stuff" to fulfill a commitment, you either procrastinate about doing it – and never get it done – or you do it half-heartedly – and never get it done well. Making it a commitment makes it a noose around your neck, something you dread doing and are sorry later that you ever promised you would do.

**Ev:** What do you suggest that I do about it if it truly *has* to be done?

**Kathy:** Get someone else to do it. This may involve bartering your talents to do a task for them in return. Or it could involve hiring someone to do it.

**Ev:** What if there's a task that has to get done and I think I'm the only one capable of doing it, or at least doing it well?

**Kathy:** You'll be surprised how often you think your experience matters more than your MO. Give people with the right talent a chance to gain the experience of doing the things you've hung on to, and you may be surprised. They'll probably do it better than you ever did.

If training is essential, give them the training – but not in doing it your way. You might show them how the government regulations require that it be done. Or maybe you can share your history of what *not* to do.

**Ev:** So I could hire a person to cut the grass, but explain how to mow around the neighbor's odd fence. I like the idea of agreeing to fix the meals if my spouse promises to do the dishes. I guess I could even suggest that I'd write the proposals for some of the other people in the department if they'd develop a system for tracking the long-term results.

**Kathy:** That's exactly how to make it work.

Check to see if you have to add things to your triangle. Now circle the commitments you've listed that you know you won't be able to accomplish during the month.

Reasons for your doubts could include:

· others not accomplishing tasks that influence your effort

· lack of proper supplies or time

· weather or forces of nature issues

While many of these factors are out of your control, you do have the ability to circle the commitment that they influence and move it into the Attempt category.

If your Attempt category is now overflowing, and you cannot realistically expect yourself to accomplish everything in it, then circle and move specific tasks into the Intention section.

Ev: Couldn't this become a form of escape?

Kathy: A *Conative Cop-Out* is something you don't commit to doing (or apologize for not doing) because of your MO, when, in fact, you could have found an alternative method for accomplishing it. Beware of moving anything out of your commitment category without trying to do it through all four of your Impact Factors. It's too easy to just look at how you initiate action, when you have a much fuller range of capabilities.

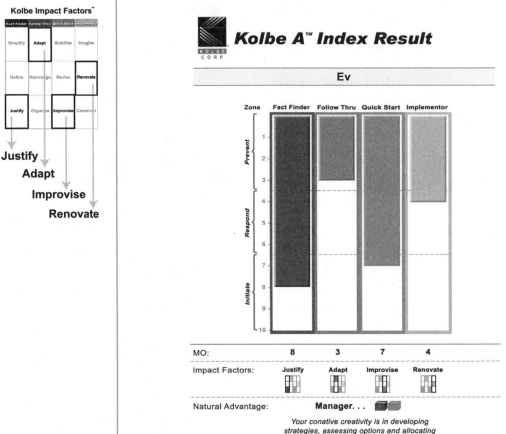

**Kolbe Impact Factors™**

| Fact Finder | Follow Thru | Quick Start | Implementor |
|---|---|---|---|
| Simplify | **Adapt** | Stabilize | Imagine |
| Refine | Rearrange | Revise | **Renovate** |
| **Justify** | Organize | **Improvise** | Construct |

Justify
Adapt
Improvise
Renovate

**Kolbe A™ Index Result**

Ev

| Zone | Fact Finder | Follow Thru | Quick Start | Implementor |
|---|---|---|---|---|
| MO: | 8 | 3 | 7 | 4 |
| Impact Factors: | Justify | Adapt | Improvise | Renovate |
| Natural Advantage: | Manager . . . | | | |

*Your conative creativity is in developing strategies, assessing options and allocating resources.*

**Ev**: I'm so glad you brought that up, because that's exactly what I was starting to do in my head. I was overlooking my preventative talents in Follow Thru as a help in fixing the meals, for instance. I'm great at multi-tasking and can be watching the news, helping the kids with their homework, and throwing a meal together all at the same time. I truly don't know how people can live up to many commitments if they don't *adapt*.

**Kathy**: Remember to think in terms of your four Impact Factors, not just your Fact Finder mode of initiation.

**Ev**: But wouldn't I have to move any Attempts that couldn't be done through my Impact Factors off my Commitment triangle?

**Kathy:** You can do that now or as they move up to the Commitment section. Just beware of your inclination to *improvise* in the Quick Start mode, and focus that energy on changing the categories in which you place the task – not on skipping any of the essential steps.

**Ev:** It's fun to see how using my talent affects the way I do a Think-ercise.

**Kathy:** My goal is to get you to put this part of the Commitment Contract into practice on a regular basis. If your instincts are to add additional layers to it, I've certainly created them for you.

**Ev:** When you say "regular basis," do you mean that I should do this weekly or monthly?

**Kathy:** For people who *organize*, this kind of system would work well. For you, being able to *adapt* it to your needs involves keeping the time frame open-ended. Regular for you could result in doing it every time you start to feel overwhelmed, or whenever you get a bunch of new projects on your plate, or at times when your instincts are telling you that things are getting out of your control.

Remember, this is a tool for tapping into your instincts, so you need to make it work within the scope of your Impact Factors – your strengths. [Details: p. 229]

**Ev:** So when I do the things I do best, I actually pay attention to what my guts are telling me.

**Kathy:** And if you do during any commotion on this flight, I'll feel especially safe sitting next to you.

The first thing I want to emphasize about the following activities is that they're absolutely *not* to be taken lightly. The purpose behind this part of the *Powered by Instinct* program is so critical to your well-being – to reducing your *Failure Factors* – that you dare not duck any part of it.

**Ev:** I have to do *all* of it? Isn't that contrary to what you just said?

**Kathy:** You don't have to do anything. You risk a great deal, however,

"If there is anything that a man can do well, I say let him do it. Give him a chance."

Abraham Lincoln

by not confirming what matters most in your life – what you're most willing to devote your resources to accomplishing. You're either willing to act with a sense of purpose or you're not. If you play around with the prescriptions for committing to very little, you'll be sending a message to yourself that you haven't made a decision to trust your guts.

**Ev:** Okay, I understand, but what if there are parts of this or other Think-ercises that I can't *justify* doing? Can I skip a step here and still follow the rule?

**Kathy:** I believe it's important to do all the steps, but it's possible to follow the rule if you commit only to the parts of a Think-ercise that you can *justify*.

I hope you're not just playing an intellectual game with me... (In which case you just won some points!). I concede that you'd be following the rule if you decided to commit only to those parts of the how-to's that meet your needs.

**Ev:** I'd love it if my kids could negotiate that point with their teachers. I'm tired of helping them with inconsequential homework.

**Kathy:** You're assuming you – and/or they – know what's good for them. That's one of the conundrums of deciding for yourself what you will and won't commit to. Sometimes we have to rely on others to advise and counsel, because we can be blind to our own opportunities and needs. Maybe the teacher has a better perspective on what homework kids that age need to do.

**Ev:** Ah, the complexities do keep growing with this rule, don't they?

**Kolbe Impact Factors™**

| Fact Finder | Follow Thru | Quick Start | Implementor |
|---|---|---|---|
| Simplify | Adapt | Stabilize | Imagine |
| Refine | Rearrange | Revise | Renovate |
| Justify | Organize | Improvise | Construct |

**Justify**

## THINK-ERCISE #11

# Calendarize!

1. Identify the percent of each day that you think you're now spending on actions related to the following list. If any are irrelevant, give them 0%. Add any missing categories, but don't use a catch-all category, such as "other."

2. Assign each of the following categories a specific amount of time you'll devote to it next week. Be sure not to allocate more hours than there are in a week.

3. Rank the categories in order of their priority in your life. Think in terms of how much time you wish you could commit to them.

4. Rank the categories in terms of the actual time they took last week.

5. Rank the categories in terms of the energy they are taking. Adjust the energy, based on your converting some of them to habit.

| Activities | Priority | Time | Energy | % wkly now | % wkly future |
|---|---|---|---|---|---|
| Job or job-search | | | | | |
| Job-related travel | | | | | |
| Significant other | | | | | |
| Immediate family | | | | | |
| Extended family | | | | | |
| Social life | | | | | |
| Travel (out-of-town, non-work) | | | | | |
| Local travel (errands, to job) | | | | | |
| Recreation (in-town) | | | | | |
| Learning (formal or informal) | | | | | |
| Personal care/grooming | | | | | |
| Health | | | | | |
| Meals (preparation/shopping) | | | | | |
| Home (maintenance/cleaning/repairs) | | | | | |
| Auto (maintenance and repairs) | | | | | |
| Personal finances | | | | | |
| Shopping (non-food) | | | | | |
| Religion/faith | | | | | |
| Community | | | | | |
| Philanthropy/charity | | | | | |
| Contemplation | | | | | |
| Sleep | | | | | |
| Doing Nothing | | | | | |

**Ev:** If I had trouble coming up with an estimate for how much time I spend on something like contemplation, what's the best way for me to give you an estimate? Should I keep a diary for a week to figure it out? Or do you have any tips for making a good guess?

**Kathy:** With your Quick Start, you should have no trouble estimating, and your Fact Finder will base that upon past experience. If I told you to keep a diary for a week, your resistance to Follow Thru would prevent you from doing it. That's why I don't give many specific instructions within Think-ercises on HOW to approach a task. I purposefully give you open-ended opportunities to accomplish the goals in the ways that work best for you.

**Ev:** This seems an awful lot like lists I've made in getting-to-know-myself courses.

**Kathy:** That may well be. You'll find the way you'll use it now could challenge your assumptions. Remember, as a person who multitasks, you only have to account for the time you have to focus separately on the task.

**Ev:** So what happens to the time I'm doing three things – is it free time?

**Kathy:** Hardly, one thing will always have your primary focus and the others will be in the background. Just ask your spouse! **People know when you're not giving them your focused attention.**

**Ev:** So I'll be sure to convey that I'm giving my "focused attention," if not my "full attention"...

**Kathy:** My husband has an MO that is probably similar to your spouse's, and I know that when we're in a restaurant, he's always taking in the conversations of the people around us. Sometimes it's fun for me to find out what he's picked up, to see if it matches what I *improvise* from their body language. Then I *rearrange* it into "What if..." scenarios. We actually do this kind of thing intermittently, while engaged in other conversations that have our focused attention.

**Ev:** So you'd list a dinner out with your husband in the Significant Other category?

**Kolbe Impact Factors™**

| Fact Finder | Follow Thru | Quick Start | Implementor |
|---|---|---|---|
| Simplify | Adapt | Stabilize | Imagine |
| Refine | Rearrange | Revise | Renovate |
| Justify | Organize | **Improvise** | Construct |

**Improvise**

**Kathy:** Unless I was focused on the "fashion show" the whole time!

**Ev:** As I go through this, I assume what you're getting at is that **the time I spend on something doesn't equate directly with the energy it takes.**

**Kathy:** That's part of it.

**Ev:** I found some of my percentages – the time I thought categories were taking – were pretty far off from the actual time I had available to slot for them next week.

**Kathy:** Does that reflect a difference in the energy you seemed to be devoting vs. the actual time you have to give to a category?

**Ev:** Maybe. I think it also has something to do with wishful thinking. Perhaps I'd hoped I'd spent more time with my family than I actually have time to spend with them.

6. **Identify five commitments you hope to fulfill next week and the time you hope to allocate to them. Identify the categories they fall into from your list.**

_____

_____

_____

_____

7. **Allocate all your waking hours for next week by the time you plan to spend in each of the categories.**

8. Keep a detailed calendar for the week of how you *actually* spend your time, and compare your plan with the reality of your week. Ask yourself:

· Did any of your top commitments get slighted?

· What took up considerably more time than you had planned?

· Did anything take less time than you scheduled?

· Were you able to give more time to your top commitments? Why?

· Did the amount of time you gave your commitments impact the amount of energy you put into them?

Be sure you figure out why your answer is true for your situation. HINT: More time does not necessarily equate to more energy.

**Ev:** If I do all this, the time I'd need to devote to it is going to cause me greater stress. I see the value in thinking about what would probably happen, but do I have to go through the process of writing down all the numbers?

**Kathy:** Do it in a way that works for you, but please realize that your answers will be superficial if you don't experience the process. I doubt there'll be much of an "Aha!" if you just read the exercise and *imagine* what would happen. It's like falling in love: you can memorize poems about it, but until you've experienced it, those poems have little meaning for you.

Now you're ready for some next steps to take control of your commitments.

9. Compare your answers for the recent week with your primary commitments over the last year.

   · Did you have more or less of them in the last week?

   · Are your most recent commitments more or less important to you, long-term?

   · How effective have you been in accomplishing the goals you committed to over the last year?

10. Think in terms of your long-range objectives. Limit yourself to three primary commitments. What system or tool could you devise that would help you stay focused on them and reduce other commitments to assure greater success in accomplishing the goals you associate with them?

> **Kathy:** I know that's a lot to think about, but it really is important. Here's the last of the Commit – but to Very Little Think-ercises.

## THINK-ERCISE #12

# Productivity Props

1. Pick the most productive time in your life and consider the commitments you were making.

· Were there a great many or just a few?

_____

_____

· Were they tied to specific goals?

_____

_____

· Were you as fatigued as you are now?

_____

_____

· Were you trusting your instincts as much as, more than, or less than you are now?

_____

_____

2. Select four props, items that represent your ability to take control over your commitments during that highly productive period.

3. Place those Productivity Props where you will see them every day, and use them as reminders of how well you can take charge of your own instinctive energy.

4. Add to your collection of Productivity Props as you enjoy future successes. Collections can be wonderful ways of reminding yourself of your strengths. If you showcase them well, they can also be terrific talking points for your strengths. Think of the fun you can have explaining their meaning to others!

**Ev:** So it's a sneaky way of getting people to recognize you for the four Impact Factors you contribute.

**Kathy:** It's up to you how you present it. Some people use props that are almost caricatures of themselves, such as clown collections for people who *improvise* and *construct*, collections of measuring devices for people who *justify*, and miniature rooms with fully coordinated trimmings for people who *organize* and *construct*.

It'll be fun to see what you pick.

**Ev:** Does it have to be a collection? Could be it just a few different things?

**Kathy:** As I said: It's up to you.

# CHAPTER EIGHT

# RULE #4

# BE OBSTINATE – IN OVERCOMING OBSTACLES

## Stick with your instincts.

**Peter Mark Roget**
**1779-1869**

English physician and lexicographer who first presented his Thesaurus of English Words and Phrases in 1852.

His overlooked genius was the classification of the English language into six categories, with three that dealt with the mind: Intellect, Volition (which listed conation as one of the three dominant words), and Affections.

In the late 1800s he was far ahead of our modern academic community in recognizing the essence of human nature.

**Kathy:** This is my favorite rule. It's what I've had to do to succeed in my own life. I've also found that it's the rule that most impacts the lives of people who act upon it for the first time. It helps people make quantum leaps in their productivity and sense of well-being. If you're not now acting with the gumption it takes to Be Obstinate, you have a treat in store for you.

**Being Obstinate, according to one of my personal heroes, Peter Mark Roget, is akin to:**

- **Tenacity**
- **Perseverance**
- **Dogged resolution**
- **Having a ruling passion**
- **Being willful**
- **Acting with determination**

[Details: p. 231]

*If you don't overcome the obstacles that keep you from having the freedom to act on instinct, you will never live up to your potential.*

**Ev:** My father would accuse me of being "a brat" if I acted obstinately.

**Kathy:** Funny how the term conjures up messages from our youth. When my mother got disgusted with my finagling for ways to do things my own way, I was sorry I distressed her. But I was determined not to cave in to what I considered the nonsense of making hospital corners on the sheets when I changed my bed linens. I knew I would kick them loose as soon as I crawled inside.

The battle of our wits usually ended with her saying: "Kathy, stop being so obstinate!" And my replying: "Mom, do you really want me to just go along with how other people do things?"

She just rolled her eyes – as if to say, "There she goes again." She was one of my biggest role models for being obstinate despite her protestations.

Both of my parents survived and excelled by being obstinate. I think they also knew that I would have to Be Obstinate or be treated as if I were handicapped, because of my being dyslexic.

**Ev:** In what way did your parents have to Be Obstinate?

**Kathy:** My mother was a homeless orphan. She was taken in by an elderly woman who hid her from the authorities so she wouldn't be taken away to an orphanage. As a result, she missed several months of school at a time throughout her grade school years. Much of what she learned during that time was self-taught. There were never any excuses, as far as she was concerned, for not learning everything the school offered – and then some.

My dad's successes came through highly creative problem solving during the Depression and war years. Later, despite his work ethic, he never let any of the pressures of running a business rob him of time with his wife and four kids. He eschewed foolish effort. He never let me forget that I was solely responsible for figuring out how to do things my own way, and that every decision had consequences – for myself and for others. He made it clear that I'd better be able to stand behind my choices. He'd make me stand up for what I believed in – even if it was why I should get out of eating canned peas (an argument I rarely won). [Details: p. 232]

My parents knew I had a quirky way of learning (fortunately, I never heard the word "dyslexic" as a child). They told me that I had a problem I would have to solve. It wasn't their problem or the school's problem. It was made perfectly clear that I'd have to figure out a solution because the learning had to happen. Then they hugged me and told me they knew I could do it.

That was one of the greatest gifts my parents gave me. **I believe that I learned the process of creative problem solving because I had to, and because of their trust in my instinctive abilities to do so.** They helped me turn my so-called learning disability into one of the greatest advantages of my life. It's not unlike my using the term, *The A.D.D. Advantage*, to describe the Quick Start/Implementor talents of so many people who get a negative label (double dis-es) assigned to their positive talents. [Details: p. 233]

**I figured out very early that I had to Be Obstinate – not apologetic about doing things differently.** I refused to watch people tie their shoe laces, because their way didn't work for me. I just looked at the bottom line. I had to tie a knot that kept the laces from coming loose, but one that I could untie quickly myself. Did it really matter whether it looked like the way my big sister tied her shoe?

**Ev:** So you were a kid that had spunk. Wasn't that more a matter of your being an extrovert?

**Kathy:** Your personality type has nothing to do with either your MO or your level of tenacity. I innovate and have a knack for expressing myself through the spoken word. But I was an extremely shy kid, and am an introvert – most of the time – as an adult. That means that my energy is drained by social situations, and replenished when I get time to myself.

**Ev:** I assume that you do lots of speaking, and you obviously enjoy personally coaching lots of different kinds of leaders. I would think that you thrive by working with people.

**Kathy:** That's true, but that doesn't make me an extrovert. You can love people, be any MO, and still need time away from others to develop your ideas. I'm not conatively fatigued being around people. This issue is affective. I feel uncomfortable in most cocktail party environments.

**Ev:** Give me a positive example of someone Being Obstinate, when personality was not the issue.

**Kathy:** Dr. Kalpana Chawla, who died aboard the space shuttle Columbia in January 2003, is a great example. She was born in a north Indian city in the 1960s. The birth of a girl brought sadness there, because they were presumed to have little merit. Her brother, Sanjay, told the New York Times that she was determined, and acted as if to say, "I'm going to tell these guys I'm not just another girl."

She became only the second Indian-born astronaut and the first woman from India to go into space. Yet she had often been told no, and was discouraged by others when she sought opportunities to use her innate abilities. She was too obstinate to be held back. The New York Times said her story is "of a girl who refused to be dissuaded, and who in her clarity of purpose did her part to reshape India's complicated gender calculus."

A former teacher described her as saying, "I have to do this thing, and I'll do it." **In her unwillingness to be constrained by the traditional paths open to women, she is a role model for being obstinate.**

I always loved Katharine Hepburn roles because it seemed she invariably played women who were obstinate – in the positive sense of overcoming obstacles. In African Queen, she had moments when it looked as if she might succumb, but it never happened. Her personality mellowed, but her self-determination, her iron will, stayed intact.

## Other role models for being obstinate include:

Galileo
Christopher Columbus
Joan of Arc
Golda Meir
Nelson Mandela
Lech Walesa
Helen Keller
Winston Churchill
Snoopy from the Peanuts comics

I don't see strong similarities in their personalities, and I certainly don't think they all would have had the same four Impact Factors as their instinctive strengths. You can be equally obstinate with any MO. Although my hunch is that people with certain MOs have to be more obstinate in some situations. Think of a preventative Implementor fighting to save the farm, or an insistent Quick Start housewife fighting for women's suffrage.

Ev: Sometimes being obstinate is just plain stupid. A teenager who won't listen to good advice, a coworker who's too stubborn to try a new approach – they could use your rule as an excuse.

Kathy: Being obstinate in overcoming obstacles is quite different from being ignorant or uncooperative. That's the negative spin on the word.

Obstinately acting on instinct – even when people tell you you're nuts, will help you thrive.

Obstinately clinging to an incorrect fact or arguing for the sake of arguing serves no good purpose. It wastes conative energy.

Ev: Being obstinate implies that you're a nonconformist and belligerent.

Kathy: Conforming to others' methods of operation leads to mediocrity.

If all people were obstinate in following their own innate abilities we'd all benefit from the variety of creative energy that would emerge.

"Classification of ideas is the true basis on which words, which are their symbols, should be classified. It is by such analysis alone that...[we] can obtain a correct knowledge of the elements which enter into formation of compound ideas..."

Peter Roget, 1852

Why wouldn't we want to fulfill the dictionary description of obstinate, which is to "firmly adhere to a purpose, opinion or course of action?" Or live up to its secondary definition: "not easily being controlled or overcome?"

Belligerence is an unattractive behavior that doesn't lead to anything very constructive. Some dictionaries use that as a synonym for obstinate, but that's not how Mr. Roget or I use the term.

**Ev:** Of course I want to adhere to a purpose, and I don't want others to have control over me. I don't want to be at loggerheads with people all the time in order to do that. Why does it have to be so confrontational?

**Kathy:** Could it be because we live in a conformist society that has not made acting on individual differences the natural state of affairs?

We wouldn't have to be so obstinate in rejecting misplaced efforts to control or overcome individual freedom of action if there weren't so many limitations on our personal liberties.

Our country has a history of obstinacy in fighting for freedom of speech and freedom to pursue happiness – but our public policies and institutions, such as our schools, do not live up to that standard. How many kids get to freely express ideas on the tests that determine whether they get into our institutions of higher learning?

"Only once did I break loose and pour forth my pent up soul...I argued for my rights and was instantly guilty of the sin of disrespect and disobedience. I became silent but unconvinced and was condemned to the sin of obstinacy."

Hughes Mearns
Creative Power

We tell kids not to talk to Mr. Stranger Danger, but there is little encouragement, much less explanation, for them on how to Be Obstinate should anyone try to control or overcome them.

**Ev:** That's not how we've been taught to parent our children. "Encourage your child to be willful" is hardly the standard in parenting guides. If that's what kids have to learn to do in order to trust their guts, then I guess we better change the way we parent our kids.

I'm as guilty as the next person of encouraging my youngsters to get along by going along. I've wanted them to be viewed as nice kids. I've thought of being obstinate as being obnoxious. But now I see what you mean: being obstinate could actually keep them from harm in some cases. Would it have been a different story if an abducted child who didn't run from her captors had practiced being obstinate?

**Kathy:** In the hope that it would, I recommend that every parent role model Be Obstinate, as well as the companion rule: Self-Provoke. Showing kids how to trust their instincts is perhaps the greatest gift we can give them. It could mean a lot more to their safety and well-being than all the other lessons we work so hard to impart to them.

It takes *having a ruling passion* to live under house arrest as Galileo did. It takes a ruling passion to carry out any mission. It didn't gain him popularity among his contemporaries, but I would imagine that he was energized by his obstinacy.

People who act with *dogged resolution* overcome the *Failure Factors.* They're too *determined* to be ruled by fatigue, fear or frustration. They do something about it. They get conative!

**Ev:** Presumably, you don't have to carry it to extremes, like Joan of Arc, being so willful that you risk your life.

**Kathy:** Sometimes you do need to be extremely obstinate in order to take the actions your guts tell you to take. **The greater the danger, the more obstinate you have to be in dealing with it.**

Whether it's fighting a war or a fire or any horrendous force of nature, you have to be very resolute in order to survive. Anti-war activists demonstrate just as much determination. We can disagree on the issues cognitively and have varying affective attitudes about them, but we ought to value the guts it takes to adhere to a purpose or course of action.

You don't have to worry that an obstinate person will fall into the hands of a cult leader or become the puppet of a dictator. Obstinate people will not give up their freedom of expression, which is a conative process that authors and artists have sacrificed for throughout history.

**Ev:** Is that why we're drawn to shows like *Les Miserables*? It seems that was a Broadway musical about obstinate people.

---

**Being obstinate is acting with:**

- Tenacity
- Perseverance
- Dogged resolution
- A ruling passion
- Willfulness
- Determination

**Characteristics of Cults and Mind Control**

- The leaders demand absolute obedience and are the sole judges of each member's faith/commitment.

- Members put the goals of the cult ahead of personal concerns, family interests, and career goals.

- Cults utilize techniques designed to effect ego-destruction, thought reform, and dependence on the cult.

**Keep in Mind:**

Trust your instincts about a group. If you are uncomfortable at any stage, get out!

Excerpted from:
Cults on Campus
Office of Student Affairs
York University

A remarkable work by several measures, *Under the Eye of the Clock* is the autobiography of Christopher Nolan, struck at birth with brain damage and left paralyzed, spastic, and mute.

**Kathy**: Yes. And what about the photo of the Chinese freedom fighter standing in front of the tank during the Tiananmen Square uprising? What a powerful image!

We cheered that guy's obstinacy. Was he being logical? No. He was doing what his guts told him to do.

We all fight our own personal battles. Some people have to Be Obstinate in order to conquer disabilities and injuries. They have to take on challenges every day of their lives – or they'd be condemned (as some do to themselves) to inactive and nonproductive lives. One of the most inspiring memoirs of an obstinate person is *Under The Eye of the Clock: A Memoir*, by Christopher Nolan. Severely handicapped from birth, he found ways to express his inner strengths – becoming an award-winning writer despite having been labeled uneducable by educators.

**Here is another example of a wonderfully obstinate person. Randy Tufts,** as a young adventurer, naturalist, and college student, came upon a sinkhole in the southern Arizona hills that his instincts told him led to a cavern filled with the secret wonders of the inner earth. He waited to explore it until his best buddy was with him several years later. Both their imaginations went wild when they found it led to magnificent subter-ranean rooms filled with lustrous structures.

He immediately knew that what would become of one of his life's greatest discoveries had to be kept a secret – for a while.

That "while" became 14 years. That while became filled with mental agonies over how to protect one of the few living caves in the world from destruction by souvenir seekers, graffiti "artists," and the careless intrusion of the climatic elements from which nature had protected it.

Randy and his partner, Gary Tenen, became the stewards of a secret treasure and natural resource. Due to their wisdom, Kartchner Caverns (which they suggested be named for the land owner rather than themselves) has been protected and developed as a mystical environment in which my family and yours can observe the purity of nature. They also preserved its integrity for future scientific study. [Details: p. 234]

"I was born to explore. My
commitment is to be a good
steward of all that I find."
Randy Tufts

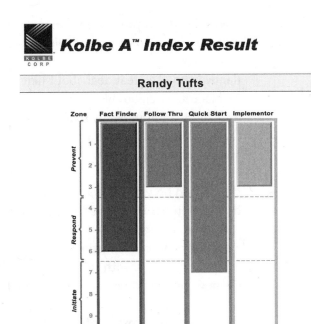

### Kolbe A™ Index Result

**Randy Tufts**

| MO: | 6 | 3 | 7 | 3 |
|---|---|---|---|---|

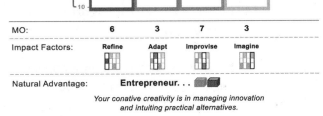

| Impact Factors: | Refine | Adapt | Improvise | Imagine |

Natural Advantage: **Entrepreneur. . .**

*Your conative creativity is in managing innovation
and intuiting practical alternatives.*

**Randy's tenacity and trust in his guts was as awe-inspiring** as the caverns themselves. He knew that he alone couldn't do what needed to be done to protect his discovery. From the start, he formed a dedicated partnership with Gary and slowly and carefully enlarged the circle of those they thought **had a ruling passion for the same goals** concerning the caves.

**Listening to his instincts every step of the way,** Randy once told me that there was a time he so feared the destruction of the cave that his gut reaction was to willfully plan elaborate subterfuges to throw everyone except Gary off the track. **He so firmly adhered to his purpose that he was prepared to never go back** to the incredibly beautiful underworld he'd sacrificed years to slowly unearth, rather than see it plundered for material profits.

During this time, Randy became a Ph.D. in planetary sciences and

**painstakingly worked toward astounding discoveries** concerning Jupiter's moon, Europa, on which he believed we may find life.

Randy learned a great deal about himself as he coped with the momentous decisions his discoveries had thrust upon him. He knew his MO and that, as perfectly suited as he was for some parts of the effort that lay ahead, his talents were just a part of the total needed to accomplish his lofty goals.

**He learned how to ask for what he needed from others. He learned that sometimes he needed to do nothing. And he learned that sometimes he needed to act on instinct – lest his highly intelligent mind overwhelm the instincts he came to understand and trust so profoundly. Then, with perseverance and an incredibly willful persua-siveness, he would convince others of his point of view.**

**Randy remained totally obstinate about his mission, and completely at peace with his most important decisions when he succumbed to a rare form of cancer.**

**Ev:** Is being obstinate truly a possibility for all of us? Isn't it easier for a single guy without family responsibilities? Or people who don't have to put financial obligations first?

**Kathy:** Here is an example of a human being who proved to me that there are no obstacles to being obstinate.

When I first met **Marcella Hunter**, she was a middle-aged Native American who had recently survived quadruple-bypass heart surgery. Minimally educated and physically handicapped from birth, she was a single parent with no job-related skills. Yet she was unwilling to turn to the welfare rolls for financial support. **She was fiercely, but quietly, determined** to be self-supporting – and to support if she must – three generations of her family.

Marcella showed up at my doorstep, eyes fixed on the ground, and said, "Help me do something to earn a living."

Obstinate is:
- firmly adhering to a purpose, opinion, or course of action

- not easily being controlled or overcome

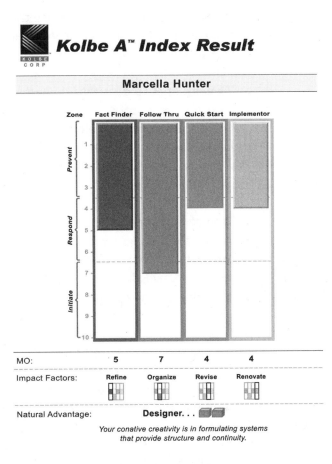

**Kolbe A™ Index Result**

**Marcella Hunter**

| Zone | Fact Finder | Follow Thru | Quick Start | Implementor |
|---|---|---|---|---|

| MO: | 5 | 7 | 4 | 4 |
|---|---|---|---|---|
| Impact Factors: | Refine | Organize | Revise | Renovate |

Natural Advantage: **Designer. . .**

*Your conative creativity is in formulating systems
that provide structure and continuity.*

For 15 years, **Marcella demonstrated on a daily basis what being obstinate is all about. With courage, commitment and conviction, she set a standard for performance** at Kolbe Corp that kept me hopeful and focused in the face of myriad obstacles. If Marcella could do it, so could I.

**No matter what the setback – there she would be, quietly giving all she had to give, purposefully using the talents bestowed upon her. Being as obstinate as she was gentle, Marcella didn't engage in gossip, put-downs, sarcasm, or second-guessing. She was who she was, and she expected the same self-determination from others.**

Marcella willfully employed her mental resources, dedicating them to her job while at work, and then to the three generations of children she raised single-handedly at home. When I asked her one year how Thanksgiving

Randy and Marcella

Vision
Mission
Compassion

dinner had turned out, she told me that she was only able to do all the cooking and clean up because she knew she would get to come back to work at Kolbe Corp.

"At work I get to do what I do best. At home I have to do it all."

**Randy and Marcella would have made a terrific team. They shared values, tenacity, wisdom – with differing, and perfectly wonderful, authentic talents. They're a part of the team which has helped me understand the simple truths concerning natural abilities.**

At his core, Randy was an entrepreneur. He was project oriented (with projects that had a very long life cycle). He was a deal maker who used facts, but didn't let them stand in his way. Highly capable of multi-tasking, he pursued myriad options simultaneously and switched gears the moment an artful dodge was required.

Randy was insistent on having the freedom to take risks – calculated risks. And just as resistant to getting bogged down by bureaucracies. He wasn't particularly handy with tools and was more imaginative than tangible with his environmental discoveries. He wasn't frustrated by not feeling free to touch the stalactites within the caverns for fear of germs that might kill the living cave.

Marcella, on the other hand, was a systems person. She had a plan and she stuck with it. She would accommodate change by carefully considering worst-case scenarios and making sure she was protecting herself, her family, and her job responsibilities from disruption.

One of the beauties of Marcella was that there was no method of operation that she would resist. Over the years she took on many tasks, moved to numerous locations within the office, and converted from manual typewriters to computers. I called her our "stripper" because she would affix glossy strips of laminated color on Kolbe index results before technology made it possible to electronically produce such personalized results.

I learned from Marcella what it was like to work with someone who instinctively accommodated to the needs around her while being totally obstinate in being herself.

"No thank you, Kathy. You know I won't do that," she would say very respectfully when I mistakenly thought a change of pace might be good for her. She was never controlled or overcome by anyone, including me.

**It takes resolve and strength of mind to take a stand for your freedom to act on your own will. Randy and Marcella exemplified those qualities.**

Dogged determination is required when the freedom to be yourself is at stake. It forces you to climb the Dynamynd. Obstinacy is a *commitment* of your conative energy. It's a *conviction* about something that matters to you.

**Ev: Obstinacy, as you describe it, would certainly take courage. But most people don't face huge obstacles such as disabilities. Surely most people don't have to go around being obstinate.**

**Kathy:** Everyone faces trials and tribulations. Sometimes only the individual knows his or her personal struggles. Without realizing it, we may be posing obstacles to a friend's use of free will, trying to get him to take a risk that goes against his grain, or making him accommodate our schedule when he needs more time to consider the options.

**Dynamynd\*: Kolbe Decision Ladder**

**Culture**

| Social Responsibility | 5 |
| Self Actualization | 4 |
| Self Control | 3 |
| Self Esteem | 2 |
| Self Awareness | 1 |

Affective　Conative　Cognitive

**Self Control**

**It takes great self-control at a minimum to stick with what your guts tell you to do in the face of criticism or opposition.** That Chinese man standing in front of the tank was exercising tremendous self-control.

When you see obstinate actions overcome obstacles, consider how you might praise those actions – in yourself as well as in others.

**Ev:** I wish there was another word for it, but I do hope that I'd encourage anyone to fight against any limitation on their freedom to trust their guts.

**Kathy:** It's easy to say that we would encourage people to fight for the freedom to be themselves, yet we become a part of the obstacle when we reward people for foolish efforts they make that force them to betray their own instincts.

"Never give in — never, never, never, never, in nothing great or small, large or petty, never give in except to convictions of honour and good sense. Never yield to force; never yield to the apparently overwhelming might of the enemy."

Sir Winston Churchill,
Harrow School
1941

"I cannot be what I'm not."
John Lennon

**We promote do-as-I-say-not-do-as-you-would-instinctively-do actions in the workplace, with ratings for potential success based on the ability to fit in or conform.**

**We select members for clubs and organizations based on similarities to us, not diversity of natural inclinations.**

**We've been taught that it's smart to do as we're told, not as we're naturally compelled to do.**

I've seen wonderful examples of people refusing to compromise their instinctive integrity who were fired from jobs or quit because they insisted on acting more authentically. I've never known anyone who regretted leaving under those circumstances. It leads invariably to better opportunities – jobs with less stress and more opportunity to excel.

**Ev:** But making a living can be more critical than making a philosophical point about your freedom to be yourself.

**Kathy:** Hey, this is about gut-wrenching decisions that impact your personal destiny. Wasted effort to do things the so-called "right way" can rob you of your chance to excel, demean your talents, and limit your potential for true success.

Those who are obstinate remove obstacles that limit their accomplishments. They make damn sure that they act through their natural advantages – with or without the approval of others. They don't wait for permission to succeed. They don't settle for mere survival. They use the power of their instincts to the fullest extent.

**Ev:** It's uncomfortable to think that I'm part of a conspiracy to make people become obstinate in order to be themselves. But I can think of many circumstances in which I've either been a silent witness or been one of the people encouraging others to **just do what they were told to do.**

Help me here. **Aren't there times when people have to do what they're told to do, even if it's against their grain?**

"When you get to the end of your rope, tie a knot and hang on."
Franklin D. Roosevelt,
Kansas City Star,
June 5, 1977

**Kathy:** I coach youngsters on how to survive classroom situations where they have to rein in their talents. They need to graduate with decent grades to get into good colleges. Diplomas from "the best" universities are tickets of admission to many careers. But some kids have to pay a high price to earn their way in.

**Ev: What do you coach them to do?**

**Kathy:** To be *strategically obstinate* in being themselves, but not to let it show. Some battles aren't worth fighting. They can do the assignment that will get them the good grade, but not study the way they were taught to; not pay attention in class, but seem to be listening; negotiate deals that let them have as much freedom in showing what they know as possible. [Details: p. 236]

They have to learn the content, but they can learn tricks for protecting their instinctive energy in the process.

The same type of strategic techniques work in the workplace. I love it when my employees negotiate for ways they can get more done! There's no reason being obstinate can't be accompanied by being honest and reasonable – and having a sense of humor.

**Ev:** Yet it seems a bit hypocritical.

**Kathy:** It's not being deceitful. Not if it is *strategic obstinance*. It's firmly adhering to a purpose or course of action without distressing others in the process.

We all need to figure out how to get to do things our way, yet not alienate or disturb others. So it's everything from reading in bed with a penlight that doesn't disturb our mate's sleep, to writing limericks in your head while at a dreadfully dull dinner party.

**Ev:** Tell me that the limerick thing isn't rude!

"To see what is right, and not to do it, is want of courage or of principle."
Confucius

**Kathy:** I'm not talking about the content of your limericks... And – if you are strategic about it – you will not do it without being able to pay enough attention to what is going on around you. You should still be able

135

to nod appropriately and be polite company. For some of us, this strategy prevents our becoming disruptive.

## You're practicing Strategic Obstinance when you:

· Go where everyone else wants to go, but do your own thing when you get there.

· Play the game others are playing, but set challenges for yourself that the others don't recognize.

· Give the "right" answer, then add your alternative recommendation.

· Wear what's required, with your personal favorite tucked out of sight.

· Plan everything to meet your standards, then get others to think it was their plan.

· Go back later and rebuild the structure more solidly, without anyone being able to see the difference.

· Whistle silent tunes.

Ev: I can think of situations when someone should not be obstinate.

Kathy: For instance?

Ev: When your personal safety is in jeopardy. Aren't there times when you wouldn't want to irritate someone else, like a person who might harm you if you don't give them your money, or someone who is detaining you – and threatening greater harm?

Kathy: Those are excellent examples of exceptions to the usual process. Certainly there are times you intentionally appear to go along with a predator as a strategic maneuver. **The idea is to act with great purpose and determination – while having the gumption to hide that behavior from the other person.**

The **exceptions to this rule are any situations where common sense** dictates a safer way of taking action than your natural inclinations. A person who resists Follow Thru structure, but who regularly needs to take medicine ought not to use his or her MO as an excuse for not following the regimen.

**There's no point in being obstinate about doing things that could improve the quality of your physical life. Just make them habits,** and down the pills at the regular intervals. Habits, once again, help you avoid using your instinctive power in ways that force you into any of the *Failure Factors.*

**Ev:** I'm glad you say that. Life shouldn't be a constant battle over doing things your way.

**Kathy:** I'm not suggesting that you become intolerant, a fanatic, or prejudiced, or that you mope when you don't get your instinctive way. If you are obstinate enough, you will never have to stoop to being sulky.

**When you are obstinate:**

- **Your intractable defense of your own methods will be persuasive.**

- **Your unyielding pursuit of your self-actualized approaches will make you invincible, even to the criticism of those whom you admire greatly and wish to please.**

- **Your instinctive powers come to the forefront.**

- **You won't procrastinate.**

- **You don't linger in discouragement and despair.**

- **You do the do-able – and even some things you may have believed were improbable.**

**Ev:** Basically, you're saying that criticism for being obstinate in acting on your instincts shouldn't faze you.

Being obstinate is acting with:
- Tenacity
- Perseverance
- Dogged resolution
- A ruling passion
- Willfulness
- Determination

**Kathy:** Kind of like Snoopy after Lucy shouts at him that he's just a dog and will never be anything more than a dog. His thought bubble? "How reassuring!"

**If Snoopy had to work like a cat to be a dog, it certainly would take foolish effort – without the desired result.**

**Ev:** Would it still take *dogged* determination?

**Kathy:** Ouch! Not as much, actually. But we'd encourage him to be *dogmatic* about it!

**Ev:** That hurt more than mine!

**Kathy:** Being Obstinate validates that you're an incorrigible loyalist to your own cause.

**Having the backbone to stand up for yourself starts with knowing who you are (your MO, your desires, and your learned abilities). Determination helps you to make better decisions because it moves you up the Dynamynd.**

Being as obstinate as I hope you'll be leads you all the way to being just as resolute in fighting for everyone else's right to be who they are.

**Your perfect, innate method of operation (your MO) is just a start. It's the gold hidden beneath the surface. You have the responsibility to mine it and transform it into something of value.**

It's up to you to convert God-given talents into observable personal assets. You do this with purposeful use of your best efforts.

**Ev:** Where does humility come in?

**Kathy:** Humility comes with the recognition that your instinctive talents are gifts you've been given, not traits you created.

Integrity comes when you take full responsibility for the stewardship of your talents – and the power they give you to create.

Dynamynd®: Kolbe Decision Ladder

Culture

Social Responsibility 5
Self Actualization 4
Self Control 3
Self Esteem 2
Self Awareness 1

Affective   Conative   Cognitive

**Social Responsibility**

Ev: What's the best way to assess whether someone needs to be more obstinate?

Kathy: Perhaps it will help if I give you some simple examples of what happens when someone makes the effort to be nice rather than rock the proverbial boat.

**When you refuse to Be Obstinate, you risk:**

· **Succumbing to the demands of others.**

· **Being indecisive.**

· **Hesitating and letting others choose the way.**

· **Abstaining from action.**

· **Compromising on the process.**

· **Vacillating.**

· **Being compliant.**

If these behaviors describe you, you may be called "charming." Or you might be called "boring."

And you'd clearly never have to worry about being called obstinate.

# CHAPTER NINE

# HOW TO BE OBSTINATE – IN OVERCOMING OBSTACLES

**Ev**: Sometimes I wonder what I'd do in a situation in which an enemy captured and tried to brainwash me. Do most people know what they'd do, or are my doubts natural?

**Kathy**: Even people who consider themselves strong-willed and very self-determined wonder what they'd do under duress. None of us can know for sure, but experts usually advise us to be willful, trust our instincts, and not let anyone control our actions.

**Ev:** Given your take on why it's important to Be Obstinate, I think I could use some goading in that direction. Sometimes I think I let people get the best of me.

**Kathy**: I have some Think-ercises that will help you. Let's get started.

## THINK-ERCISE #13

# What's So Great About Being Obstinate?

Quickly think of as many positive descriptions or synonyms for being obstinate as possible. Give yourself no more than three or four minutes to do this. Setting an egg timer or having someone watch the time for you would be helpful.

1. _____

2. _____

3. _____

4. _____

5. _____

6. _____

7. _____

8. _____

9. _____

10. _____

Evaluate whether others would consider the things you came up with as positive or negative. Then, show your words and phrases to at least four people to get their take on whether these are constructive behaviors. If they don't agree that you're describing positive approaches, try to convince them of the benefits of acting in the ways you've described.

Is there a pattern to the types of people you asked and the way they responded to your words? Degree of optimism, employment issues, health, personal history, geography, gender, and age could be among the factors you observe.

_____

_____

_____

What causes people to react differently to the same words?

_____

_____

_____

Rate how obstinate you believe each of these people to be about acting on their instinctive powers. Use a scale from 1-5, with 5 being Very Obstinate and 1 being Not at all Obstinate.

| Name of Person | At work | With family | Socially | Health |
| --- | --- | --- | --- | --- |
|  |  |  |  |  |
|  |  |  |  |  |
|  |  |  |  |  |

## Levels of Obstinacy:

After talking with these people, do you have a greater or lesser conviction regarding the importance of Being Obstinate – in Overcoming Obstacles? Why?

_____

_____

Were you able to convince any of them that they need to be more obstinate?

_____

_____

If so, how were you able to do that?

_____

_____

Ev: I'll do the part of this that involves other peoples' reactions when I'm back home. That'll be interesting to guess who will respond in what ways. I'm going to ask my spouse, a close friend, my oldest kid, and a colleague at work. Two people I'd love to have do this are my father and my boss. I doubt that will happen though.

Kathy: Who do you expect will be the most obstinate about not agreeing that it's good to Be Obstinate?

Ev: It's easier to say who will wildly applaud the idea – my kid, of course.

Kathy: That can be a good news-bad news situation.

**Ev:** In my case, my oldest child is not involved in drugs or what I consider a dangerous peer group. The obstinacy is more directed toward what's probably a healthy rebellion against anything we parents suggest would be appropriate dress or courteous behaviors.

It would be nice to have more peace in the household, but I know I'm very fortunate that I don't have to worry about seriously dangerous actions. I hope I'm not overlooking the other side of it – the possibility that my kid is too compliant or submissive. I hope this Think-ercise will help us talk that through together.

**Kathy:** Why do you think it would be a problem to get your father and boss in on this?

**Ev:** I guess I just don't want to appear to need their help. That puts me in a position of weakness – at least in my mind.

**Kathy:** What if you asked them to interpret the answers you got from others – without betraying anyone's confidentiality?

For instance, you could ask why they think a young person would think persevering is more important to trusting his or her instincts than three adults you showed the same list of words.

**Ev:** Something like that might work. I'd sure like to make the point to these guys that when I'm obstinate about something it might just be a very positive thing.

**Kathy:** It sounds as if you could benefit from another Think-ercise.

## THINK-ERCISE #14

# Confidence Clinchers

Think about times you have or have not been obstinate about very important actions you needed to take.

Note two times when you were *very obstinate and it worked to your benefit.*

1.

2.

Note two times when you were *very obstinate and it worked against you.*

1.

2.

Note two times when you were *not at all obstinate and it worked out well.*

1.

2.

**Note two times when you were *not at all obstinate and it worked against you.***

1.

2.

**Draw your own conclusions. Are you more effective when you are obstinate? If not, why not?**

_____

_____

_____

**If so, what are you going to do to Be Obstinate more often?**

_____

_____

_____

Ev: This last part, my self-evaluation, is particularly interesting. I can imagine being very hard on the people who don't agree that being obstinate can be a good thing. Yet, it was easier to think of times when I wasn't obstinate than to give examples of when I have been obstinate.

**Kathy: Perhaps that's because you still have some difficulty separating being abrasive from being obstinate.** Remember, you can be cooperative, gentle, an introvert, calm, and considerate – and still be obstinate. Remember me telling you about Marcella?

Try looking at how others handle the types of situations in which you wish you'd been more obstinate. An easy way to do that is by watching some TV.

The key question you'll be considering as you watch three different types of shows is whether or not it's generally in a person's best interests to Be Obstinate. In order to do that, you'll need to **clearly distinguish between when people or characters are showing determination to act in ways that are true to themselves and when they're going along with the way others want them to act – even though it's against their grain.**

Ev: Do I have to do this by watching TV? I really don't like spending time watching it.

Kathy: Are you being obstinate?

**Kolbe Action Modes**

**Fact Finder:**
The instinctive need to gather information

**Follow Thru:**
The instinctive need to organize information

**Quick Start:**
The instinctive need to deal with unknowns

**Implementor:**
The instinctive need to deal with tangibles

Ev: I have an attitude about watching TV, so I guess refusing to do it makes me more belligerent than obstinate. It would be different, wouldn't it, if my instincts were to stay out of doors and not sit around long enough to watch TV. Wouldn't refusing to watch it for that reason be more of a case of being obstinate because I'd be protecting my instinctive needs?

**Kathy: Yes. That's great insight into the differences.** I'd give an Implementor insistent person a pass on having to watch all of a show or having to sit down and make notes while watching. That's because highly insistent Implementors (with 8-10 in the Action Mode) need lots of freedom to move. **People should always feel free to adjust the way they do an assignment.**

Ev: What about insistent Fact Finders?

Kathy: Those with 8-10 in Fact Finder on their Kolbe index often get their information from reading rather than watching TV. They might do this exercise by reading magazines or books.

It wouldn't be as effective, however, because it's tough to separate emotions from thoughts and from actions. It's especially difficult when you can't see facial expressions, body movements, or eye contact.

There's a certain eyeball test to whether someone is being obstinate. I've just given it away. When you're truly obstinate, you literally hold your ground. You look people directly in the eye and lean toward the action rather than away from it.

**Ev:** You've actually studied that?

**Kathy:** I wish there were ways to statistically prove something that's so subjective. **Years of close observation convince me these are consistent signs of being determined to act on your instincts.** I'll be interested in your observations. Don't forget, you can email me your findings anytime at info@poweredbyinstinct.com.

**Ev:** I keep going back and forth between seeing the importance of not caving in when you need to Be Obstinate, and not wanting to come across as abrasive. Is there a Think-ercise that will help me approach confrontations in the best possible way?

**Kathy:** The best way to learn to stand your ground without sinking an otherwise positive relationship is to practice away from personal relationships.

# Character Critic

Before watching each of the types of shows listed, read the entire Think-ercise so you can find out what is most important to observe.

## 1. Sitcom or Drama

This is a chance to react to people being obstinate – or not – without any bias because of your personal relationship with them.

Don't try to analyze or judge your reactions as you watch the show. Just jot down a few words (and the character's name) next to some of the phrases listed below. It's not necessary to write something next to every phrase.

Base your reactions on what the characters in the show do, not what you think of the script or acting.

An example would be your reaction to a person feeling sorry for himself because others tease him about his weird ears. You jot down something like the following:

· That's enough...self pity, Harold.

· It's about time...Harold got new friends.

· Haven't they thought about...Harold can't do anything about his ears.

Try it yourself with a sitcom or drama:

· That's great_____

· That's enough_____

· Thank goodness _____

· It's about time _____

· Don't even go there_____

· It would have made more sense if _____

· Next time _____

· What's wrong with _____

· It's a good thing _____

· If you ask me _____

· It was funny even if _____

· I can see myself _____

· The price that person paid was _____

After you watch the show, go back to your notes and add more complete comments regarding your reactions to how the characters in the show acted, reacted, and interacted. Don't limit yourself to these phrases. Add your own.

Evaluate whether you generally are determined to act, react, or interact in the ways you suggest for the character.

_____

_____

Evaluate whether you're generally determined to avoid acting, reacting, or interacting in the ways you considered negative.

_____

_____

Review your notes. Ask yourself how obstinate you are about doing things you would recommend for others.

_____

_____

**Write a phrase that describes your level of self-determination or obstinacy.**

_____

_____

_____

**Note examples of when you acted with great determination in similar situations.**

1. _____

2. _____

3. _____

4. _____

5. _____

**Did your willfulness in these situations have a positive or negative result?**

_____

_____

_____

If there were any negatives, were they in people's attitudes toward you or in the results themselves?

_____

_____

Would you rather be effective or have people like you affectively? _____

_____

_____

Did any of the characters on the TV show make the choice between being effective and being popular?

_____

_____

How might you rewrite the script to make the point that being obstinate would make the character more (or less) effective?

_____

_____

_____

_____

## 2. Reality TV show

After watching at least some of a reality TV show, complete the following statements regarding your reactions.

I was particularly sorry that _____ wasn't more obstinate when _____

_____

I kept wishing _____ would stand up for him or herself by_____

_____

When it did (or didn't happen) I was _____

_____

I've been in situations like that, and I've handled it by_____

_____

If I were advising _____, the things I would emphasize to help him or her be more obstinate would be

1. _____

2. _____

3. _____

4. _____

**The most obstinate person on the show was** _____ **because,** _____

_____

_____

_____

**That self-determination helped (or hindered) that person because others on the show reacted to that persistence by**

_____

_____

**If I were that person I would have been more (or less) obstinate because** _____

_____

_____

**It took** _____

_____

**for that person to Be Obstinate.**

**Do you think it changed the level of trust he or she had in her instincts?**

Why? _____

_____

_____

_____

_____

## 3. News Show

**Was there an item on the news that had anything to do with a person being obstinate about acting on instinct?**

_____

**What was the outcome?**

_____

_____

**Had you been able to talk with the person about being more obstinate, do you think you might have changed the outcome?**

_____

_____

_____

When government officials, organization spokespeople, or others give advice, or try to convince you of something, does it matter if they appear obstinate – or not? Give an example:

_____

_____

_____

_____

_____

**Did anyone on the show (live or on tape) seem more abrasive than obstinate? Why?**

1. _____

2. _____

3. _____

4. _____

5. _____

6. _____

7. _____

8. _____

**What could that person do to change your impression?**

1. _____

2. _____

3. _____

4. _____

5. _____

**Does that give you any ideas for how your actions influence the way others view your ideas? What can you do to both Be Obstinate in trusting your guts, and be effective in influencing others to react positively to your actions?**

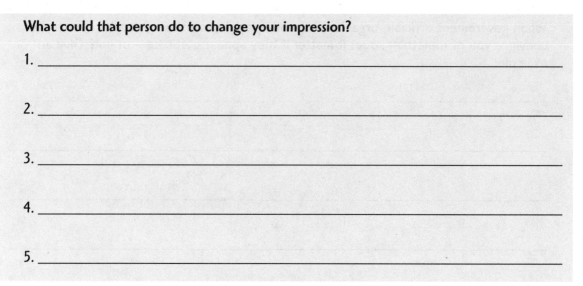

The human mind is Three-Dimensional

It has three equal parts

- **Cognitive**: thoughts, intelligence, learned behaviors, knowledge, recall, skills

- **Affective**: feelings, emotions, personality, preferences, desires, attitudes, values

- **Conative**: purposeful actions, drives, urges, natural abilities, innate talents, MO

**Ev:** I think I get it!

**Kathy:** Okay. Can you come up with a Think-ercise for me?

**Ev:** Okay. I'll give it a shot. And I'll do it in the style of an insistent Implementor. I'll start by capturing my affective desire, then move into the conative action for a couple of the assignments, and do the thinking/editing part at the end. That'll get my mind fully into it. I can do this!

# THINK-ERCISE BY EV

1. Make of list of words or phrases that describe how you feel when you have to work against your instinctive grain.

2. Collect cartoons, photos, or drawings from magazines that illustrate your frustrations and/or the situations that cause them.

3. Display the cartoons on your refrigerator or stick them on your mirror, with comments, color-highlighted markings, or a mustache-type addition to a photo or drawing to inject your own feelings.

4. Re-do the cartoon or drawing so it turns the situation around to your advantage. Give it a positive outcome that results because of an action, not just an attitude or opinion.

5. Evaluate why the cartoon or drawing is so poignant. Draw a counter-cartoon, one that illustrates a can-do solution in a similar situation.

Communication Methods by Action Mode:
- **Fact Finder:** written word
- **Follow Thru:** charts and graphs
- **Quick Start:** spoken words
- **Implementor:** props, models and demonstrations

**Kathy:** I like it. You've covered all three parts of the mind, in the order that integrates them into tools for creative problem solving. What could you do to make the tasks more welcoming for people who hesitate to draw?

**Ev:** I'd add this:

**You can either add your own drawing or find a cartoon or drawing that illustrates the points in steps 4 and 5.**

I think I'd also add that they could find dialog in a play or something with just words if they prefer. That might work better for insistent Fact Finders, because they are word-oriented people and might think the pictures are silly.

**Kathy:** You're right about those who *justify* being drawn to the written word. That doesn't mean they wouldn't love the comics. The tangibleness of something to stick on the refrigerator adds value for the initiating

Implementors. Follow Thru's who *organize* would probably place all this neatly into a notebook or file, if they really got into it.

Where you strayed from the correct use of the Kolbe Concept was in your assumption that a conative talent in Fact Finder would cause a person to think of using cartoons as being silly.

**Ev: Oh, yeah. What a person thinks about is cognitive. And whether they like something or not, or feel it is silly, it is affective, which relates to their personality type. So I would cut out the cartoon because I liked what it said, but how I changed it would depend upon my MO.**

**Kathy**: You're getting really good at this.

## THINK-ERCISE #16

# Quit Your Complainin'

· Pick three things you usually do that you're fed up with because they force you to go against your instincts.

· Refuse to do them any more.

· Decide whether they have to be done at all. If so, get someone else to do them.

· Now get real. If no one else will do them, figure out how to do them differently.

· If none of these alternatives is truly possible, consider the worst-case scenario: Challenge someone else to figure out a solution to the problem.

· If no one will help find a solution, find six other things you won't do so you can buy the energy to deal with these issues.

· If that upsets people around you, ask them what alternatives they see.

· If they don't see any alternatives, tell them that you don't either and stick to your guns.

---

Insistent Implementor
words:

Form
Shape / Mold
Craft
Render
Build
Repair
Construct
Fix
Demonstrate
Practice

**Ev: This is great. Perfect for the straight-talking Implementor types. Right?**

**Kathy**: Be careful not to stereotype the insistent Implementor as a personality type because they're less verbal and more what-you-see-is-what-you-get kind of people. Remember that your MO has nothing to do with your IQ either. Unfortunately, most academic tests (including the SAT) are geared to those who *justify* and are biased against Implementors. [Details: p. 237]

**Ev**: I have to keep telling myself that being obstinate is not affect, and that people DO it according to their MOs. Give me examples of how people act differently being obstinate through their Impact Factors.

**Kathy**: Here are some examples:

· A preventative Fact Finder won't *justify*.

· An initiating Fact Finder will insist on specifics before agreeing to bottom lines.

· An accommodating Follow Thru *is* willing to follow up to see that everyone completes the form.

· A preventative Implementor won't touch the equipment without a disclaimer if it breaks.

**Ev**: I have a lot of thinking to do about this rule. People may get tired of me asking them questions about it.

**Kathy**: Or they may get inspired.

# Kolbe Impact Factors™

| Fact Finder | Follow Thru | Quick Start | Implementor |
|---|---|---|---|
| Simplify | Adapt | Stabilize | Imagine |
| Refine | Rearrange | Revise | Renovate |
| Justify | Organize | Improvise | Construct |

# CHAPTER TEN

# RULE #5

# DO NOTHING – WHEN NOTHING WORKS

## Take charge of time outs

**Ev:** This rule sounds a lot like Rule #3, Commit – but to Very Little. What's the difference?

**Kathy:** Rule #3 deals with the levels of energy you commit to specific purposes.

**Do Nothing – when Nothing Works means shutting off all use of your instinctive energy. It helps you shut off the energy leaks that go toward nonpurposeful actions. It removes the mental clutter in your life.**

This is mental house cleaning. Just get rid of the nonsense that you store in your brain.

**Ev:** It's tempting to get rid of at least half the things I have to do. Couldn't this rule be badly abused – used as a cop-out?

**Kathy:** The following conditions REQUIRE that you Do Nothing:

• **Your instincts are to take no action – in order to protect yourself.**

• **Your instincts aren't sending you clear signals of what to do.**

• **You're trying to do too much, and need to cordon off types of actions you can avoid completely.**

**Ev:** I can't think of a time when my instincts told me to Do Nothing. It seems like they either tell me to run like Hell in the other direction, or that I need to try one more thing to make something work.

**Kathy:** How about those times when your instincts told you to stop talking, but you just keep digging yourself a deeper hole? Or you knew at a gut level that you should stop exercising because it hurt too much...

**Ev:** ...but I foolishly kept going, and paid for it later.

**Kathy:** I'll bet you're more aware of the need to recharge your energy. That's just a matter of giving yourself permission to Do Nothing for a while so it doesn't become DIRe.

**Ev:** I can use you as my excuse for begging off.

**Kathy: Too bad we need excuses for protecting ourselves from mental burn out.**

**Ev:** But most people just don't understand that not making a decision is a rational option.

**Kathy:** If you don't take control and Do Nothing as a preventative measure, you can get to the point where you have no choice. You're out of juice. Nothing works for you.

Avoid such DIRe situations. Do Nothing often enough that you prevent the problem.

That constant treadmill you describe that you're on degrades your natural talents. Stop putting out energy without getting enough back. Take time to replenish your instinctive power.

DIRe Syndrome can be caused by:

• Over-thinking
• Heightened Emotions
• Mind-altering Substances

**Ev:** My calendar is filled with appointments. I have one deadline after another. How can I just tell everyone that I'm going to be doing nothing for a while?

**Kathy:** Would you rather suffer from the Failure Factors? When you're running on empty, you're not ready, willing, and able to handle a crisis to the best of your ability. That's not a safe situation. In today's world you simply cannot operate without being *Powered by Instinct.*

**Ev:** If I follow all the other rules for trusting my guts, couldn't I just keep going?

**Kathy:** It takes acting on all *5 Rules* to fully trust your guts. Having too much going on in your life – even if it's all positive – causes static in your mind. How can you hear your instincts when you have mental tinnitus?

**Ev:** What's tinnitus?

**Kathy:** It's a physical hearing problem that causes constant ringing in the ears, making it difficult to discern specific voices or sounds. [Details: p. 238]

**Ev:** So I've got **tinnitus of the mind. That, I assume, blocks out the messages I need to hear, the ones my instincts try to get through to me.** I know I need to pay attention to my gut reactions in order to do my best, be safe, and all the other benefits we've discussed that come from listening to these internal powers. So this is serious. How do I make it go away?

**Kathy:** As the rule says, you need to set aside time to Do Nothing.

**Ev:** You mean that literally?

**Kathy:** You need to do absolutely nothing that requires conative or purposeful action. You can turn off this *doing domain* to reenergize your limited number of ergs without disrupting the signals from your instincts. So this does not put you in an unprotected state.

**Definition of tinnitus:**
a sensation of noise (as a ringing or roaring) that is caused by a bodily condition and can usually be heard only by the one affected

**Mental tinnitus:**
a condition of having too much going on in your life, thus causing static in your mind

165

Remember, *doing* is the conative action that results from using the power of your instincts. When you run out of ergs, your instincts are still intact. They're always true to form, but will operate on a low battery if you don't recharge their power periodically.

When you're living with uncertainty, it's especially critical that you keep some of this power in reserve.

**Ev:** What if that means not doing things that might bring positive results?

**Kathy:** People don't usually think of doing nothing as a sacrifice, but it can be just that. **It's not easy for highly committed people to stop striving.** You have to Be Obstinate about saying "no" to invitations, some kinds of opportunities (including things you may want to do), and responsibilities you can avoid. You have to set some goals aside and take time for rest and relaxation.

**Ev:** So I wouldn't do this unless my *Failure Factors* were in a seriously high range?

**Kathy:** You should also Do Nothing – when Nothing Works preventatively. Don't let yourself get into a state of fatigue. It puts you in harm's way because it dulls your instinctive reaction time and alertness.

You stay *Powered by Instinct* when you periodically Do Nothing, including when you:

- Sleep

- Daydream

- Watch stupid TV

- Read for pure pleasure

- Have idle chat

- Mess around in the garden

"Half our life is spent trying to find something to do with the time we have rushed through life trying to save."
Will Rogers
New York Times
April 29, 1930

- Toss a ball

- Paddle in the water

- Doodle

- Cook without a cause

- Aimlessly listen to sounds

- Play with kids or animals

- Contemplate

- View a sunset

- Meander

I believe that our senses are to our minds as calories are to our bodies. You need to take time to touch, smell, listen to, watch, and taste the environment around you. That's why a variety of good foods matter, as do sounds of music and laughter and birds and water. Everything that allows the senses to penetrate your mind helps energize you for future activity.

Ev: Some of the specific activities you give as examples puzzle me. Can you actually Do Nothing while engaged in all these activities? Or do you start thinking about how they fit into some project or cause?

Kathy: I find it quite easy to Do Nothing, but that doesn't mean I'm not thinking at the same time. In fact, all of the hard charging executives and major authors who are my clients report that they do some of their best thinking while doing nothing. Since they're not taking responsibility for producing or creating anything while they're doing nothing, it's a chance for them to get into the cognitive dimension without their thoughts having to be purposeful.

When you Do Nothing, you can think about anything you want to think about. What a luxury! Especially for anyone who's constantly on

"Why is it I get my best ideas in the morning while I'm shaving?"

Albert Einstein

167

**Definition of Pensive:**
Musingly or dreamily
thoughtful (adjective)

deadline or having to meet a multitude of requirements. **When you Do Nothing, you're not checking things off the list, or not evaluating *what you're doing*, so you can be pensive about things you may otherwise not give much consideration.**

For those whose minds were stimulated in school and at home, doing nothing is an acquired ability. I used to feel guilty about watching stupid TV, for instance. Now I enjoy doing it – as long as I'm doing a couple other doing nothing things along with it.

While I'm watching stupid TV shows, I'm playing computer games on my laptop and enjoying idle conversation with my husband.

**Ev:** And he doesn't resent that?

**Kathy:** Why should he? He's doing similar types of nothing.

**Ev:** What happens if one of you starts a conversation that involves decision making, perhaps about your schedule?

**Kathy:** If one of us really needs the downtime, we'll say so and ask for that discussion to wait.

Doing nothing reduces the *Failure Factor* of fatigue and increases your ability to trust your instincts. It's well worth the occasional inconvenience of shutting off the conative spigot. Sometimes the hardest part is having to gear up again.

**Ev:** How much time should I spend doing nothing?

**Kathy:** There are those who advocate scheduling whole days of doing nothing on a fairly consistent basis. For others, grabbing a few minutes each day, and some half days on weekends (with no honey-do lists) works quite well. Two-week vacations seem necessary for other people to totally refresh their mental stamina.

That doesn't work for me because I get too many ideas and start to feel like a caged animal that needs to get out and run. I get bored and frustrated when I Do Nothing for more than a few days at a time.

**Ev:** So you Do Nothing intermittently and others do it more consistently. How do I know what will work for me?

**Kathy:** You need to figure out your personal cycle, how long it takes you to rejuvenate or replenish your mental energy when it's at different stages of depletion. Once you pay attention to it, you'll discover that catnaps can work when you're just a bit fatigued. When you've maxed out your mind – when you've hit the proverbial mental wall – it's even difficult to get the full night's rest you may need.

If you've had to switch entirely into the thinking and feeling domains because your instincts were of zero help, they may not let go very easily. You've lost the control you have when you're *Powered by Instinct*.

**Ev:** So I enter the world of tossing and turning all night because I'm worrying and overthinking instead of being able to get conative and do something about solving problems.

**Kathy:** We've all been there. It happens a lot less if you use this rule for trusting your guts. By the way, it's great that you're using the word "conative." I like that. It means you're tying instinctive power to the resulting conative actions – the things you do on purpose.

**Ev:** I am? It actually just popped out.

**Kathy:** That's the point. You've internalized it so you don't have to think about it consciously as being "the right word," but it is.

**Ev:** But my Fact Finder need to be precise is just getting comfortable with using it. Won't it take me longer than a person who can live more easily with generalizations to test the results of doing nothing?

**Kathy:** Yes, the pattern of how people adjust for downtime is as different as the pattern of MOs.

People who *organize* as one of their Impact Factors need to plan on doing nothing. When people who *improvise* plan to Do Nothing, it can add to their frustration – which makes the people around them see it as out-of-character behavior. We ought to be able to Do Nothing without giving up being who we are.

45% of American workers feel they are asked or expected to work on too many tasks at once, according to a study of 1,003 employees by the Families and Work Institute, New York.

**Efforts**: Conative actions you take to solve problems.

**Best efforts**: Actions that use your four Impact Factors or instinctive abilities.

**Foolish efforts**: Actions you take that you know are not your best efforts.

**Wasted efforts**: Energy you use to take action that goes against your grain, or is contrary to your best efforts.

Doing nothing is in everyone's character, but – as with everything else that ties to instincts – when you go against your grain, the results require added, ineffective wasted effort. And it certainly is counterproductive to turn doing nothing into effort.

**Ev**: Do you actually see people do that?

**Kathy**: Oh, yes. I'm sure you have too. It's like watching people making an effort to have a *really* fun time on New Year's Eve. It may be one of the reasons so many people now decide to stay home on December 31st.

**Ev**: I'm not sure I can separate doing nothing from doing something half-heartedly. You said earlier that "close enough is good enough." Or are you suggesting that just going through the motions is a way of doing nothing?

**Kathy**: There are times when you can get things done without a high level of commitment – without striving. For instance, you could round-off the numbers, rather than calculating precisely the resources you'll need for a project. Can you think of anything like that in your life?

**Ev**: I've purchased supplies when I sure didn't try to account for every inch that I'd need. I used to spend hours researching the lowest airfares for holiday trips. Now I figure my time and energy are worth something, so I get a reasonable price and just book it. There was a time when I had to finish a crossword puzzle or I felt like a jerk. That's behind me, too.

**Kathy**: What about a job-related situation?

**Ev**: Some reports are never going to see the light of day. They need to be there for the record, and are worth doing for that reason. But they don't have to be done all that well.

**Kathy**: Are you striving to make those reports accurate?

**Ev**: Yes. In that sense, I do them well. But I don't print them out in color or worry about designing fancy charts or cover pages.

**Kathy**: So they don't constitute doing nothing.

**Ev:** Well, almost. I can do that kind of thing at home at night, while I'm watching stupid TV, as you call it.

**Kathy:** Things you can do without using much mental energy are fringe benefits, not unlike two-fer offers ("Two for the price of one"). They still count as doing something, even if they don't take much work. You'd be surprised how answering a lot of e-mails or returning several calls can use up your ergs for a while. You need to be certain that you have some total and complete Do Nothing time, as well.

Rule #5 involves numerous words that start with R. **When you truly Do Nothing it's refreshing, relaxing, reenergizing, rekindling, and recharging.**

My favorite is re-creation. Recreation is all about reenergizing us for the next round of our creation.

**Ev:** Ah, another one of those fascinating "word things."

**Kathy:** Be sure that your recreation doesn't slip into being part of the "effort ethic." You have to make it into totally nonproductive fun in order for it to assist you in recharging your instinctive batteries.

**Ev:** What would I do recreationally that would interfere with it being downtime?

**Kathy:** If you work at improving your golf game, golfing is not recreational time for you. If you do comparative pricing, shopping isn't downtime. If you work at getting a tan while lying on the beach, then even that doesn't count as totally doing nothing.

**Ev:** So what society defines as doing nothing may not fit what I need to do in order to truly *do* nothing?

**Kathy:** I never said doing nothing was easy. It actually takes some thought. And, by the way, emotions are certainly allowed when you're doing nothing.

**Ev:** Well, then. Is making love doing nothing?

**Kathy:** It all depends on how much mental energy you put into it! It's a definite conative activity for some people.

**Ev:** So that's why people come home tired from a honeymoon?

**Kathy:** Could be. People come home tired from most vacations because they involve so many logistics. Now just getting through the airport takes more mental energy than a day's work, as we certainly know.

The expenditure of instinctive energy when traveling makes most people need to come home and Do Nothing for a while before they can be fully productive. That's one reason people feel so disoriented when they first get back from an exhausting trip. I hope you take time to Do Nothing after you get off this plane.

**Ev:** I wish I had said "no" to the dinner with my client. I'm dreading my upcoming vacation because it involves more travel. Would you suggest people travel less on vacations?

**Kathy:** It depends on the purpose of the vacation. If you need a vacation to recharge your mental energy, traveling is a questionable alternative. But if you're traveling to a foreign country to broaden your perspectives, or traveling to see friends and family, the energy can be well spent. You'll need time to recuperate, however. Schedule time so you can Do Nothing for a day – or whatever length of time you need – after you get back.

**Ev:** Should all business travel come with comp time, to compensate you for the effort you had to put forth in the process?

**Kathy:** Ideally, yes. Realistically, that's tough to do. You come back to voice mail that's run out of space and stacks of things waiting for decisions. Even if the time to Do Nothing were made available, frequently it just puts off the inevitable drain of your energy.

What we all have to do is learn to pace ourselves as much as possible every day and every week – to turn off the conative effort whenever we get a chance – and to take control by being obstinate about what makes no sense for us to do. We have to learn what's a Stop Action situation for us.

> "During [these] periods of relaxation after concentrated intellectual activity, the intuitive mind seems to take over and can produce the sudden clarifying insights which give so much joy and delight."
>
> Fritjof Capra, physicist

**Ev:** How will I know that I'm in a Stop Action situation?

**Kathy:** You'll learn to trust your guts to warn you.

When your instincts are silent, and give you no direction for taking action, I believe you're wise to Do Nothing until it becomes clear what direction to take.

**Ev:** So no message from your guts means stop everything?

**Kathy:** You can keep on practicing by habit. However, if the situation requires an immediate response to prevent a problem and your guts tell you to Do Nothing – then stop any voluntary action. Your instincts can save you from moving too soon, too fast, too far – just as they can get you moving when you must.

**Ev:** I remember a *New Yorker* article about an officer in a police department who had a knack for knowing when not to shoot.

*"It was a gut reaction not to shoot..."*
John Yarbrough in
*The New Yorker*
by Malcolm Gladwell,
August 5, 2002

**Kathy:** That was John Yarbrough with the Los Angeles County Sheriff's Department, who has been studied because of his uncanny ability to save himself and others by sensing when to hold his fire. He said of one situation: "If you looked at it logically, I should have shot him. But logic had nothing to do with it. Something just didn't feel right. It was a gut reaction not to shoot – a hunch that at the exact moment he was not an imminent threat to me." That inaction saved the life of a kid with a gun who also didn't shoot.

**Ev:** I guess the DIRe situation is more obvious. At least I wouldn't be afraid of misreading the signals.

**Kathy:** My best advice is simply to Do Nothing when your guts tell you that it's the best solution. That could:

- Stop arguments
- End useless reworking of data
- Prevent buying at the wrong time
- Avoid turning off the right road
- Decrease the chance of errors

**Three Failure Factors:**
- Fatigue
- Fear
- Frustration

This often requires use of the Impact Factors that are in the Preventative zone in one or more of the modes. You might have to stop the analysis paralysis when you're considering a major purchase. If you don't naturally *simplify*, doing nothing is a way to get back on track.

Or it could mean tossing out the system you've used for years to purchase a car. It now makes sense to get on the Internet as a part of the process. In your case, that would be a great chance to exercise your natural ability to *adapt*. For a person who isn't inclined that way, it could be an added hassle, so it might be better to hold off to see if there's someone else who could help out in that arena. You are inclined to immediately grab hold of an innovative approach, but some people have to stop and *stabilize* before they add risk to their plate.

**Ev:** Sorry, I'm going to interrupt you there. I think that it's quite necessary for you to help me Do Nothing.

**Kathy:** All right, then. It would be nice if we could just hit the refresh key, as we can on a computer. It's precisely because of the difficulty of reading the Stop Action signals that I won't attempt to cover them in detail in this discussion. Check out www.poweredbyinstinct.com for more information on this subject.

I think it will work for you to do some brief Think-ercises that will help the concept of doing nothing sink in.

# CHAPTER ELEVEN

# HOW TO DO NOTHING - WHEN NOTHING WORKS

**Ev:** I'm confused about the difference between action that helps you Do Nothing and action that results in getting nothing done.

By doing nothing I could get more done, couldn't I?

**Kathy:** As confusing as it sounds, you're right. Give me an example of how you do nothing.

**Ev:** Exercise works fairly well for me when I don't want to think.

**Kathy:** Remember, Do Nothing is not the same as Think Nothing. You can reenergize your conative ergs while you're thinking. As long as your exercise is non-striving – you aren't preparing for a marathon or racing a clock or trying to achieve another goal – you could be doing nothing while going through the physical motions.

**The key is to focus on the purpose of the rule. You need to Do Nothing in order to recharge your instinctive energy. It helps you trust your guts to Do Nothing because it allows you to replenish your natural creative powers. You're not only saving your mental energy, but you're also allowing quiet to prevail, giving yourself a greater opportunity to hear the messages from your guts.**

**Ev:** I have a lot of required reading for work, but I also read novels. I spend a lot of time reading the newspaper and news magazines.

**Kathy:** That's being very true to your Fact Finder MO. One of the patterns I find in highly insistent Fact Finders is that they spend hours with the Sunday newspaper.

**Ev:** I feel as if I'm going through a sort of withdrawal when I'm on vacation and can't get my hands on a newspaper for a couple of days. If that's my MO, does that mean that I'm using up a lot of my instinctive power when I read the newspaper?

**Kathy:** Only if you're clipping out stories or highlighting them for your own or others' files. Most of the time, you're not operating at a commitment level when you're reading the paper. In fact, it's more of a **conative comfort zone – a way of doing something that doesn't take much energy.**

Retreating to the lowest levels on the Dynamynd is a way to do less or use fewer ergs. The higher an activity is on the Dynamynd, the more energy you're exerting.

## THINK-ERCISE #17

# Sensory Input

Complete the following thought: When I Do Nothing, I am able to:

1. _____

2. _____

3. _____

4. _____

5. _____

6. _____

7. _____

How many of the things you listed dealt with your senses of sight, sound, smell, touch, or taste?

**For any that didn't, add a sensory element that would help you reenergize. The goal is to get rid of tinnitus of the mind – that undercurrent of noise that blocks out authentic communications.**

Ev: Clearly, I need to get outside, to observe more closely, to pay attention to smells and sights and sounds. I should take time to touch things, not just look. I should be more aware of my surroundings.

**Kathy**: Erma Bombeck, a wonderful humorist, wrote a touching list of things she would do if she had her life to live over – after she found out she was dying from cancer. Some of them included:

I would have gone to bed when I was sick instead of pretending the earth would go into a holding pattern if I weren't there for the day.

I would have taken the time to listen to my grandfather ramble about his youth.

I would never have insisted the car windows be rolled up on a summer day because my hair had just been teased and sprayed.

I would have cried and laughed less while watching television and more while watching life. But mostly, given another shot at life, I would seize every minute...look at it and really see it...live it, and never give it back. Stop sweating the small stuff.

**Ev**: I wonder how many people, at the end of their lives, wish they had spent more time doing nothing – or at least not sweating the small stuff?

**Kathy**: I hear that sentiment a great deal from people who others consider highly successful. Since success is the freedom to be yourself, and that means trusting your instincts rather than the opinions of others, only you are truly able to measure personal success.

While we can see signs of fear, fatigue, and frustration in people, we rarely know how deep it goes.

In my work, I've been very close to a number of highly visible high performers. Like Erma, they often seem so "well put together" that it's hard to imagine they suffer self-doubts. Yet I often hear from such people agonizing regrets and personal longings to be able to do the one thing they haven't achieved: tap into their depths, their instinctive powers, in order to truly be who they are. They just hadn't taken time to Do Nothing in order to achieve that elusive goal.

## THINK-ERCISE #18

# Think, Feel and Do Nothing

Next time you're feeling brain-dead but still have to solve a problem or be productive...STOP! And:

· Go outside and sit in the grass, among leaves, twigs, and other things that have fallen from growing vegetation of some sort.

· Sense their color, smell, and the sounds they make when you kick them or brush them together. Without trying to make them into anything or get them to do anything, think about how they came to be in their present state. How did the leaf look and feel when it was a bud? When it was last attached to the tree? How different might it have felt or smelled?

· Observe the different colors of any grass growing in your line of vision. How many different shades of green do you see? Are there reds or blues? Browns? Consider how many different crayons you'd have to use to capture all of the colors of the grass.

· If there's no grass available because of the season or your environment, feel the difference it might make to have grass around. What do you think of grass in little pots on restaurant tables?

· What difference does having trees make?

· Is the biggest difference in the sight, the smells, or the sounds?

· Which senses benefit most from trees?

· What happens when none are around?

· What different feelings do trees give in different seasons?

· Which do you prefer?

**Ev:** I guess none of that would require my conative energy. I can see how it could be refreshing to do this unless I was a botanist.

**Kathy:** What if you were a botanist? Do you think that thinking about the sensory elements and getting involved with them would be mentally exhausting? Do you think botanists take enough time to smell the roses?

**Ev:** I'm not sure. I think it depends on whether you were doing this as research or to write about the experience, rather than to just soak it in.

**Kathy:** That's a good way of looking at it. You're doing something when it has a purpose. If you're just soaking in the atmosphere or the senses, it can be reenergizing.

**Ev:** Doesn't that mean that you're doing it for the purpose of reenergizing?

**Kathy:** Terrific question. How would you answer it?

**Ev:** I'd know why I was doing it, but I wouldn't strive for any particular result. I'd think of it as meandering through the woods, as compared to walking through the woods to get to grandmother's house.

**Kathy:** If you had access to a beach or swimming pool, I'd suggest that you:

Get in the water, but don't swim laps or do anything competitively. Literally go with the flow, stop and just feel the difference between the place just where the water touches your body and where it stops touching.

· Is it a straight line?

· How thick is the line?

· How does it move as you walk, stop and splash, and twist your body?

· How much can you control its movement?

See how long you can entertain yourself by concentrating on sensations tied to that line.

**Ev**: You could do something similar in a bathtub or with the flow of water in the shower.

**Kathy**: Yes.

**Ev**: But what if you are not a water person or a plant person?

**Kathy**: I think we underutilize places like art museums and other public facilities for such sensory experiences. If it doesn't take too much of your striving energy to get to an art institute of some sort, just wandering around and taking it all in can be very nurturing. For that matter, if you don't have to go to a fruit stand or farmers' market to buy for a big feast, that can be one of the best places to smell an incredible variety of scents that open up your senses. For some strange reason, one of the places that comes to mind when I think of fun sounds to take in is a bowling alley.

**Ev**: See, that college experience left an indelible mark on your mind.

**Kathy**: Maybe that one-place-only sound of the bowling ball rolling down the wood until it slams into the pins knocked some sense (interesting word) into my brain so that I've never forgotten the experience. Maybe the importance of sound is why some of us study better with music playing.

**Ev**: With all the applications for my instincts, it's no wonder I wear them out. But, if I back out of arguments, lower expectations, and decrease the level of energy I put into a decision, isn't there a danger that I'll just become a lazy slug? I'm trying to figure out how to Do Nothing in a responsible way and I'm having a hard time connecting the dots here.

**Kathy**: While I want to teach you how to Do Nothing – when Nothing Works, I don't want you to mistake that for being lazy. If you're not doing anything that has purpose, you won't need to use this rule. Doing nothing, by itself, is not the goal. To trust your guts, you need to Do Nothing only when you're already doing so much that matters to you that something has to give way.

Just don't ever think that it's so important to Do Nothing that you don't step up to the plate when something you value is at risk. Stay and argue rather than protect your ergs – if you care about finding a resolution to the differences with another person.

**Ev:** Let's say I've done that and my mind is so tired I can't decide what to do next. Now I really *have* to Do Nothing, but my mind is all revved up and I can't settle it down. What do I do?

**Kathy:** That's when counting sheep comes into play! It always seemed so silly to me when people said to do that in order to fall asleep. Until I realized that it's a way to turn off both the cognitive and conative juices. It puts you into a mental stupor. You not only drop the replaying of what you coulda, woulda, or shoulda said, but you also bring nothing conative to that mindless task. It helps you shut down all mental systems.

**Ev:** Doing nothing means not taking purposeful action. You said that it was okay to think, as long as I wasn't taking action at that time based on my thoughts. So why couldn't I read non-fiction that would give me good background for my work, as long as I didn't take notes or do anything with the information as I was reading?

**Kathy:** You're right, that would qualify as nonactive, Do Nothing time. Just be careful not to be making commitments about what you'll do, because **the act of making a commitment is conative.** Keep in mind that there's a difference between purposeful action and meaningful behavior. We can engage in action that's without purpose – but that's very meaningful emotionally to us.

I think about issues relating to *Powered by Instinct* while I'm watching sports, talking with friends, and especially when I'm playing with the grandkids. But I'm not doing anything about it at the time. I'm having fun. I'm thinking, but I'm not striving. So I'm doing nothing, but not getting nothing done.

**Ev:** Couldn't you be cleaning up from dinner – getting something done – but in a "mindless way?"

**Kathy:** Yes of course.

**Ev:** Aren't those things you suggest I put into the habit category also mindless, Do Nothing types of things?

**Kathy:** Sure.

**Ev:** So I'm becoming more hopeful that I can Do Nothing quite often!

**Kathy:** I'd probably be a theorist run amok if I suggested that there may be levels of doing nothing.

**Ev:** Don't tell me that you're going to introduce a reverse Dynamynd, one that takes us to the depths of inactivity.

**Kathy:** Ah, the Do Nothing Dynamynd, a one-sided (because you still think and feel) pillar that you drive into the ground.

**Ev:** You sure would be driving your theory into the ground if you did that!

**Kathy:** So let's just say that you can Do Nothing while engaging the other domains of the mind, as long as you disengage conatively. To avoid making foolish efforts – you may find it easier to do things that are totally mindless, which would put you into a trance-like state.

**Ev:** Do you recommend meditating?

**Kathy:** It works for some people to set aside specific times and places for meditation – which is a way of putting yourself into a state of doing nothing. If it helps you accomplish that goal, fine. But if you find yourself *trying* to meditate, it won't be effective.

**Ev:** What about listening to music?

**Kathy:** There are some fascinating theories that originated in Bulgaria about how certain types of music can increase the rate of learning. [Details: p. 239]

There's also interesting research on the impact of music on preparing the mind for learning math and certain types of science and technology.

**Ev:** So you're not the only one who has seen the benefits of using the senses to improve productivity?

**Kathy:** Certainly not. Too often people think that being an artist or performer is the only way to be creative. These endeavors do involve sensory experiences for the performer and audience, often energizing the conative part of the mind; but being a fisherman can be equally creative, as can any other pursuit that engages all three dimensions of the mind.

I can't emphasize enough that every mentally healthy human being is equally capable of being creative.

• **We create differently because of our MOs.**

• **We create more or less productively because of the extent to which we reenergize through the senses.**

• **We create more or less joyfully, depending upon the amount of freedom we have to be ourselves.**

To be ourselves, we have to stop long enough to hear the inner truths that come from our instincts and then commit to acting upon them with the full power those instincts provide.

# CHAPTER TWELVE

# WHY THE 5 RULES MATTER

## Acting with Purpose, Passion, and Persuasion

**Ev:** Why have instincts suddenly become such a hot topic?

**Kathy:** I think our culture has been given a wake-up call about paying attention to instincts. We know now that in a crisis we have nowhere else to turn.

**Ev:** Does this mean we'll see more serious applications of our knowledge about instincts? Will *trusting our guts* become a more accepted way of dealing with problems and opportunities?

**Kathy:** I count on instincts to pull humanity through wars, economic crises, natural disasters, health epidemics, and societal binges. We've always done it. Now it's acceptable to say we're doing it.

**Ev:** What's the impact of that change?

**Kathy:** Recognition of the importance of instincts has been missing in the discussion of health, education, parenting, relationships, job training, people management, and every other endeavor that is influenced by what makes people tick. Now a more in-depth analysis

**Definition of Instinct:** term used generally to indicate an innate tendency to action, or pattern of behavior, elicited by specific stimuli and fulfilling vital needs of an organism.

185

of the implications of instinct can take place.

**Ev**: You think instincts are that far-reaching?

**Kathy**: Instincts are our mental energy, the power behind our decision making, productivity, and creativity. They are the basis of our equality *and* our individuality. Is that far-reaching enough?

Writing about instinct goes back to the early philosophers. Acting on instinct goes back to the beginnings of humankind. Instincts have retained their power – and given us ours – throughout the ages. They are the only resource we can count on under any circumstance – now and in the future. [Details: p. 240]

Our instincts will keep us grounded. And give us an ever-present power to solve problems. As long as we have our instincts we are capable of coping with any disaster. That's what using our wits is all about.

These natural advantages are the core of who we are individually and collectively. And I see no evidence that their power is diminishing. They are so deeply imbedded that neither emotional abuse nor intellectual brainwashing can alter them. They are the way in which we've been hardwired.

**Ev**: It would be nice to think that *something* isn't spinning out of control.

**Kathy**: Even cloning is not a threat to the uniqueness of individual instincts. Your MO isn't tied to your DNA, but your MO is to your mind what DNA is to your physical being.

We've seen no evidence of genetic links in MOs from parent to child. Your kids could well have a natural advantage that drives them to do things quite differently than you do them – which proves God has a sense of humor.

**Ev**: Or just enjoys watching us live with challenges every day.

**Kathy**: As with so many other things in life, raising kids wouldn't be as difficult if we understood the instincts that make them do things they way

> "We are what we repeatedly do."
> Aristotle

186

they do. We could actually build on their strengths instead of cajoling or nagging them to do things our way.

The *5 Rules* are very important in parenting, as they are in every major undertaking in life. There is a Kolbe Y (Youth) index for kids under 16. Sometimes, when parents see their kid's result, they understand why there have been years of stress between them. It helps to know the intrinsic need that is driving behavior, and to see that your child is not just being obstreperous, acting spoiled or simply trying to drive you crazy. [Details: p. 241]

**Ev:** Would that help explain why so many teens seem to get involved with drugs? Are they rebelling? Or just trying to dull the pain of not being understood?

**Kathy:** I did a study with the cooperation of a psychologist who dealt with substance abusers and found that an abnormally high percentage of them were in a state of conative crisis. Evidence of this shows up in their inability to report their authentic MO when completing the Kolbe index. We all can go through periods of duress and uncertainty in our lives in which a Kolbe Transition result will register. Teens are in Transition twice as often as adults. **Substance abusers in the study group were in Transition three times as frequently as the general population.**

We have a lot of work to do to fully understand the implications of these results. We need to use what we know about human instincts to reduce all the factors that work against our ability to act on natural advantages, whether it is teenage angst or substance abuse. And we have to figure out which is the cause and which is the effect.

**Ev:** Seems like you've done a lot of research for a person who isn't running a research institute.

**Kathy:** I make no claim to being a brain scientist, as I've said, but there's no way I could help people use their instincts to their advantage – or for the betterment of our schools, workplaces, and personal relationships – without doing my homework. I had to know, for instance, that the Kolbe index result was truly measuring conation, and not mistakenly lapping over into the identification of personality or intellect.

---

**Test retest reliability**

Reliability refers to the quality of a measurement and its ability to yield consistent results. Test-retest studies of the Kolbe index revealed that for 90% of test-takers, modes of insistence remained the same.

**Validity**

Predictive validity studies were undertaken to correlate Kolbe results with performance measures. In a meta-analysis the observed correlations were compared to established population values. The measure of effect size when Kolbe was used as a selection instrument was .67 with anything over .5 considered significant.

**Credibility**

Kolbe Wisdom has been widely used and accepted at the most prestigious universities, at the highest level of major multinational corporations, and by esteemed professionals in the psychological community.

**Ev**: How did you do that?

**Kathy**: I compared results for hundreds of people on cognitive tests with their results on the Kolbe index. Then I did additional studies comparing personality profiles with the Kolbe index results. I found no significant correlations with either of the other validated types of mental assessments, so I knew I was measuring a factor that was different from those mental domains.

Once I was satisfied that the results made further study worthwhile, I donated thousands of Kolbe indexes to independent researchers who replicated those studies, with the same results. [Details: p. 242]

**Ev**: Based on what you've learned from these studies, your database, and your personal observations coaching individuals and organizations, I hope you can give me a simple answer to this question: What area of my life will be most improved by following the *5 Rules for Trusting Your Guts*?

**Kathy**: Your personal safety and well-being.

**Ev**: That's because if I Act before I Think, I'll get out of dangerous situations faster?

**Kathy**: Yes. Following these *5 Rules* helps you sense danger before it's physically apparent. The implications of that in terms of your health are dramatic.

Having a sense of something is the result of your instincts reacting to a message that cannot yet be defined in objective reality. Being intuitive is knowing without knowing how you know.

Instincts drive conative action.

**Ev**: What about people who misinterpret instinct and don't understand that it has an action component?

**Kathy**: When you use the *5 Rules for Trusting Your Guts* you allow such reactions to surface, have the self-determination to take the risks that could save your own life – or, at the very least, get to someone who can

"I think that somehow, we learn who we really are and then live with that decision."
Eleanor Roosevelt

help you soon enough to make that possible.

No one will be able to thwart your will or misinterpret the warnings you voice because of your gut instinct.

**Ev:** Instincts aren't always responses to negative things or crises. I've been surprised to realize just how much they can help bring more joy into my life.

**Kathy:** They help you react to positive opportunities, too, such as finding that a particular financial opportunity makes sense or that the person you just met might be the ideal partner you've been seeking.

**Ev:** I still want to be sure that I don't just jump at a chance because my guts say it might work.

**Kathy:** Remember, I said that you do not stop thinking when you *trust your guts*. You simply allow decisions to be made instinctively before you get too bogged down in the traditional or learned approach. Sometimes you need to Do Nothing, so you can have a moment of quiet when your instincts can be heard.

Many medical breakthroughs have been the result of someone following the principles behind the *5 Rules*.

The Jacuzzi would never have been invented if a child named Ken Jacuzzi hadn't been born with physical disabilities. Ken's father was determined to reduce his son's pain. And this led to his experimenting with water treatments. After initial attempts, he used his technical expertise to adjust the right combination of water movement, temperature, and force. That's when thinking did its job.

If Ken's father, Roy, had thought before he acted, Ken and millions of other people might not have benefited from his creativity – or from the Jacuzzi and its therapeutic benefits. Nothing he knew could have told him what to do because nothing previously existed that gave his son much relief from pain.

**Ev:** What is the education community doing to help students build on their instinctive strengths?

**Kathy:** Apart from the rare individual teacher, nothing. A lack of awareness of conation as the third dimension of the mind causes professionals to misjudge many situations.

When so-called learning disabled kids act before they think, they're often told they are wrong – again. In truth, many such minds have contributed to our most astonishing solutions. Had they not trusted their guts, we might not be benefiting from their creativity. [Details: p. 245]

Did a teacher ever tell you to guess at the answer before she taught you the "correct way?"

**Ev:** Not that I can remember.

**Kathy:** If it ever happened, you'd recall that lesson best. Yet, acting before you are taught the so-called right answers is not a part of most lesson plans.

**Ev:** Teachers ought to give kids a chance to *discover* right answers, not just sit in boring lectures.

**Kathy:** Don't blame teachers for inhibiting creativity. Expecting, even demanding, that we adhere to a restrictive form of problem-solving permeates our society. Doctors tell us to trust our instincts, but some of them still characterize any symptom they can't verify as "psycho-somatic."

**Ev:** Yes, and I love it when a manager tells you that you're in a "brain-storming session," then rates your gut responses for their reasonableness.

**Kathy:** Most courtroom lawyers pick juries based upon knowledge of the demographics of prospective jurors. Think of how much better off they'd be if they knew the MO of each juror – or at least had practiced trusting their guts so they made wise decisions, not just statistically correct calculations.

If only people would trust their guts they would save so much pain and create so many opportunities. One of the stories that has always troubled

> "Children may turn away from the instinctive creative spirit within them to cope with others or even themselves...."
>
> Hughes Mearns
> Creative Power

me is that of a friend of mine who received a marriage proposal from a young man who lived three states away. She told him she wanted a year to think about it, a year she'd spend teaching in her hometown. When I told my father about that, he said, "If you have to think that hard, the answer is 'No.'" He was an expert at cognitive testing, but he knew when you needed to trust your guts.

**Ev:** Did she marry the guy?

**Kathy:** Yep. And it was a disaster. He once hit her so hard she ended up in the hospital. I've always believed that her guts sensed something wrong with him from the beginning, but "on paper" he looked good.

Our instincts drive our creative potential. Not acting on them condemns us to saying, "If only I had trusted my instincts..." over and over again. **If you don't trust your guts, you'll only meet the common standards and use common solutions.**

**You're nothing special if you are not yourself.**

- **You won't buy or sell at just the right moment.**

- **You won't return the "look" that takes the relationship in the right direction.**

- **You won't say "Yes!" before the opportunity passes, or "No" just in the nick of time.**

**Ev:** I've noticed how often actions are stopped in their tracks by action plans. That's another oxymoron.

**Kathy:** Imagine the little engine that could having to convince the railroad authorities that he understood and accepted his liabilities before he climbed the mountain.

**Ev:** So health, education, and business could all benefit from being *Powered by Instinct.*

**Kathy:** And government too. Presidents put their own strengths at the

191

public's service when they act spontaneously. What they ad lib often serves them better than prepared speeches. George W, not noted for his eloquence, said what was in our hearts when he called out an unscripted "We can hear you!" to workers at Ground Zero.

**Ev:** There's a great show tune about "Doin' What Comes Naturally..."

**Kathy:** Easy to sing about it, but it's tough to do when parents, teachers, bosses, trainers, and spouses tell you how you *ought* to act. It makes you stop and think.

**Ev:** Help me out with some more examples of how I can respond naturally to people and situations, without overanalyzing.

**Kathy:** Here are some examples:

- You get a last-minute invitation. It sort of throws your schedule off a bit, but you sense you'd be missing out on great fun if you didn't accept. Do it.

- You are disgusted with the way a meeting is being conducted. Speak up or walk out.

- The price is the lowest you've seen, and your guts say now is the time to make a move. Make it.

- Everything about the job feels right except that it doesn't fit your resume. Take it.

- Your pet doesn't have specific symptoms, but you sense she is sick. Get her to the vet.

- You have been taught how to study but it doesn't work for you. Do it your way.

- The salesperson says it looks great on you, but you keep tugging at the seams. Take it off.

**Ev:** Those are helpful examples, but doing this could lead to tension and even arguments between me and the people in my life.

**Kathy:** It probably will – initially. Trusting your guts doesn't guarantee approval. In the extreme it could get you labeled eccentric, noncon-formist, and iconoclastic. Oddly, it's also a significant factor in what's called charisma.

We watch people who act authentically with a certain fascination. There are people you admire because they are what-you-see-is-what-you-get folks and you agree with them.

John Wayne was popular – and not necessarily because of his acting abilities or his looks. He tended to play characters who would take action without waiting for a buy-in from all the guys around him. His character didn't just talk-the-talk, he walked-the-walk and didn't let anyone hold him down.

## Dos and Don'ts for the 5 Rules

1. **Don't compromise or sacrifice your instincts. Everything else springs from this. Remember, you are perfect. Perfectly you. Ignoring or suppressing your instincts takes greater effort than working through them to achieve your goals.**

2. **Don't be satisfied with happiness. Like fame, it's fleeting. Happiness isn't inconsequential – it's just not enduring – or as endearing as unmitigated joy. It's a self-esteem snack at best. Go for joy. Beethoven knew this when he decided to write "Ode to Joy" rather than "Ode to Happiness."**

3. **Do base your desires on your intrinsic needs. Do you truly need what you want, or is it a passing fancy? The things that are in line with your instincts will have the greatest lasting value.**

If you **don't** trust your guts:

- Your grammar and syntax are correct but people aren't reading what you write.

- You're wearing an acceptable outfit, but you don't look like yourself.

- Your experiment went without a hitch, but you didn't prove anything new.

- You practice in your head what you're going to say, but the meeting ends before you've made your point.

- You've been thinking about tossing in more spices, but now the chicken is overcooked.

- You've evaluated the relationship and decided it's worth giving another chance, when you find out she just got engaged.

**Ev**: Most of those examples deal with worrying about the consequences of being wrong while opportunities are passing you by.

**Kathy**: You could also be analyzing how to make something work, while the resources to do it are withering away:

- "I could make a great sauce with those herbs, if I could just find the recipe."

- "If you'll just let me think about it for a little while, I can explain why I can make it work."

**Ev**: I get it. You do admit, though, that following some of the 5 Rules could easily cause you to fail?

**Kathy**: Which is one of the best reasons for following them!

If you don't fail, you haven't dared to stretch your mental muscles. A healthy dose of failure ought to be required in any business, family, school,

"An essential aspect of creativity is not being afraid to fail."
Sir Isaac Newton

or other place where honest communication and productive performance are essential.

The greatest glory in using the three parts of your mind (thinking, feeling, and doing) to solve problems is in the process. It brings the joy of self-discovery with the thrill of charting your own path. Being *Powered by Instinct* does not demean the intellect. It gives it the opportunity to operate at its highest levels.

Ralph Waldo Emerson says it best:

> *"All our progress is an unfolding, like the vegetable bud. You have first an instinct, then an opinion, then a knowledge, as the plant has root, bud and fruit. Trust the instinct to the end, though you can render no reason."*

Your best bet for keeping up the good work is to Do Nothing – so you can maintain the creative pace. If that seems nonsensical, think about the times you hit a mental wall, stopped what you were doing, went for a walk in the woods, or ate a great meal. Or listened to your favorite music. Or just took a nap. When you went back to the drawing board, *voila*: a solution seemed to appear from nowhere. Of course, it wasn't from nowhere. It was from your instinctive warehouse, which had been replenished.

You don't have a mental energy gauge on your forehead, so you have to pay attention to the **signs of burnout**.

- **When you want to make a decision but just can't work up the energy to do it, you're running on empty.**

- **When you care about the outcome but haven't the foggiest notion how to achieve it, you've used up your conative reserves.**

- **When you know you know the answer but you don't even try to prove it, there's no power hooked up to your mind.**

You have all it takes to fulfill your desires and convert thoughts into deeds, as long as you're physically and psychologically healthy (which includes not being on mind-altering drugs). In order to maintain your creative strengths, you have to re-create the drive when it's depleted.

Re-create is the root of recreation. Don't get caught up in recreational outlets that become striving efforts, or you forfeit the opportunity to use them for rest and relaxation. There's a reason the military provides R & R for its personnel.

- **Too bad those on the front lines have to wait so long to get it.**

- **Too bad more corporations don't follow universities in the policy of offering sabbaticals.**

- **Too bad teachers get personal days, but students don't (at least, not officially).**

- **Too bad more communities – and extended families- don't offer respite weekends for financially strapped single parents.**

Instincts are the common sense we trusted when we went against the advice of others and came out better than they did.

"In the truest sense, freedom cannot be bestowed; it must be achieved."
Franklin D. Roosevelt
September 22, 1936

Learning theories that took us down a strictly cognitive path in education betrayed our need to act on instinct, thwarted our wills, and left us with undue stress about our futures. The flower children brought us into the era of emotions, but could still not provide us with answers without incorporating instinctive truths. *Being who we want to be does not always free us to be who we truly are.*

*Powered by Instinct* brings out the best in whoever you are. That, in turn, offers the following essential benefits:

- Increased awareness of natural abilities

- Greater joy in what you do

- Improved performance with less effort

- Increased resistance to stress

- Enhanced creativity

- More effective problem solving in less time

- Improved ability to communicate why you need what you need

- Humility because you know your natural ability is no greater or less than that of any other human being

*Powered by Instinct* is based upon a revolutionary program that enhances performance without asking you to change a thing about yourself.

The secret to its worldwide success is that it helps you discover and use the inalienable strengths within you – the undeniable third dimension of your mind.

Well, we're being asked to prepare for landing. Time flies when I'm sharing this mission.

Ev: I've had quite a journey. I'm eager to find out where *Trusting my Guts* will take me.

Kathy: Let me know. You've got my email address: kkolbe@poweredbyinstinct.com

Ev: And you've got my MO, so you probably know where I'm headed.

Kathy: I hope it's off to a place called *Freedom to Be Yourself.*

# GLOSSARY OF TERMS

**Accommodate:** A mid-range positioning of 4-6 units in a given Action Mode describing the ability to bridge differences between those on the outermost limits who initiate solutions or prevent problems in using the same Action Mode.

**Action Advantages:** Ambition, Alertness, Achievement.

**Action Modes:** As identified by Kathy Kolbe, four distinct clusters of behavior able to be measured which result from engaging our striving instincts: Fact Finder, Follow Thru, Quick Start and Implementor.

**Affective/Affect:** Known for centuries as one of the three parts of the mind. Pertains to or arises from feelings or emotions as measured on personality or social style instruments. An emotion or tendency (noun); to influence (verb).

**Best Effort:** See **Effort.**

**Cognitive/Cognition:** Known for centuries as one of the three parts of the mind. Deals with knowledge, competencies and intellectual processes as measured on IQ or skills tests.

**Commitment:** Guarantee that the necessary instinctive power will be allocated to accomplish a goal.

**Commitment Contract:** Process of determining and guaranteeing appropriate levels and types of efforts will be given to specific activities within a specific time.

**Conative/Conation:** Known for centuries as one of the three parts of the mind. Action derived from instinct; purposeful mode of striving, volition. Can be measured by the Kolbe Conative Index.

**Conative Stress:** The result of a compelling need being denied when one's natural drive is thwarted, creating unproductive pressure on the individual.

**Conflict:** As defined by Kathy Kolbe, conative stress that results from natural differences of four units or more in how people function in any one Action Mode.

**Creative Process:** See **Kolbe Creative Process.**

**Dire:** An exciting horror, dismal, oppressive or a warning of disaster or desperately urgent.

**DIRe Syndrome:** syndrome that can be caused by overthinking, heightened emotion and mind-altering substances.

**Dynamynd Decision Ladder:** A hierarchical model of the graduated, sequential steps that lead to higher levels of thinking, feeling and taking action in the creative problem solving process.

    **Culture Dynamynd:** A model for assigning the status on the Dynamynd Decision Ladder for a category of people who are affiliated, but who do not make decisions interactively.

    **Individual Dynamynd:** A model of the specific behaviors an individual exhibits when making decisions at each level of the Dynamynd hierarchy, in each of the three dimensions of the mind: cognitive, conative, and affective.

    **Leader Dynamnyd:** A model of the levels of decision making required of leaders as they develop higher standards of performance for themselves and others whose decisions they influence.

    **Team Dynamynd:** A model of the levels of decision making – in all three dimensions of the mind – available to a group of people who work interdependently.

**Effect:** The result of using your instinctive energy (noun); to bring about (verb).

**Effort:** Conative actions you take to solve problems.

    **Best Effort:** Actions that use your four natural Impact Factors or instinctive abilities.

    **Foolish Effort:** Actions you take that you know are not your best efforts or working against your MO or instincts. See Wasted Effort.

    **Levels of Effort:** The degree to which we decide to employ our mental energy or engage our instincts as represented on a scale: See Will. Lowest level – Intention, Middle level – Attempt, Highest level – Commitment

    **Wasted Effort:** Energy you use to take action that goes against your grain, or is contrary to your best efforts. Working without using your natural talents. See Wasted Effort.

**Erg (Mental Erg):** Unit of energy.

**Facilitator:** A person with all four Action Modes in the mid-range. Also termed Mediator.

**Fact Finder:** The Action Mode that deals with detail and complexity, providing the perspective of experience.

**Failure Factors:** Fear, Fatigue, Frustration.

**Follow Thru:** The Action Mode that deals with structure and order, and provides focus and continuity.

**Foolish Effort:** See **Effort.**

**Going Against Your Grain:** Making efforts that do not use your instinctive talents.

**Impact Factors:** The twelve ways (4 Action Modes x 3 Zones of Operation) of taking instinctive action when problem solving. Each of us takes action in all of the four modes and our uniqueness derives from the combinations of modes and the zones in which we fall.

**Implementor:** The Action Mode that deals with physical space and ability to operate manually, and provides durability and a sense of the tangible.

**Initiation:** The instinctive way of approaching a solution to a problem through any Action Mode. A measurement of 7-10 units of conative energy in any Action Mode. Also referred to as insistence.

Insistence: See **Initiation**.

Inertia: Loss of productivity caused by uniformity of action among people in an organization.

Instincts: Mental energies which are: universal, intrinsic, individual talents, seminal, valid across cultures, needs, innate, natural, authentic, inborn tendencies to strive or initiate action through probing, patterning, innovating, and demonstrating.

Ipsative: The Kolbe index is an ipsative instrument. 'Ipsative' means 'measured against itself.' An ipsative result is not compared to other results and then put in the context of an average or expected result (as is done with 'normative' instruments). An ipsative score expresses results in terms of the relative strength of need rather than absolute terms and each person thus provides his or her own frame of reference.

Knack: A person's instinctive way of dealing with detail, structure, risk and tangible effort.

Kolbe Creative Process: The mental process that results in the development of something that has not previously existed; also the mental process that naturally takes place when the mind is focused on solving a particular problem.

Kolbe Concept: Unique expression by Kathy Kolbe of her theory of individual performance driven by instinctive behaviors. Consists of psychometric measurements identifying natural talents and providing a pathway to higher productivity and greater satisfaction.

Kolbe indexes:

Kolbe A Index: An instrument designed by Kathy Kolbe that quantifies the degree of natural talent an individual possesses in each Action Mode.

Kolbe B index: Formerly known as the Kolbe J index, an instrument designed by Kathy Kolbe that measures self perceptions of job requirements.

Kolbe C Index: An instrument designed by Kathy Kolbe that indicates the conative requirements for success in a job as described by any third party, frequently a supervisor.

Kolbe R index: An instrument designed by Kathy Kolbe to identify how one person wishes the other person would take action in a personal relationship.

Kolbe Y index: Youth version of the Kolbe A index designed by Kathy Kolbe for a fifth grade reading level.

Kolbe Wisdom: Creating solutions through intelligence, integrity, and trusting your instincts.

Leisure: Activity that does not involve striving. See **Recreation**.

Levels of Effort: See **Effort**.

Mediator: See **Facilitator**.

Mental Energy: Internal power sources available to drive one's Instincts toward goal-directed activity.

Mental Tinnitus: Static in the mind resulting from over commitments, which makes it difficult to discern what your instincts are trying to tell you. See **Tinnitus**.

Modus Operandi (MO): A numerical representation of one's instinctive way of taking action as measured across the four Action Modes.

Natural Advantage: Description of the natural way of operating based on the combination of talents derived from a Kolbe A or Y result.

Obstinate: Having tenacity, perseverance, dogged resolution, a ruling passion, being willful, acting with determination.

Prevention: The instinctive way of resisting certain activities in an Action Mode as a unique method of problem solving. A measurement of 1-3 units of Mental Energy in an Action Mode. Also known as resistance.

Provoke: To goad, inspire, push, direct, trigger action, make happen, cause.

Quick Start: The Action Mode that deals with originality and risk-taking, and provides intuition and a sense of vision.

Recreation: Free time activity that involves striving. See **Leisure**.

Resistance: See **Prevention**.

Responding: Having from 4 to 6 units of mental energy in an Action Mode, indicating an ability to use the mode as needed.

Rue: To feel sorrow over; repent of; regret bitterly and to wish that something had never been done.

Strain: As defined by Kathy Kolbe, conative stress resulting from a person's unrealistic self-expectations of how he or she needs to perform.

Theory of Equality: Every individual is endowed with equal Will and is, therefore, equally capable of creating solutions.

Three Parts of the Mind (3-Dimensional mind): The mind controls the actions stimulated by the Will and transmitted by the striving instincts. Every Individual has three mental faculties:

   · Cognitive or intellectual, which controls thought
   · Affective or emotional, which controls feelings
   · Conative or functional, which controls actions

Think-ercise: Exercises that involve the use of all three parts of the mind to do creative problem solving.

Tinnitus: the presence of sound in the ears when no external sound is present to cause it. See **Mental Tinnitus**.

Transition: The loss of ability to express or recognize one's own conative nature; loss of sense of self. Kolbe results resemble that of a Facilitator, but are distinguished on the bar chart by an asterisk under the Action Mode(s) that is out of sync.

Wasted Effort: See **Effort**.

Will: The power of control the mind has over whether, or to what degree, to engage the striving instincts. Although an intellectual awareness of the need to employ these instincts or an affective concern for their use may exist, free will makes that determination. See **Levels of Effort**.

Work: What happens when something is accomplished. It is seemingly effortless.

Zones of Operation: The perspective through which a person naturally uses a striving instinct – what they will do, won't do or are willing to do. In Kathy Kolbe's expression the zones include initiation (insistence), prevention (resistance) and response (accommodation).

# Details

## CHAPTER ONE – TAKING OFF:

### Kathy Kolbe and Kolbe Corp, Detail: p. 8

Freud, Jung and Skinner may be more famous, but it was Kathy Kolbe who solved the ancient riddle of human behavior by unlocking the mystery of the conative part of the mind.

Throughout history scholars believed there were three distinct parts of the human mind - the cognitive (knowledge or intelligence), the affective (motivation and emotion) and the conative, (volition or action) but it is only Kolbe, an award-winning and internationally-recognized theorist and expert on human behavior, who has contributed original research on conation in the last 100 years.

Kolbe amassed over 500,000 case studies to support her breakthrough theory, which proved not only the existence of conative modalities, but also identified four specific conative Action Modes® derived from human instinct and defined these modes as the source of the human modus operandi (MO). Her work shows why we don't always do what we know we should, and proves that no one can change the basic way a person acts.

An entrepreneur, educator and best-selling author, Kolbe pioneered programs that apply her work regarding instinctive abilities to improving performance in individuals and organizations in endeavors ranging from athletic and academic achievements, to relationship and financial successes. By helping people understand why they do what they do, she has improved their ability to manage stress and other health-related issues, make better career choices, and control the primary source of interpersonal conflicts.

On her road to success, Kolbe had to meet and overcome many personal obstacles including dyslexia and a car accident that left her with severe physical injuries and brain damage that cost her the ability to read and write for nearly a year. She approached these problems as challenges and overcame each situation. Eventually, Kolbe gained national recognition as an author and publisher of books for gifted education and was showcased in Time magazine's "Man of the Year" article that featured Can-Do people. Her high-energy passion for uncovering the best that a person has to offer draws a wide and varied audience. Leaders respect her painstaking research – spanning three decades and several continents – in business, education, psychology, religion, sports, health, and government.

Kolbe's first book, *The Conative Connection*, shook the very foundations of conventional wisdom regarding the mind by identifying its third – and most elusive – dimension, the conative actions that are derived from instinctive drives. *Pure Instinct*, her breakthrough business book published by Times Books (Random House), details her experience with high performers in the corporate arena and her techniques for helping them to maximize their potential.

With *Powered by Instinct: 5 Rules for Trusting Your Guts*, Kolbe is fulfilling her promise to people around the world who have wanted her to write this book for them. In the book Kolbe delivers five practical, results-oriented rules for putting the power of natural strengths and talents to work in everyday life. The book will help readers find the joy in acting on their authentic, instinctive abilities and personally benefit from Kolbe's years of proven wisdom.

Kathy Kolbe founded Kolbe Corp which has been in business for nearly three decades. Professionals from 23 different countries have been trained and licensed to deliver Kolbe applications. Kolbe Certification training has taken place in multiple countries around the world on five continents. Through Kolbe Corp's Internet websites thousands of people from all over the world have completed a Kolbe index and purchased products and services.

Kolbe Corp's database includes input from students, teachers and parents. Professions represented range from Administrative Assistant to Zone Manager and include military, clergy, medical technologists, athletes, psychiatrists and psychologists among many others. Industries cover the full gamut from agriculture to underwriting, and the level in an organization ranges from unemployed to self-employed, to CEO of major corporations.
*Source: Kolbe Corp Research Files*

# Research Summaries re: Stress Correlation, Detail: p. 11

The following cases are illustrative of the direct correlation between symptoms of serious stress such as absenteeism and turnover in the workplace when various Kolbe measurements identified employees who were mismatched in their jobs.

## Absenteeism
In a study completed in 1992, 50 staff-level employees were selected by a national food processing company to study absenteeism. The employees were all rated on a three-point scale for absenteeism during 1990. The results showed 16% of the employees fell in the medium to high range of absenteeism, representing more than one week of unexcused absences during the previous year. Of that number, 62.5% were experiencing conative tension or strain, a rate more than three times that of the rest of the group.

## Turnover
This study compared the percentage of turnover between two groups of professionals within an internationally recognized accounting firm. Group One consisted of 30 professionals whose Kolbe results indicated that they were mismatched for their positions. Group Two consisted of 57 professionals whose Kolbe results indicated a good match with their positions.

The turnover rate for Group One, where the Kolbe scores indicated a job mismatch, was significantly higher than that of Group Two, where the Kolbe indicated a good job fit.

Group One – Mismatch        47.5% Turnover
Group Two – No Mismatch     22.8% Turnover

A number of individual cases relating to stress in the workplace can be found in the Kolbe Statistical Handbook on the www.kolbe.com website which should be consulted for more detail. *Source: Kolbe Corp Research Files*

# Summary of Academic Research and Comments from Educators, Detail: p. 12

- American Graduate School of International Management – Predictive validity of major studies programs/Test-retest reliability studies

- Arizona State University – Prediction of Hiring success of major corporations based on selection criteria of IQ, personality and conative makeup

- Claremont Graduate School – Longitudinal study of the impact of Group Decision Support Systems on a public sector task using Kolbe assessments to understand group dynamics

- Brigham Young University – Predictive validity of synergy of student design teams

- Cal State Northridge – Application of conative talents in crisis situation/Conative makeup of juvenile offenders

- Case Western University – Correlation of Kolbe Conative Index (Kolbe A index) with Kolb Learning Style Indicator (LSI)

- Oregon State University – Self regulation of high school students in managing their learning based on their Kolbe result

- Pepperdine University – Predictive validity of Kolbe result applied to a student population

- Prescott College – Predictive validity showing conative makeup of students in this experiential education environment compared to students in more traditional learning environments

- Stanford University – Conative makeup of teams as a predictor of group synergy

- Texas A & M University – Effects of conation on individual and group task completion/Effects of conative stress on students' self esteem

- U of Arizona – Forming effective teams using the Kolbe Concept in a workplace environment

- U of California Los Angeles – Predictive validity of makeup of senior law enforcement officers compared to general population

- U of Chicago – Ability to predict team behavior and team outputs of students in New Product

Laboratory/Prediction of project team effectiveness

· U of Colorado – Conative reason behind dropout rate of third year medical students in surgical residency

· U of North Texas – Relationship of conative behaviors to success in treatment of diabetes

· U of Pennsylvania – Conative connection in addictive personality

*Source: Kolbe Research Files*

## Educators' Comments, Detail: p. 12

"I truly believe this system needs to be an integral basis for all aspects of education. I will not continue teaching if I cannot use the Kolbe method in my job."
*Mickey Anderson, Vancouver, Washington School District*

"By providing clear and practical applications, Kathy Kolbe helps us understand how we can communicate more effectively both interpersonally and professionally."
*Elizabeth, Berry, Ph.D. Professor of Communications, California State University, Northridge*

"I have just finished a review of your work on Conation and continue to be enthusiastic, even amazed, at its basic simplicity and far-reaching implications for personnel and management productivity. In my 30 years of experience with all levels and forms of education, public and private, pre-collegiate and collegiate, vocational and classical, I have run into little which combines the elements of originality and validity. Conation meets that dual challenge."
*Ralph Bohrson, former Program Manager, Ford Foundation*

"By focusing on the way people behave, rather than how they think or feel, Kathy Kolbe offers a simple yet powerful tool for self-exploration. Our students have learned more about themselves and about teamwork using the Kolbe A index."
*Harry Davis, Ph.D., Deputy Dean, Graduate Business School, University of Chicago*

"I only wish that I could ask everyone I encounter to become a Kolbe card-carrier; I would make fewer mistakes when forming faculty workgroups."
*Cynthia Desrochers, CELT Director, California State University Northridge*

"The inevitable outcome of reading this book is the desire to share its wisdom with colleagues and friends. This is a 'must read' for leaders desirous of obtaining maximum productivity, quality, and creativity."
*Forrest Gale, Ph.D., Professor of Engineering Management, Defense Systems Management College*

"I never felt that my personal gifts were validated until this CEO appointment. But if someone had told me four years ago I'd be here now, I would have laughed. It wasn't a career track I was on."
*Judeth Javorek, CEO, Holland Michigan Community College*

"Managers have been using this technique intuitively but now they actually have a quantity to measure- that can really demonstrate and prove how to best structure teams and how people will work and won't work."

*Robert Keim, Ph.D., Director, Division of Information Management and Systems Technology,*
*Arizona State University*

"... used the Kolbe system to select and place team members, which resulted in such a high performance division that the Board was astonished by the amount of productivity. We used Kolbe to assess instinctive strengths, and freed people to work according to those innate abilities."

*Marilyn Kourilsky, Ph.D., Vice President Kaufman Foundation,*
*University of California at Los Angeles*

"Kathy Kolbe's detailed examples, so rich, so vivid, so meaningful, so illustrative. The possibilities are endless. I'll build better teams."

*Hank Laskey, Ph.D., Associate Professor, Bloomsburg University*

"Having the on-going personal attention of Kathy Kolbe conducting the Kolbe Certification Training. increased (my) confidence professionally regarding my abilities as well as being able to identify the sources of my recent stress. It would be extremely beneficial as part of the informational core requirements of my current doctoral program."

*Monique Lewis, Occidental College*

"Kathy Kolbe has done for business what Timothy Gallwey did for tennis. She has provided remarkable insights for helping each of us understand how we play our inner game."

*Richard Mason, Ph.D., Carr P. Collins Distinguished Professor,*
*Southern Methodist University*

"Professionally I anticipate working with students, educators and business in a totally new way—including research. Personally, this is a new and exciting tool! The facet of knowledge provided psychologically is invaluable."

*James Mullarkey, Waukesha County Technical College*

"Kathy Kolbe's Kolbe A index is a powerful tool to aid us in understanding and overcoming the struggles that emerge when we cannot achieve unity between what we do and who we are. The implications for its use in researching the psychology of meaning and character formation are vast."

*Morrie Olsen, Ph.D., Clinical Research Coordinator, Treatment Research Center,*
*University of Pennsylvania*

"Kathy Kolbe has created a book that is a godsend to managers trying to pull together the human resources needed to get their jobs done. This is one of the most useful and best books of the year."

*Jerry Porras Ph.D., Professor Stanford University Graduate School of Business*
*Co-Author of Built to Last*

"We have been persuaded by the data, that we have available an instrument that is not only minority bias free but an instrument, which may under the 1991 law be one of the few instruments available which is bias free and a consequence, is a viable and important instrument for anyone involved in the selection process to consider."

*Ryan Thomas, Ph.D., Brigham Young University*

"I had been in education for 30 years and for all those years I kept feeling 'Why am I such an odd duck?' Once I got into Kolbe, I understood why I always felt out of step and I thought it's not that I'm such an odd duck, it's just that I have a different sort of talents. Once I understood, I then had a language to express it to my school board and fellow administrators. It helped me in delegating tasks. What it's taught me is that everybody's different and we need to use teaching techniques that allow every kid in the classroom to use their natural talents. The validation is just terrific."

*Mark Yehle, Ph.D., Superintendent*

# Historical Reference re: Instincts, Detail: p. 13

Aristotle "starteth" the question that has led to a discussion of instinct and its companion principle of "will," according to a seventeenth-century treatise by Ralph Cudworth. "What is it that first moveth in the soul and setteth all the other wheels on work?" he paraphrased Aristotle as having asked. "What is that vital power and energy which the soul first displayeth itself in, and which in order of nature precedes all its other powers, it implying them, or setting them on work?"

Such philosophical discussions on the nature of instinct gave way to heated debate two hundred years later, as the new field of psychology attempted to define instinct in scientific terms. "Actions we call instinctive," wrote William James in 1890, are "as fatal as sneezing." He argued against the notion espoused earlier that century by Lindley Kemp that "unlike animals, when it comes to man, we find ALL is actions placed under the control of reason. Man is, indeed, devoid of instinct. . . He observes and reflects, and acts in accordance to the decisions of his mind." Although James, Freud, Jung and others brought the issue of instinct into the hallowed halls of academia, their lack of "proof" of the existence of this unconscious energy weakened their theories.

Modern psychologists could have written Kemp's nineteenth-century book on instinct. There is a current contempt among academicians for those suggesting instinct as a source of human activity. James hadn't softened such opinions by saying that, "the older writings on instinct are ineffectual wastes of words, being their authors never came down to this definite and simple point of view [that behavior is energized by instinct], but smothered everything in vague wonder."

Both those in agreement with and those who oppose a human instinct model to explain unlearned behavior have used the same simplistic argument. Lack of proof to the contrary was assumed as evidence for both sides. The battle over instincts' power to determine human action has raged since the eighteenth century, when philosophers in the Age of Enlightenment turned to reason as the sole basis of human action.

James's protestations seemed to give encouragement to philosophers and psychologists of the late nineteenth and early twentieth century who rejected the notion that human beings were purely rational creatures. Freud, for instance, identified sex and death (or self-destruction) as instinctual. Jung added the herd and nutritional instincts. William McDougall, the foremost social psychologist of the early 1900s, identified twelve urges, including seven primary proclivities: fear, repulsion, pugnacity, curiosity, self-abasement, self-assertion, and parenting. The momentum built as H. W. Warren offered twenty-six instincts, and Woodworth threw in one hundred and ten, under the general headings of organic needs, responses to other persons, and play instincts.

By 1926, Luther L. Bernard had enough. His criticisms were instrumental in turning modern scholars away once again from the study of instinct. "There is scarcely any conduct employed in the social sciences about which there is so much diversity of usage and uncertainty of meaning as there is concerning the term instinct." He enumerated the problems as:

1. There was no agreement on the nature of true instincts.
2. The discussions of instinct were too vague and conceptual.
3. Instincts weren't visible and therefore couldn't be a part of scientific study.
4. There were no accurate methods for classifying instincts in terms of overt manifestations.

Bernard was writing at a time when IQ testing was beginning to allow behaviorists to study the cognitive part of the mind in quantifiable terms. In the 1890s Alfred Binet had discovered the measurable qualities of faculty; it was presumed to be the only mental faculty that mattered. Researchers came to believe human behavior was premeditated, that we acted only according to learned patterns. If there was any discussion of instinct, they tried to connect it with motivation, since both remained non-quantifiable components of the performance equation.

There have always been a few learned voices who have realized the limitation of a scientific approach to understanding instinct, for whom this has not lessened a belief in instinct. I like to refer my academically oriented friends to a statement by the philosopher George Berkeley, who said it took "a mind debauched by learning to carry the process of making the natural seem strange, so far as to ask for the WHY of any instinctive human act.
*Source: Pure Instinct, by Kathy Kolbe*

# Abraham Maslow Biography and Hierarchy of Needs Summary, Detail: p. 14

*The Right to Be Human*, Edward Hoffman, Ph.D., McGraw-Hill, 1988

"Maslow often emphasized his notion of instinctive needs – our naturally good tendencies....which can easily be crushed in early upbringing." Ibid; pg. 127.

"Maslow: 'Man is ultimately not molded or shaped into humanness [...]The environment does not give him potentialities and capacities; he has them in inchoate or embryonic form, just exactly as he has embryonic arms and legs. And creativeness, spontaneity, selfhood, authenticity...are potentialities belonging to his species-membership just as much as are his arms and legs, brain and eyes.'

For this reason, he urged his colleagues to grapple with the complexities of human instinct and the [partially] hereditary-determined needs [and] urges...of mankind." Ibid; pg. 215

"Most important to the impact of Maslow's later theoretical system, this work convinced him that we have certain inner needs unrecognized by Freudians and members of other psychological schools of thought – especially the need to experience meaning and purpose in life...Maslow, relying on his intuition...sensed the real issue to be the woman's sense of meaningless and wasted talent...he wrote: 'Any talent, any capacity was also a motivation, a need, an impulse'..." Ibid; pg 133.

"Maslow also emphasized that each of us has an intrinsic core of personality – what he called a "real self" -unique and yet possessing traits in common with all humans. Reflecting his belief in the biological essence of human nature, he also assured his audience: 'Cultural differences, although seemingly very marked, are actually only superficial. As one goes deeper into personality, it is apparent that men have more in common than in difference'." Ibid; pf 198.

"...we shall probably have to make room for some notion of fundamental or natural 'tendency-to-have-a-certain-type-of-personality' with which each human comes into society – and which the society will have to take as a fundamental datum, perhaps to build upon, perhaps to repress, or warp, or reshape." Report to the annual convention of the American Anthropological Association in New York City, 1938.

## Equality of Instincts, Detail: p. 16

Everyone has the same amount of instinctive power and an equal need to act freely according to those instincts. Each of us has talent in all four Action Modes. Our particular zones of operation, determined by our instinctive patterns of behavior, are with us from birth. Every possible combination of Operating Zones provides the same potential for achievement.

Our instinct-driven talents are the one way in which we are all created equal. Yet the opportunities to use these talents often differ significantly. Quick Start females and minorities – those with the right instincts to start their own businesses, for example – may well have more difficulty getting bank loans than less well-suited white male candidates for small-business loans. Men with an inclination to initiate designs are often unfairly labeled effeminate because of gender stereotyping of talents. While the distribution of instinctive abilities is the same for males and females, whites and minorities, the young and the elderly, opportunities are rarely so equal.

The data in over 100,000 case studies, including Kolbe A index results from every continent and a wide variety of workplaces and educational settings, show that Kolbe A index scores are unbiased by age, race, gender, national origin, or disability. Women are as likely as men to initiate action in any mode. As many minorities naturally innovate as do whites. People who prevent rigid structures as youngsters will do the same as they age. Therefore those who limit opportunities for any segment of the population because of false presumptions regarding innate abilities can now be proved wrong. The equal energy of striving instincts gives every human being the same potential for productivity. The form that talent takes is differentiated by nothing other than individual differences in Operating Zones.

At long last, the fact that instincts are unbiased makes it possible for us to characterize individual differences without unfair discrimination. When we measure the actions that are based upon instinctive needs, there are no good or bad results. There are only right answers on the Kolbe A index because it identifies internal strengths. An insistent Fact Finder is no better or worse than someone who prevents getting bogged down in details. Responding to change doesn't make you a more valuable human being than someone who responds to technical needs.
*Source: Pure Instinct, p.19 by Kathy Kolbe*

## Supporting Data from Statistical Handbook

Dr. Robert T. Keim of the Decision Systems Research Center of Arizona State University conducted an extensive study on bias and the Kolbe instrument in 1990, in which he examined 4030 Kolbe results which were broken down into 17 groups reflecting common conative patterns similar to job selection criteria.

Study samples were drawn from the database of Kolbe Corp. Because the Kolbe index has been predominantly used in the corporate management environment and with smaller entrepreneurial firms, the number of middle-aged white males is over-represented. For the same reasons, the number of insistent Implementor profiles used in analyses represent a smaller percentage of the database than is reflected in the general population. The database included profiles obtained from respondents worldwide, but a preponderance of the profiles are from individuals currently residing in the United States.

Dr. Keim initially performed analyses of variance with each of the four conative instincts as dependent variables and the independent variable being race, gender, or age. In 65 out of 68 analyses of variance, the results showed that at the .05 level of significance the differences in scores on the Kolbe could not be attributed to the dependent variables of race, gender, or age. For the three values where the initial analysis of variance did not provide conclusive results, a Chi Square analysis was conducted by computing a Chi Square base-model value for each with gender, race, and age. Subsequent analyses of variance and Chi Square values were computed leaving out each of the independent variables. Comparisons between the base-model values and the subsequent values demonstrated that in no case do the independent variables of race, gender, or age explain differences in scores. Dr. Keim concluded that "at the Alpha=.05 level the Kolbe is not biased by gender, age, or race."

## Gender

Evaluation of the intensities by Action Mode for a group of 1447 males and 1125 females who took the Kolbe index in Ms. Kolbe's book The Conative Connection revealed remarkably similar distributions.

| Gender | Mode | Mean Score | Std Deviation |
|--------|------|-----------|---------------|
| Male | FF | 6.164 | .372 |
| Female | | 6.136 | .344 |
| Male | FT | 3.665 | 1.071 |
| Female | | 3.621 | 1.074 |
| Male | QS | 7.547 | .625 |
| Female | | 7.575 | .607 |
| Male | IM | 2.882 | .896 |
| Female | | 2.917 | .925 |

The results again support that neither gender is more likely to follow a particular pattern of scores. The frequency table is presented below:

| Mode | Gender | % Initiate | % Accommodate | % Resist |
|------|--------|-----------|---------------|----------|
| FF | Male | 34.14 | 53.28 | 12.58 |
| | Female | 33.60 | 52.80 | 13.60 |
| FT | Male | 19.56 | 51.69 | 28.75 |
| | Female | 22.22 | 53.33 | 24.44 |
| QS | Male | 38.77 | 32.07 | 29.16 |
| | Female | 40.71 | 33.78 | 25.51 |
| IM | Male | 12.23 | 48.86 | 38.91 |
| | Female | 8.36 | 47.38 | 44.27 |
| TOTAL | Male | 26.17 | 46.48 | 27.35 |
| | Female | 26.22 | 46.82 | 26.96 |

## Age

For the sake of simplicity and due to an informal demarcation line used in business and industry separating those workers 40 years of age and under from those over 40, the database was sorted into these two age groups for evaluation. Because of a significant difference in the size of each sample, the table below reports the percentage of each group classified by their scores into Natural Advantage categories.

| Natural Advantage | % 40 and Under | % over 40 |
|---|---|---|
| Fact Finder | 9.84 | 9.04 |
| Fact Finder / Follow Thru | 20.20 | 19.27 |
| Fact Finder / Quick Start | 5.74 | 6.70 |
| Fact Finder / Implementor | 1.65 | 1.38 |
| Follow Thru | 3.10 | 2.84 |
| Follow Thru / Fact Finder | 7.11 | 5.98 |
| Follow Thru / Quick Start | 0.58 | 0.47 |
| Follow Thru / Implementor | 1.40 | 1.27 |
| Quick Start | 15.91 | 20.24 |
| Quick Start / Fact Finder | 7.42 | 9.35 |
| Quick Start / Follow Thru | 1.32 | 1.49 |
| Quick Start / Implementor | 2.91 | 2.78 |
| Implementor | 2.17 | 2.01 |
| Implementor / Fact Finder | 1.23 | 0.83 |
| Implementor / Follow Thru | 1.11 | 0.41 |
| Implementor / Quick Start | 0.82 | 0.74 |
| Mediator | 17.49 | 15.19 |

## Race

As with the age groups, the disparity in group sample sizes between whites and non–whites identified in the Kolbe database was such that the most obvious meaningful comparisons are to be seen in frequency data. The table below details the similar percentage of each group who were classified by Kolbe results into Natural Advantage categories.

| Natural Advantage | Whites | Non–White |
|---|---|---|
| Fact Finder | 10.03 | 11.95 |
| Fact Finder / Follow Thru | 22.17 | 28.15 |
| Fact Finder / Quick Start | 6.26 | 4.09 |
| Fact Finder / Implementor | 1.52 | 2.78 |
| Follow Thru | 3.04 | 3.44 |
| Follow Thru / Fact Finder | 6.00 | 9.66 |
| Follow Thru / Quick Start | 0.53 | 1.31 |
| Follow Thru / Implementor | 1.40 | 1.47 |
| Quick Start | 16.79 | 7.04 |
| Quick Start / Fact Finder | 8.01 | 4.58 |
| Quick Start / Follow Thru | 1.58 | 0.82 |
| Quick Start / Implementor | 2.66 | 1.31 |
| Implementor | 1.78 | 1.64 |
| Implementor / Fact Finder | 0.00 | 0.00 |
| Implementor / Follow Thru | 0.99 | 0.49 |
| Implementor / Quick Start | 0.53 | 0.65 |
| Mediator | 16.70 | 20.62 |

## National Origin

Comparisons between those born in the United States and natives of countries other than the USA reveal the most startling information from a statistical viewpoint. When a mode-by-mode distribution of insistence, accommodation, and prevention is compared for respondents of US and non-U.S. origin, the results show there are no statistically significant differences. The study included 10,124 respondents of U.S. origin and 1,182 of non–U.S. origin. The charts below reflect the percentage of respondents in each mode by zone of intensity. Country of origin clearly does not influence the distribution of Kolbe results.

| | % Initiate | | % Accommodate | | % Resist | |
|---|---|---|---|---|---|---|
| | U.S. Origin | Other | U.S. Origin | Other than U.S. | In the U.S. | Other than U.S. |
| FF | 39.29 | 40.61 | 51.10 | 50.00 | 9.61 | 9.39 |
| FT | 20.89 | 26.40 | 55.81 | 52.37 | 23.30 | 21.24 |
| QS | 36.08 | 32.66 | 35.40 | 34.35 | 28.52 | 32.99 |
| IM | 6.87 | 6.60 | 49.03 | 48.39 | 44.09 | 45.01 |
| TOTAL | 25.79 | 26.57 | 47.83 | 46.28 | 26.38 | 27.16 |

### General Selection Study

In a subsequent selection-bias study performed in 1992, 24,416 Kolbe results were studied. The Kolbe results were cross-tabulated by each of 51 professions and 10 professional levels. In each profession and level in which there was an adequate minority sample (30 or more) the data was analyzed to determine whether the Kolbe would have selected any minority group (determined by the federally protected categories of race, gender, and age) less than 80% as frequently as the most frequently selected group (the criteria for adverse impact established by the EEOC). In no category in which there was an adequate minority sample would the Kolbe have adversely selected on minority status. There was no evidence that the Kolbe would have an adverse impact on any minority group if used as part of a properly designed selection process.
*Source: Kolbe Corp Statistical Handbook available at www.kolbe.com*

# Three Parts of the Mind, Detail: p. 16

The Kolbe Wisdom is based on historical, philosophical, and psychological research. The following is but a summary for those who wish to put the significance of this breakthrough in identifying conative Action Modes into its proper perspective.

That the mind has three distinct parts is the "Wisdom of the Ages." The Ancient philosophers Plato and Aristotle spoke of the three faculties through which we think, feel, and act. George Brett in his "History of Psychology," said, "Augustine was not far from the same standpoint...his language at times suggests the same three-fold division of knowing, feeling and willing."

Like Plato's Rationalism, Spinoza's Homic philosophy focused on an understanding of the three-faculty concept as a necessary prelude to the quest for ideal self-actualization.

Johann Nicolaus Tetens (1736-1805), sometimes called the "Father of Psychology" because of his introduction of the analytical, introspective method to psychology, believed that the three faculties of the mind not only existed, but were an expression of an underlying "respective spontaneity of the mind."

Immanuel Kant's tripartite division of the mind gave psychology the support of the most influential philosopher of his day. In his "Critique of Pure Reason" (1781), "Critique of Practical

Reason" (1788), and "Critique of Judgment" (1790), he discussed them transcendentally rather than empirically. In his classificatory scheme, pure reason corresponded to intellect or cognition; judgment to feeling, pleasure or pain, therefore affection; and practical reason to will, action, or conation.

In the 18th and 19th centuries, the trilogy of the mind was the accepted classification of mental activities throughout Germany, Scotland, England, and America. In the first half of the 20th century, it was American psychologist William McDougall who was its primary proponent.

As Ernest R. Hilgard notes in "The Trilogy of Mind: Cognition, Affection and Conation" (1980), McDougall "assumed that his reader was familiar with the classification of cognitive, affective and conative, as common-sensical and noncontroversial."

In McDougall's "Outline of Psychology (1923), he refers to the three-faculty concept as "generally admitted." He said, "We often speak of an intellectual or cognitive activity; or of an act of willing or of resolving, choosing, striving, purposing; or again of a state of feeling. But it is generally admitted that all mental activity has these three aspects, cognitive, affective, and conative; and when we apply one of these three adjectives to any phase of mental process, we mean merely that the aspect named is the most prominent of the three at that moment. Each cycle of activity has this triple aspect; though each tends to pass through these phases in which cognition, affection and conation are in turn most prominent; as when the naturalist, catching sight of a specimen, recognizes it, captures it, and gloats over its capture."

In the late 1940s, Raymond Cattell attempted to explain conational modalities in a complex set he called the "dynamic lattice." What McDougall had called instinct or propensity, Cattell termed an "erg." An erg, Cattell said, was an innate psychological/physical disposition, or inborn disposition, which permits its possessor to acquire reactivity to certain classes of objects more readily than others, to experience a specific emotion in regard to them and to set on a course of action which ceases more completely at a certain specific goal activity. His dynamic lattice analyzes the interconnections among "ergs" (conative) and sentiments (affective) to show purposive sequences.

His philosophy of dynamic psychology stressed the importance of motivation or fundamental energy in psychic life. Only by looking at man in dynamic rather than static conditions did he feel conation could play its appropriate role.

In the context of our rapidly changing environment, conation becomes a key element in the interpretation of human behavior. For centuries, philosophers and scientists have talked about it, but the dynamic requirements which lead us to strive under ever more challenging conditions has required an entrepreneurial mind to not only research the historical perspective of its existence, but to produce operative models with practical applications.

As to proving empirically the existence of specific traits, Albert Mehrabian in Analysis of Personality Theories says: "One cannot observe a habit, a need, or a trait. One only infers these from observable behavior [...] conceptual labels subsume several classes of behaviors [...] factor analysis makes it possible for theorists to evolve a set of habits which satisfy these assumed properties [...] to identify clusters of behaviors."

Jung's type theory (1912) involved four subclasses-thinking, feeling, sensation, and intuition – which cut across his major categories of introvert and extrovert. Freudian writers Friedman and Goldstein found this classification arbitrary and had difficulty in "operationalizing" the function type constructs.

The difficulty, it would seem, arises from a lack on Jung's part of incorporating the conative as a clearly delineated aspect of the mind. That may well be why his main distinction between introversion and extroversion has been the more lasting contribution of his work.

McDougall, as so many others aware of conative traits, expressed the need for giving them specificity. "At the standpoint of empirical science, we must accept these conative dispositions as ultimate facts, not capable of being analyzed or of being explained. When, and not until, we can exhibit any particular instance of conduct or of behavior as the expression of conative tendencies which are ultimate constituents of the organism, can we claim to have explained it (the purposive process)."

The case has been made for defining Modes within the conative domains. That Jung and others have not separated out the conative and that, therefore, instruments based on such theories have not thoroughly measured such Modes may have to do with the very conative nature of those philosophers and psychologists who have held the mind as their domain. The conative Modes of most Ivory Tower philosophers and psychologists, those who could strive in the research environment, would lead to this bias.

E. R. Hilgard traces the retreat from discussion of the three-faculty concept directly to McDougall:

"With McDougall the history of the trilogy of the mind appears to have ended"

Hilgard goes on to say, "When we look at contemporary psychology from the perspective of cognition, affection, and conation, it is obvious immediately that cognitive psychology is ascendant at present, with a concurrent decline of emphasis upon the affective-conative dimensions... some price has been paid for it. Information processing and the computer model have replaced stimulus-response psychology with an input-output psychology. In the process, some dynamic features such as drives, incentive motivation, and curiosity have been more or less forgotten."

B. S. Woodworth in his statement relating to the study of volition said, "We have nothing in this line that can compare with the immense amount of work done on the relation of perception to the stimulus perceived, or [...] that can compare in completeness with the work done and still being done in all departments of sensation."

That neuropsychiatrists have only recently taken a closer look at the crucial role the Supplementary Motor Area (SMA) plays in the volitional process might be seen, according to Antonio R. Damasio, Department of Neurology, University of Iowa College of Medicine, Iowa City, Iowa, in his commentary "Understanding the Mind's Will" (1985), " as the fate of higher-order integrative systems."

Jean Piaget, many years earlier, had referred to conation as the mental domain most difficult to differentiate and, thus, he laid it aside as, until now, have the neuropsychiatrists. Piaget used his concept of disengagement to refer to the degree to which cognitive activity is independent of affective and conative relationships. But as Damasio points out, the "anatomical and functional knowledge about the SMA and its vicinity will permit us to model the neuronal substrates of the will and thus overcome a persistent objection of those who favor a dualist position regarding mind and brain." [his emphasis in original]

As Richard Snow says, "Historically, the concept of 'conation' was coordinated with cognition and affect, the three comprising the main domains of mental life. There has been recent interest in the interaction of cognition and affect... But the conative seems to have dropped out of modern psychology's consciousness. It deserves reinstatement and research."

The Kolbe Concept builds on the historical, philosophical, and psychological foundations to place conation in its proper contemporary perspective by identifying the individual's Kolbe Conative Modes.
*Source: Wisdom of the Ages by Kathy Kolbe*

# CHAPTER TWO – RULE #1 ACT – BEFORE YOU THINK

## Three Parts of the Mind explanation, Detail: p. 21

Right-brain/left brain mythology so permeates our thinking about the mind that you hear about it in automobile commercials, banks ads, and sitcoms. The psychological community has led us to believe that we either think or feel, denying the obvious – we have to decide to act on our thoughts and desires. As far back as Plato and Aristotle there was a recognition of the third part of the mind, the one that manages our drive or urge to act, react, and interact. It's not that Freud and Jung didn't know about it; they just didn't focus on it. Their work was in the less elusive domains of human behavior.

Many have miscalculated the nature of our inclinations toward action, confusing them with mere physical movement or sidestepping research on instincts because there was no standard for identifying and measuring them, let alone enhancing them. According to Maslow's biographer, this author of the commonly accepted Hierarchy of Needs didn't recognize the importance of instinctive action until after he had written his major works. Piaget, the great learning theorist, admitted the significance of the conative part of the mind (conation is the term for actions taken on instinct), but said it was so intertwined with the cognitive and affective that he would not attempt to disengage it.

But disengage it we must, if we are to understand human nature. Otherwise we will continue to believe that we must change our way of doing things in order to improve our lives.

The explanation of the Three Parts of the Mind will differentiate instinctive needs from personal preferences, solving the problem that plagued Piaget. This clarification will explain why learning theories that took us down a strictly cognitive path in education betrayed our need to act on instinct, thwarted our will, and left us with undue stress about our futures. The backlash of the flower children mentality brought us into the era of emotions – no less an answer without incorporating instinctive truths. Being who we want to be does not always free us to be who we truly are.

Powered by Instinct presents a new model for the mind. Each part is a mental domain, and each is an integral part of the blossoming of your ultimate success. It identifies the following characteristics of each domain:

- Cognitive: thoughts, intelligence, learned behaviors, knowledge, recall, skills.
- Affective: feelings, emotions, personality, preferences, desires, attitudes, and beliefs.
- Conative: Actions, drives, urges, natural abilities, inclinations, pattern of doing.

*Source: Writings of Kathy Kolbe*

## Kolbe Creative Process, Detail: p. 23

The Creative Process is the path that integrates otherwise separate elements of the mind's capacity: the abilities to act with motivation, determination, and reason. We do not all create through the same instinct-based Operating Zones, nor do we have equal levels of motivation, determination, and reason. Differences in these levels allow for an almost infinite variety in how we use the creative process.

Most dictionaries define creativity as the ability to bring into being an idea or thing. It is an extension of productivity. It is the highest and best use of our talents. Because we all have the same amount of instinctive power, I believe we were born with an equal capacity to create. The Creative Process, as I define it, is the path that integrates otherwise separate elements of the mind's capacity: the abilities to act with motivation, determination, and reason.
*Source: Pure Instinct by Kathy Kolbe*

## Safety Expert Looks at Gut Instinct, Detail: p. 24

**Cognitive psychologist Gary Klein has studied people who make do-or-die decisions. His advice? Forget analysis paralysis. Trust your instincts.**

A student of human intuition, he had the courage to bet his career on the hunch that people have grossly underestimated the power of gut instinct. When observing emergency situations, he came to the conclusion that frequently lives were saved by critical decisions being made that ignored the conventional rules. He noted that rather than pondering the best course of action or weighing the options, the emergency medical technician or fire fighter plunged right in and took action. When queried later about why they did what they did, their only response was they knew it was the right thing to do.

Some said they were drawing on experience but for Klein, this was not a satisfactory answer. Instead of weighing lots of options, he theorized that fire commanders, for example, make an instinctive decision – say, to attack a burning house from the rear – and then compare it with alternatives. "I thought I'd come up with a daring theory," says Klein. "But the fire commanders insisted that they never considered options of any kind. As it turned out, my theory was way too conservative." The commanders simply trusted their guts.

"We used to think that experts carefully deliberate the merits of each course of action, whereas novices impulsively jump at the first option," says Klein. But he concluded that the reverse is true. "It's the novices who must compare different approaches to solving a problem. Experts come up with a plan and then rapidly assess whether it will work. They move fast because they do less." *Source: "What's Your Intuition?" by Bill Breen FastCompany, Issue 38, September 2000, P. 290.*

# Chapter Four – Rule #2 Self-Provoke

## Dynamynd®: Kolbe Decision Ladder, Detail: p. 51

**Dynamynd Decision Ladder:** A hierarchical model of the graduated, sequential steps that lead to higher levels of thinking, feeling, and action taking in the creative problem solving process.

**Individual Dynamynd:** A model of the specific behaviors an individual exhibits when making decisions at each level of the Dynamynd hierarchy, in each of the three dimensions of the mind: cognitive, conative, and affective.

**Culture Dynamynd:** A model for assigning the status on the Dynamynd Decision Ladder for a category of people who are affiliated but who do not make decisions interactively.

**Team Dynamynd:** A model of the levels of decision making – in all three dimensions of the mind – available to a group of people who work interdependently.

**Leader Dynamynd:** A model of the levels of decision making required of leaders as they develop higher standards of performance for themselves and others whose decisions they influence.

## Dynamynd®: Kolbe Decision Ladder

### Individual

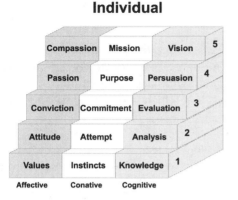

## Dynamynd®: Kolbe Decision Ladder

### Culture

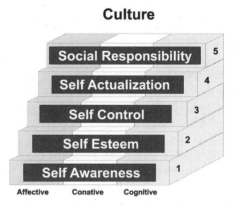

## Dynamynd®: Kolbe Decision Ladder

### Team

## Dynamynd®: Kolbe Decision Ladder

### Leader

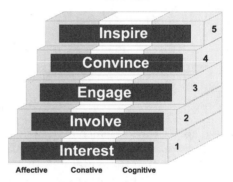

The Dynamynd clarifies how you have to go beyond simply having the amazing mental faculties found in the tripartite mind. It's a tool used to coach people on maximizing their use of these attributes. Your self-fulfillment and contribution to society can be tracked by assessing the levels you achieve in each of these aspects of your mental makeup. For instance, in the cognitive arena, you can build on knowledge by applying it, then stretch further to analyze information, evaluate it, and ultimately, to visualize its consequences. (See Bloom's taxonomy).

I believe that a similar hierarchy influences your control over the affective and conative domains. To have a personality type is fine, but you need to understand how that leads to your preferences. Only then can you take responsibility for your values and develop a passion for what matters most to you. Many people stop short of developing a sense of passion. That keeps them at a very self-centered level in the affective domain.

While self-centered has a negative ring, it is the same as self-actualization or self-fulfillment within the Dynamynd. This is a passage on the mental hierarchy for each domain, which is a necessary pathway toward development of leadership capabilities.

221

There are several ranges within the Dynamynd. If you aspire to make a difference in the world, to be socially responsible, you must pass through all of these levels. Only after a passion has shown up on your affective radar, can you arrive with a compassion for others. Only those who demonstrate this capacity become authentic leaders.

Paralleling its mental siblings, the conative hierarchy begins with self awareness, a level which has been difficult to achieve without knowing your MO. Through your free-will, you can gain control over your use of this drive, directing it toward specific goals. Ultimately you could be acting on a mission that helps others. It's up to you to select the levels at which you choose to operate, and then to work to achieve them.

It is certainly possible to be at different points in each domain. Lucy, on the I Love Lucy show had a personal mission to get on Ricky's show. This was also her passion. On the cognitive side, she certainly didn't analyze the consequences of her actions, keeping her barely at level two.

Mother Teresa seemed to be at level five in all three domains. The Seinfeld team pulled off "a show about nothing," as was the stated goal. They maintained a mental "1" across the board. (By the way, that's tough to do. Just try not thinking about, caring about, or doing anything about anything significant!)
*Source: The Writings of Kathy Kolbe*

# Impact Factors, Action Modes, and Zones of Operation,

Detail: p. 59

Because there are 12 ways in which actions impact outcomes, I call them the Kolbe Impact Factors (IFs). Individuals have four of the IFs that are their natural talents or MO (modus operandi). When they use these methods they are making their best efforts. Because everyone has the same number (4) of these innate abilities, and all of the IFs are equal in potential impact, everyone is capable of contributing equally to the problem-solving process. The 12 IFs stem from four Kolbe Action Modes, which tie to the basic ways in which people instinctively strive.

The Action Modes are:
- Fact Finder: methods for gathering information
- Follow Thru: methods for sorting information
- Quick Start: methods for dealing with unknowns and change
- Implementor: methods for handling the physical environment.

Each Action Mode has three Zones of Operation, which determine how the individual acts when using it.

- Initiating zone: how they insist on beginning the problem-solving process
- Accommodating zone: how they respond to people and situations
- Preventing zone: how they avoid or resist problems

Individual's MOs are made up of one IF from each Action Mode. It is possible to have as many as three IFs in the Insist and Prevent zones, and all four in the Accommodate zone.
*Source: The Writings of Kathy Kolbe*

# A Description of the Kolbe Action Modes, Detail: p. 61

**Energy from each striving instinct triggers a different set of actions. These lead to four consistent or characteristic ways of performing; what I term an Action Mode. The observable way an Action Mode expresses the subconscious power of a striving instinct depends upon its natural Operating Zone. The three zones span a scale from 1 to 10.**

Action Modes are the talents over which you have conscious control. As I will explain more thoroughly in Chapter 3, they are the conative abilities that link the internal force of instinct with quantifiable performance. They determine how you will, won't, and are willing to function, based on the necessities of your instinctive makeup. You may know you should review your file notes before making a call, yet you usually fail to do so. You wish you would keep more organized records, but when you do, you can't find where you put them. What you "should" do will always be overpowered by a conflicting instinct-driven need.

<u>Fact Finder</u> is the Action Mode that results from using the instinct to probe. It includes a spectrum of behaviors relating to gathering information. Some people have to define their options and examine possibilities in great depth. They become experts or authorities in specific areas. Others are generalists who attack a broader scope of pursuits. The three Operating Zones put an entirely different spin on the Fact Finder Action Mode.

| <u>Operating Zone</u> | <u>Fact Finder Actions</u> |
|---|---|
| Initiating | Details, strategies, research |
| Responding | With specifics, editing, assessing pros and cons |
| Preventing | Analysis paralysis, or minutiae |

Each zone indicates a differing degree of thoroughness necessary for an individual. Some people simply have to give you every detail of the movie plot. They are the ones who ask questions until they have the last piece of information, who operate with practical strategies based on historical evidence or personal experience.

Other people use information to satisfy someone else, responding with sufficient specificity yet not delving any more deeply than necessary into the details. For instance, they may wonder who is fourth, fifth, and sixth in presidential succession. But for all their wondering, they won't search for the answer if they don't know it already. If a debate gets going over the issue, some people will need to cut off the discussion and move on to another topic. These people prevent situations from becoming immersed in specifics. Even if they raised the question – and find it interesting to consider – they'll get frustrated if the discussion gets bogged down in what they consider trivialities.

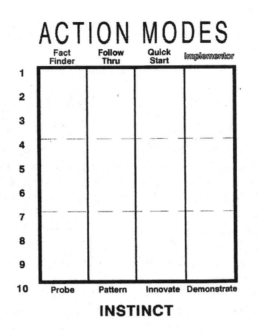

# ACTION MODES

| | Fact Finder | Follow Thru | Quick Start | Implementor |
|---|---|---|---|---|
| 1 | | | | |
| 2 | | | | |
| 3 | | | | |
| 4 | | | | |
| 5 | | | | |
| 6 | | | | |
| 7 | | | | |
| 8 | | | | |
| 9 | | | | |
| 10 | Probe | Pattern | Innovate | Demonstrate |

## INSTINCT

<u>Follow Thru</u> is the Action Mode that results from using the instinct to pattern. It determines how you relate to structure. Its characteristics range from acting sequentially to sporadically. An insistent–Follow Thru baseball player goes through a ritualistic pattern or series of sequential steps in preparing for a game. An accommodating player tries different systems, occasionally turning to one recommended by a teammate, and then switching to another. Routines will be bothersome for a resistant Follow Thru, even when they prove effective. The amount of structure people need is forecast by their Operating Zone in the Follow Thru Action Mode.

| <u>Operating Zone</u> | <u>FollowThruActions</u> |
|---|---|
| Initiating | Systems,procedures, design, order |
| Responding | By adjusting to existing plans, maintaining classifications |
| Preventing | Getting boxed in, being overly structured |

Some people naturally put things into a system. They have an urge to straighten the picture, to flow-chart the options, and to organize people and materials. The first thing they do when faced with a problem is to sort out the possibilities. They take inventory of all the information accumulated by initiating Fact Finders.

Then there are those who will live within the system and follow the procedures. These accommodating Follow Thrus put things back where they belong. They may not need to have phone messages given to them in alphabetical order, but they will maintain such structures.

Those in the preventative zone in Follow Thru rebel when they feel boxed in by schedules or routines. They resist having to stay within the parameters of policies and procedures, and instead create their own alternatives. Sometimes their resistance to filling in the form can lead to open-ended comments that improve productivity.

**Quick Start** is the Action Mode that results from using the instinct to innovate. It deals with your perspective on risk, and ranges from being highly negotiable to irrevocable. Insistent Quick Starts cut deals that are flexible and crammed with options. Yet their estate planners may have the risk-averse approach of irrevocable wills and trusts. These differing perspectives on risk are clearly defined by the following zones in the Quick Start Action Mode:

| Operating Zone | QuickStartActions |
|---|---|
| Initiating | Change, deadlines, uniqueness |
| Responding | By mediating between the vision and the given |
| Preventing | Chaos, a crisis atmosphere |

People who initiate Quick Start projects create the chaos that others have to clean up. But in the process these change makers add vision and risk to the mix. Always negotiable, they defy the odds and intuit possibilities that would otherwise go untried. Because they instigate the unusual, people who operate in the initiating zone of Quick Start are natural promoters and entrepreneurs.

Accommodating change is no problem for people who respond in Quick Start. For instance, they'll go along if you change your mind at the last minute and want to see a different movie. Don't expect the same of those who operate in the preventative zone of Quick Start. They keep changes from getting out of hand, trying instead to reach agreement on what will stay the same. What some consider enhancements, they sense could cause a potential crisis. Their resistance to risk can save the day.

**Implementor** is the Action Mode that results from using the instinct to demonstrate. It determines how we relate to objects and physical space. It functions through use of three-dimensional or tangible implements or tools. Its perspectives range from concrete to abstract. A person who views the world through tactile efforts needs to plant a garden in order to find joy in it. A resistant Implementor can find as much fulfillment in writing a poem about a garden, the abstract notion being as important as the tangible reality. The degree to which people have to see something in order to believe it is determined by where they fall in the Operating Zone in the Implementor Action Mode.

| Operating Zone | Implementor Action |
|---|---|
| Initiating | Constructing, transporting, manipulating, and protecting tangible goods |
| Responding | By using machinery or implements for either tangible or intangible effort |
| Preventing | Need for tangible evidence or physical proof |

Those who initiate solutions by using tools and implements are the hands-on Implementors. While others discuss the video they just saw, these folks are probably tinkering with the VCR. Their need for physical movement and space keeps them from staying in one place for very long. They tend to build solutions rather than talk about them.

People who respond through the Implementor mode are able to deal with both tangible and intangible solutions. If others need to put together a concrete demonstration they'll help build it, but they don't need to see the prototype in its final form in order to make a decision.

Prevention of Implementor action indicates an ability to create from abstract concepts such as words and numbers without having to use three-dimensional forms and models.
*Source: The Writings of Kathy Kolbe*

# CHAPTER SIX – RULE #3 COMMIT – BUT TO VERY LITTLE

## Meta-analysis of the Impact of Strain and Tension on Absenteeism and Job Turnover, Detail: p. 92

As illustrated by the following research, if an individual employee is in a job that represents a poor conative fit, she may experience strain due to unrealistic conative self-expectations or tension due to the unrealistic conative expectations of others.

### Absenteeism
In a study conducted in 1992, 60 employees from a national marketing firm, half of whom had the highest absenteeism in the company and half of whom had the lowest absenteeism were studied. Each employee completed an individual Kolbe A index and a Kolbe B index for their own position. The supervisor of each employee also completed a Kolbe C index for the employee's position. The results of the study indicated that fifty percent of the high absenteeism group were experiencing conative stress while only 20% of the low absenteeism employees were experiencing similar stress. Years of employment and gender were analyzed to ensure that they were not confounding factors in the results. The results indicated no differences in absenteeism in this study between those who had been employed more than two years and those who had been employed fewer than two years nor were there significant differences based on gender. While some other factors may have contributed to absenteeism, neither length of employment nor gender proved to be significant factors, but 30% of the difference in absenteeism was attributable to conative factors.

### Retention
Dr. Richard S. Deems, an independent Kolbe consultant, conducted a study in 1991 in which he used the Kolbe A index to predict branch manager turnover in a national financial services company. His study included all 483 branch manager trainees hired in 1991 who were divided into three approximately equal groups: 1) a control group which was not given the Kolbe, 2) a study group of trainees given the Kolbe whose scores fell outside the recommended range but whose managers were trained in conation to respond to the conative dissonance, and 3) a study group of trainees whose scores fell within the recommended range. At the end of six months, 11.7% of the

group that had not used the Kolbe had left the company for job-related reasons, 5.5% of those who were conatively mismatched, but whose managers tried to mitigate the conative dissonance by using the trainee's Kolbe results had left for job-related reasons, and none of the conatively-matched trainees left for job-related reasons. Dr. Deems concluded, "Selection within the recommended Kolbe range resulted in 100% retention of the desired Branch Manager-trainees." *Source: Research Files of Kolbe Corp*

## Use of Time by Action Modes, Detail: p. 95

**Fact Finder:** Gauges how much time something will take through experience and expertise; puts events into a historical perspective.

**Follow Thru:** Sequences events and provides continuity, paces oneself; sets a rhythm for effort and coordinates with others.

**Quick Start:** Predicts and deals with events ahead of time; focuses on future by forecasting what could be, anticipates change.

**Implementor:** Grounded in the here and now, wanting the moment to last; creates quality products that will endure through time.

## Conative Stress: Conflict, Strain, and Tension, Detail: p. 97

### Conflict

When two people with contradictory instincts interrupt each other's progress by insisting on their own paths to problem solving, conflict occurs. Potential conflict is identified by comparing their Kolbe A index results (the individuals' conative realities). The potential for conflict exists when there is a difference of four or more units in an Action Mode.

It can lead to complementary synergy when both people enjoy the freedom to be themselves within the relationship, with neither attempting to impose his or her will on the other. Most successful teams are comprised of people who complement each other conatively. They bring differing talents to the table.

By seeking outlets for talents that provide mutually beneficial results, conflict can foster complementary accomplishments. What one person avoids doing, the other may willingly contribute to the cause.

Prescription: humor, humility, trust, barter, respect, understanding, managing mental energy.

### Strain

When an individual tries to live up to false self-expectations, the result is strain. Strain on the job is identified by comparing Kolbe A index results to Kolbe B index results (an individual's job-related self-expectations). A difference of four or more units in an Action Mode indicates the existence of strain. Strain is self-inflicted. It's caused by trying to "improve" in the Action Modes in which you are naturally resistant. Or trying to deny your own creative bent, it comes with trying to emulate someone conatively different from you, or yielding to pressure to be someone other than who you are. It can be as dangerous to your well-being as a blood transfusion of a mismatched natural type. It can keep you from fulfilling your destiny.

Prescription: acceptance, overcome guilt (good/bad or right/wrong), express creative self, change expectations, barter, outlets, confirm expectations as reality, targeting mental energy, trust.

## Tension

When external obstacles posed by people or circumstances force an individual to work against his instincts, the result is tension. Tension is identified by comparing Kolbe A index results to Kolbe C index results (job requirements as determined by someone else—usually a boss or supervisor). A difference of four or more units in an Action Mode indicates the existence of tension.

Prescription: remove from situation, communication to change requirements, barter, manage mental energy.

Strain is the most difficult form of conative stress to allay. It stems from a betrayal of your own instincts and means that you are ignoring internal urges in favor of external rewards. It indicates an attempt to bypass your striving Instincts and act only according to detrimental motivations. Therefore it interferes with your Creative Process. A person suffering from strain limits her potential for success by not valuing, understanding, or using innate capabilities.

## Strain: A Form of Self-Denial

Denying your time-defined needs is the surest way to cause strain. For instance, a resistant Quick Start will be frustrated by the pressure of working against tight deadlines. Other sources of strain include:

1. Trying to live up to false self-expectations by:

- believing you can change who you are if you try hard enough
- confusing hard work with achievement
- undervaluing your ability to take action
- not recognizing a resistance as a strength
- attempting to rein in your instinctive impulses until you can rationally think things through
- thinking you aren't contributing unless you initiate action

2. Trying to live up to other people's expectations by:

- trying to do things the way you are told to do them
- trying to be just like someone you admire
- believing others know what is best for you
- promising you will do things differently
- taking criticism of your methods to heart
- knowing it annoys someone when you are just being yourself

3. Trying to function within the system by:

- trying to conform
- believing you can contribute best by altering your approach
- doubting what you have to offer is needed
*Source: The Writings of Kathy Kolbe*

## Definition of Conation, Detail: p. 98

"Conation (koh NAY shun) n. Conation is the area of one's active mentality that has to do with desire, volition, and striving. The related conatus (koh NAY tus) is the resulting effort or striving itself, or the natural tendency or force in one's mental makeup that produces an effort. Conative (KOHN uh tiv) is the term in psychology that describes anything relating to conation. All these words come from the Latin conatus, past participle of the verb conari (to try). The Scottish philosopher William Hamilton (1788-1856) considered conation to be one of the three divisions of the mind, the one that included desire and volition, the other two being cognition (perception, awareness) and feeling... Conation differs from velleity (the wish without the effort)."
*Source: Dictionary of the 1000 Most Obscure Words in the English Language*

# CHAPTER SEVEN – HOW TO COMMIT –
# BUT TO VERY LITTLE

## Commitment Contract program, Detail: p. 111

The Kolbe Commitment Contract program is all about managing time and mental energy. This program offers managers a tool that improves communication with other managers, superiors, and down line employees.

Each of us has a limited amount of Instincts, or mental energy, that we can commit to tasks. Once that energy is expended, we cannot create more without having some downtime. Therefore, how we allocate that energy is extremely important.

Kolbe A index results represent HOW actions are taken. Each MO (Mode of Operation) reveals the way an individual uses his or her Striving Instincts to complete tasks or engage in the Creative Problem-Solving Process. Every person has a limited amount of energy.

The Kolbe Commitment Triangle combines the WHAT and WHEN surrounding tasks. There are two key issues to be addressed regarding tasks in the Commitment Triangle:

Do I have the time?
Do I have the energy?

## II. Levels of Effort & Priorities

There are three LEVELS OF EFFORT you can assign to any action. These determine the amount of instinctive energy you give an action:

1. Commitment is the highest level, causing you to focus energy on assigned tasks. It is a guarantee that you will use your mental energy to accomplish a goal or task.
2. Attempt is the second level, where you try to accomplish a goal but don't use your full mental energy.
3. Intention is the third level, which implies no current allocation of effort.

Realize that Commitments are Guarantees. The expectation is that you will do what you say you are going to do. Implicit with a Commitment is a deadline for completion. Attempts represent an "at-ready" status; they will get done if there is mental energy to spare. Intentions are those tasks that are on the radar screen.

Commitment Triangles are a task-oriented, rather than a goal-oriented program. A goal is affectively driven (what you WANT to happen) while a task is conatively driven (HOW you will make it happen).

## III. How to Complete a Commitment Triangle

1. Use the Commitment Triangle provided or simply draw a big triangle.
2. Define the time period in which the tasks need to be completed. This could be a day, a week, a few weeks, but no longer than a month.
3. At the top write everything you are doing in the defined time period. These are items on your "to-do" list — the specific tasks that you will do to reach your goals. Start with the highest priorities.
4. Draw a line under what you are committed to doing within the defined time frame.
5. Draw a line under what you will attempt to do within the defined time frame.
6. The remainder will be what you intend to do within the defined time frame.

## IV. How to Use a Commitment Triangle

### Step 1. Edit by Priorities

Evaluate whether or not an item is really a Commitment, Attempt or Intention. Assign the task a number according to the priority of the customers, whether internal or external, that you must serve. If the majority of your commitments are not to your number 1 or 2 customers, you need to rethink your priorities.

### Step 2. Edit by Time

Circle everything in the commitment portion you don't have time to do in the given time frame. Be realistic. You must confront the limitations on your time. You cannot do more than is humanly possible. Remember, a Commitment is an obligation to do something. If you circled items in your triangle, you have two choices: either move the tasks down to Attempt or Intent, or off the triangle to someone else.

### Step 3. Edit by Energy
Draw a line through everything that you are unlikely to do, either because you are not instinctively suited to it, or because it will cause you stress.
Either move these crossed-out items down to Attempt or Intent, or take them off the triangle if they can be delegated to someone else. Be sure to communicate to others what you do not have the energy to accomplish. Perhaps tasks can be altered, delegated, or replaced. It may be that another task suited to your MO will accomplish the same goal.

### Step 4. Negotiating Tasks in the Triangle
Management is in the role of managing employees' Commitment Triangles. It is a manager's job to negotiate the commitment back and forth to free employees to do what is important to the manager. The manager must help employees re-prioritize Commitments when resources are limited.

### Step 5. Completing Tasks
As you complete a task, remove it from the triangle and shift the remaining items up from Attempts and Intentions to Commitments and Attempts. If an item remains an intention indefinitely, consider removing it altogether.
*Source: The Writings of Kathy Kolbe*

# CHAPTER EIGHT – RULE #4 BE OBSTINATE –

# IN OVERCOMING OBSTACLES

## Peter Mark Roget Biography, Detail: p. 121

Note from Kathy Kolbe re: Roget
Roget is one of my greatest mentors. His purpose was to classify and arrange words according to the ideas they express. He didn't create a mere alphabetical listing of words and their synonyms. That's the modern day trashing of his work of genius, in which he organized language around a classification reflected in nature.

As a scientist, Roget structured language in a network he said was analogous to the "natural filiation" of plants and animals. The first three of his classifications related to space, time, and matter. The last three he said were "those in which the mind is concerned, and which comprehend intellect, volition, and feeling." Roget, in the early 1800s, planted the seeds for my articulation of the Dynamynd, or the three dimensional mind.

He protected his system for decades, and then his work was carried on by his son. Now, however, there is a New Roget's Thesaurus that actually trashes his purpose, and undoes his system of classification into the mere alphabetical listing he found so lacking. It's an example that makes me ever more determined to articulate the reasons behind my use of language.

By the age of fourteen Roget was studying medicine at Edinburgh University, graduating five years later. From 1808-40 he concentrated on medicine, paying particular attention to the senses. During this time, in 1814, he also invented what he called a 'log-log' slide rule to calculate the roots and powers of numbers. This formed the basis of slide rules that were common currency in schools and universities until the age of the calculator over 150 years later. He was elected a Fellow of the Royal Society the following year.

In 1848 he retired from his position as Secretary of the Royal Society, a position he had held since 1827 and embarked on the project that has made his name, Roget's Thesaurus of English Words and Phrases. As early as 1805 he had compiled, for his own personal use, a small indexed catalogue of words that he used to enhance his prolific writing. When he retired he picked this up and published the first edition in 1852.

A book of synonyms with 990 classes of words that allows easy access to words of similar meanings, it has never since been out of print. In successive editions supervised by him, his son, his grandson, and others, it has remained a standard reference book that has sold 32 million copies since its first publication 150 years ago.
*Source: "Historic Figures" series presented by the British Broadcasting System*
*www.bbc.co.uk/history/historic_figures/roget_peter_mark*

## E.F. Wonderlic Biography, Detail: p. 123

Kathy Kolbe has frequently written and spoken of her background in psychometric testing. As the daughter of E.F. Wonderlic, her earliest memories were of fence-posting (counting and tabulating) data from test results generated through the family business.

The Wonderlic Personnel Test was developed in 1937 by Eldon Wonderlic as part of his doctoral thesis in industrial psychology at Northwestern University. The focus of this scholarship was determining a relationship between intelligence and job performance. As companies began to hear about the test, they sought access to it and a fledgling business was born.

A great leap forward in the company's development occurred during World War II when the Wonderlic Personnel Test was nationalized by the U.S. Government and used to establish the suitability for training of both military personnel and employees in the rapidly growing defense industry. A huge amount of data was generated during these years on performance in all sorts of jobs and when this data reverted to the Wonderlic company after the War, the foundation for growth had been assured.

Today the Wonderlic Test is given to three million people each year in all types of industries. The purpose of the test, which is written on a sixth-grade reading level, is to measure a person's general cognitive ability through a combination of math, vocabulary, and reasoning questions. There are 16 different forms of the test in 20 different languages.

By most standards E.F. Wonderlic is considered The Father of Personnel Testing, for he was the pioneer who took IQ testing out of an academic environment and brought it into the workplace. Wonderlic Inc. remains in the hand of other family members but Kathy Kolbe has taken personnel testing in a completely different direction. While her father focused exclusively on the cognitive part of the mind, Kathy Kolbe has pioneered the rediscovery of the conative dimension of the mind. Today her work is more accurately identified as integrating the three parts of the mind, bringing her once again into close contact with her father's original work.
*Source: Kolbe Archives*

## Learning Disabilities, Detail: p. 123

*Impulsive? Distracted? Quick Start? Experts say you suffer from ADD By Kathy Kolbe*

Are you easily distracted, highly intuitive and spontaneous? If so, are you a person insistent in Quick Start who acts on instinct? According to an article in The Wall Street Journal, it means you suffer from a "disorder." Attention Deficit Disorder (ADD) is a hot topic in publications like *Time*, *The Wall Street Journal*, and newspapers across the U.S.

Are you intolerant of routine? Do you have difficulty getting organized? You may be labeled ADD. Combine the hands-on explanations of initiative in Implementor with initiating Quick Start, plus the avoidance of orderly approaches due to Follow Thru prevention and your instincts would set you up for yet another negative stereotype.

*The Dayton Daily News* reports the following as common characteristics of adults with ADD. Are these behaviors necessarily negative?

· tend to start many projects but have trouble following through
· say whatever comes to mind, regardless of timing or consequences
· have difficulty following rules and proper procedures
· easily distracted and frequently tune out or drift away in conversation

Although the Kolbe A index validates these behaviors as the individual's instinctive strengths, psychologists diagnose people with this profile as having an "affliction." ADD gives a negative label to these positive attributes. Kolbe's theory is that we all have control over our instinctive behaviors. So, even though this type of MO comes naturally to some people, they also have the willpower to decide when and where to use them. An easily distracted person can also be called highly-flexible when the individual is in a situation that rewards who he or she is. Certainly there are people who have ADD – they are the people who have no control over these behaviors.

Other characteristics of ADD like "chronic low self-esteem, insecurity, and a sense of underachievement" may be psychological problems coming into play. Or, the individual could be working in a situation that goes against his natural grain. The stress alone would cause feelings of insecurity, particularly if the person's MO is in contrast to those around him.

Possible misdiagnoses of ADD are tragic. The person's greatest talents are being labeled a disorder. While tips for coping with the affliction may help people manage themselves the way others want them to, they will surely be pushed right into conative crisis – more stress and failure will follow. Our culture is biased in favor of people who are insistent in Fact Finder and Follow Thru. Schools and corporate training programs ask students to "choose the best answer" and "fill in the blanks." These tasks don't allow for innovation and hands-on implementation, yet we need those talents in our society.

Employers may soon face greater problems with ADD as there is a real risk that it may come under the American Disability Act. People with ADD already qualify for lengthy extensions in timed tests. The questions this law raises are obvious. "If a medical student requires extra time to pass an examination on cardiac arrhythmias, for example, who will give this physician extra time in a real-life cardiac crisis?" asks Richard Vatz in The Wall Street Journal.

What can be done? The more researchers study ADD, the less certain they are as to what it is, or whether it is a thousand different medical and non-medical situations all called by the same name. Do your own research. If an employee, client, friend, or family member is diagnosed with ADD, give them the Kolbe A index™. Validate their strengths and give them positive reinforcement instead of a negative label.
*Source: www.kolbe.com*

## The Story of Kartchner Caverns, Detail: p. 128

In the rugged hills of the Whetstone Mountains, about 40 miles south of Tucson, Arizona, amateur cavers Randy Tufts and Gary Tenen found the "motherlode." More precious to them than gold was their 1974 discovery of an untouched natural treasure, a living cave with growing calcite formations, hidden under the desert floor for more than a million years.

Equally amazing are the steps Tufts and Tenen took to protect their remarkable find from vandalism and destruction. Rather than trumpeting the news of their discovery, the two men, then in their mid-20s, adopted a 14-year code of silence, going so far as making selected friends and loved ones sign documents of secrecy, so as to protect the caves.

The road to discovery was a long one. In 1966, Tufts and a few of his college buddies were feeling frustrated by their lack of success in finding an "undiscovered" cave. On one of their many weekend trips into the Whetstones, they bumped into a miner digging in the Lone Star Mine, in the Coronado National Forest just west of the private Kartchner ranch. They asked the miner if he knew of any caves in the area. He didn't, but he did tell them about a nearby sinkhole where he had observed some high school kids exploring the terrain.

After many hours of searching, Tufts found the sinkhole and, in it, an opening leading into a small chamber. The two cavers found no evidence of the existence of a larger cave and, concerned that the sinkhole might be unstable, they abandoned further exploration. While Tufts had no expectations of finding a cave, out of habit, he marked the site on his topographical map.

On an autumn day seven years later, Tufts, while caving in the same area, decided to further explore the sinkhole. While wandering near its perimeter, he discovered a second tunnel and hypothesized about the possibility of a passage between the two holes. When Tufts and Tenen returned the next weekend for further exploration, they found the small chamber as they remembered it.

Searching more carefully this time, the two men found a small opening in the rocks. From it, amid the cool air of the chamber, seeped a whiff of warm guano-scented air. Tufts and Tenen knew they were on to something big. They wasted no time squeezing into the narrow opening—and discovered a second chamber. The cavers continued their search of the chamber, finding a 10-inch high crawl space, which extended into a narrow twenty-foot tunnel. The tunnel ended abruptly at a wall, marred only by a small hole. As Tufts peered through the blowhole, a breeze extinguished his carbide light.

After enlarging the blowhole enough to squeeze through, Tufts and Tenen crawled through a 50-foot long guano-covered tunnel. Then suddenly, they emerged into a 300-foot long passage, one high enough for them to walk upright. The cavers stood stunned, surrounded by fragile glass-like soda straws, formations that grow into stalactites as the droplets of water seep through limestone and calcium carbonate. There were no footprints, or other evidence that a human being had ever entered this wondrous cave. Carefully, the young men retraced their steps—knowing that touching one of the mineral formations could destroy a structure that took a million years to create.

They emerged changed, weighted down by the awesome responsibility of protecting their discovery—a living cave dripping with an awesome variety of mineral and rock formations, undiscovered by humans since its formation. If the word got out, the cave could be vandalized or damaged by enthusiastic amateurs. They decided to keep it a secret until they could decide what to do. The weight of the responsibility of their discovery continued to grow. The pristine cave was too accessible, only nine miles from a major highway. Tufts and Tenen decided that the only way to protect the cave was to develop it as a commercial attraction, or get federal or state protection. By this time, using aliases, they had visited other tourist caves, making comparisons of their discovery and learning about the cost of commercial development.

In 1978, they went to visit the landowners. By then, Tufts and Tenen had been trespassing on the Kartchner ranch for four years. The family was at first annoyed, but then they heard about the cave. Sworn to secrecy, the Kartchner family worked with the cavers. Despite all the secrecy, however, the caving world is a small one and rumors inevitably spread. When curious spelunkers trespassed on the ranch, the pistol-packing Kartchner brothers rode up on horseback to escort them off the property.

The Kartchners, who owned the ranch since 1941, couldn't have anticipated that the development and commercialization of the cave would cost more than $28 million. They brought in then-Governor Bruce Babbitt, who viewed the cave and, under a veil of secrecy, helped to guide the property into public ownership.

Babbitt led the cavers and ranchers through the legislative process of designating the cave as a state park. In 1988, when the state of Arizona bought the land, only six members of the legislature knew that the dummy legislation actually authorized the creation of the James and Lois Kartchner Caverns State Park. Tufts and Tenen had seen their dream come to fruition.
*Source: The Private, Selective Newsletter for the Active/Adventure Traveler Vol. 4 No. 2 Nov., 1999*

## Strategic Use of "Learning Styles", Detail: p. 135

Much research has been done on differing learning styles, all of which support the notion that people of equal intelligence and motivation internalize information differently. Whether in training or educational programs, conative characteristics can help explain why some people (Fact Finder–insistent folks) are compelled to write it down and others (Quick Start initiators) excel in oral presentations. The topic in which you are training isn't the decisive factor; it's the person's MO. A case in point is John Chiatalas, an attorney with Sandoz Corp. While his wife, Nancy, was at home struggling with a serious illness and the special needs of their three physically and mentally challenged children, he was working full-time and going to law school at night. He was able to maintain his energy by trusting and using his instincts, having a determined purpose and the support of his family. John (whose Kolbe A index result is 7-2-9-3) was literally off and running to meet economic needs and to reach the professional goals he and Nancy agreed were important for him.

"I used a time-compression system," John explained, "simply because my Quick Start needed to have some sense of urgency. I am a shortcut person; I circumvent obstacles." Then, describing how his resistance to Follow Thru caused him stress when outlining and studying in the recommended way, he said, "My other responsibilities kept me too busy to spend all that time getting organized." He then mentioned some waffle-soled shoes and a tape recorder with a power booster. John had created a Quick Start technique for doing two things at once: exercise and study. During lunch hour at the corporate job he'd don his cushioned shoes – which magnified his stride – and a headset that played back his taped notes 40 percent faster than normal speed. Now he could jog farther and review material faster. And he made it to the courthouse to deliver his last-minute filings (remember the 2 in Follow Thru) just on time.

Reggie Behl has taught Quick Start "Sketching for the Traveler" at the Smithsonian Institution in Washington, DC, the Museum of Natural History in Los Angeles, and the Museum of Natural History at the University of New Mexico. She, like sculptress Helen Blair Crosbie, finds there is an artist in everyone, but that equal creative gifts are nurtured through different methods. "Anyone can learn to draw," Reggie said. "You just have to use your inclinations."

Teaching business people, engineers, and others has allowed her to see the diversity of natural talents among them. "Some students can't draw a vertical line, so I tell them to let that be their style. 'Don't fight it, use it.' Some people aren't complex Fact Finders – that's their charm."

Reggie is a trainer who enables people to learn by unmasking their own best efforts. "Some people fight their instincts," she said "and need to loosen up. I bombard them with seeing, selecting, and making choices – relying on guts – with no time to think. Then they just have to react. They get very excited when they see the results. Within a group you can see twenty different responses to the same thing. It's hard to get rid of habits in my two-day workshop, but they learn a lot about themselves they can put to use afterward. Once they tap into their natural way of expressing themselves, their talent for doing whatever they want to do develops very rapidly."

People often associate learning styles with gender and race stereotypes. But the lack of bias in Kolbe A index results indicates that differences in how people react to training or education is not because of innate differences by gender, age, and race. For instance, since there are as many female Fact Finders as males, both genders can be trained equally well to use natural abilities for defining strategies.

Barbara Barrett (Kolbe A index result, 7-3-6-4), an attorney who was at the top echelon of the Civil Aeronautics Board and who was the number-two person at the Federal Aviation Administration, noted, "Cross-cultural community courses are in some cases teaching that women and minorities learn in different ways. This information is presented as truth rather than explaining that environment builds different expectations." She stated that even in these times when college students promote "politically correct" notions of equality, "I was quite surprised to hear students repeat the stereotype that women just think about things differently. We're training women to believe they have to go into human resources, public relations, accounting, and law, and not manufacturing and engineering."

Barbara is amused that aircraft engineers don't expect she'll know the technology of F-18 planes, when, in fact, she's an expert. "But then," she acknowledged, "I'm often viewed as a novelty." In the corporate setting there's a notion that women must be trained as the nurturers because, she pointed out, people like Clarence Darrow have promoted the idea that women don't have the nature of litigators. "By exercising a little more gumption, I got in," Barbara said of her ability to overcome stereotypes and be trained as a jet pilot, litigator, and political strategist.
*Source: Pure Instinct p. 176-178 by Kathy Kolbe*

# CHAPTER NINE – HOW TO BE OBSTINATE

## SATs , Conative Biases and MO/IQ Correlation Studies,
Detail: p. 161

Several studies were done attempting to determine correlation between results for any of the conative modes identified by the Kolbe Index A and any of the four index scales of the Meyers-Briggs Type Indicator (MBTI). No statistically meaningful correlation was found.
*Source: Kolbe Corp Research Files*

## Admissions Exams

Because education is used so often as a prequalification for jobs, it is especially important to consider the basis on which candidates are selected or rejected for educational opportunities. To be admitted to most colleges or universities, students must achieve acceptable scores on college admission exams. Many firms interview only potential hires from certain universities, so the test cutoff scores used by particular academic institutions have great importance for future job candidates. A primary source of such tests is the Educational Testing Service (ETS), which developed the Scholastic Aptitude Test or SAT (recently renamed the Scholastic Assessment Test), as well as a multitude of other exams for graduate and specialized educational placement.

In order to do well on the SAT, the test taker needs to have had prior educational opportunities, since it assesses knowledge and skill. Not only does this tend to discriminate against minorities, it primarily measures the potential for success in another academic situation, not on jobs. Such instruments, which are a major factor in determining future job opportunities, need to be considered in terms of their ability to predict on-the-job performance. They are heavily dependent on linguistic skill and therefore biased in favor of insistent Fact Finders. They are biased against Implementors and Follow Thrus. So they are inappropriate tools to select or reject people for jobs that are not dependent upon book learning for results. They reward Fact Finders through their emphasis on word definitions, analogies, and reading comprehension, as well as mathematical computations. They don't reward the Implementor talent for constructing manual solutions, since they're strictly paper-and-pencil exams. The SAT, for instance, rewards guessing and encourages skipping questions. Therefore it can lower scores for an insistent Follow Thru who needs to answer in an orderly way. As a recent Follow Thru initiator said after taking the SAT, "I had to finish one page before I could go on to the next, even though I knew I was being penalized for it."
Source: Pure Instinct p. 135-136, by Kathy Kolbe

# CHAPTER TEN – RULE #5 DO NOTHING –

# WHEN NOTHING WORKS

## Tinnitus as a Hearing Problem, Detail: p. 165

Tinnitus is the presence of sound in the ears when no external sound is present to cause it. It can be perceived as a ringing, hissing, roaring, pulsing, whooshing, chirping, whistling or clicking sound. The sound can be heard in one or both ears, and ranges from a mild short-lived experience to a distracting chronic problem.

About 50 million Americans have experienced tinnitus to some degree. All age groups are affected, but most cases occur in people between 30 and 50 years of age. And half of all tinnitus sufferers experience hearing loss in addition to tinnitus. The causes of tinnitus are not well known,

but exposure to damaging decibel levels of sound is the most probable cause.
*Source: www.webmd.com*

# CHAPTER ELEVEN – HOW TO DO NOTHING – WHEN NOTHING WORKS

## Information on Accelerated Learning Theories, Detail: p. 183

Developed in the 1970s, Accelerated Learning is based on the work of Dr. Georgi Lozanov, a professor of psychiatry and psychotherapy from Bulgaria now living in Austria. His early program, which focused on teaching a foreign language, included relaxation, visual arts, and music. Students learned from one hundred to one thousand new vocabulary words a day with 98% retention or better. He called his new method Suggestology, based on the theory that suggestions can and do affect the outcome of learning.

According to Lozanov, Suggestology is an organized way of augmenting natural learning. It builds on those methods that allow us to learn most effectively and efficiently, emulating some of the ways we learned as a young child. Suggestology recaptures that natural learning process and accelerates the understanding and retention of content.

**Core Elements:**

**The Physical Environment**
Every effort is made to create a comfortable learning environment. Lighting, temperature, color, plants, and décor are taken into careful consideration. Seating arrangements are open and flexible.

**Music**
Appropriate and effective use of music enhances the learning environment. Baroque music helps students relax and focus. Upbeat music energizes students.

**Peripherals**
Peripherals are posters and visuals that reinforce lessons. The information, or suggestion, contained in the peripherals is taken in by the subconscious mind while the student is consciously focused on the teacher or an activity.

**Teacher**
The teacher must establish credibility with the students and be well trained in Accelerated Learning. Tonality of speech (pitch/tone/tempo/loudness/softness) is a technique used to capture the students' attention and emphasize key points.

## Positive Atmosphere

Emotional safety is established and the tone is friendly and joyful. Positive emotions influence the learning process and enhance retention. Careful languaging emphasizes positive statements and avoids negative statements. The teacher builds strong rapport and relationships with the students.

## Art and Drama

The teacher uses props such as puppets, costumes, hats, and artifacts to illustrate lessons. Dramatics, including role-playing and storytelling, make lessons come alive.

## Active and Passive Concerts

These elements are used in classic suggestopedic classrooms. Accompanied by selected music, the teacher dramatically reads a story imbedded with information and main points from the lesson. Using the proper voice tonality is a crucial part of effectively telling the story.
*Source: www.newhorizons.org/strategies/accelerated/deporter*

# CHAPTER TWELVE – WHY THE 5 RULES MATTER

## Wisdom of the Ages, Detail: p. 186

It was (and is) common to think that other animals are ruled by "instinct" whereas humans lost their instincts and are ruled by "reason," and that this is why we are so much more flexibly intelligent than other animals. William James took the opposite view. He argued that human behavior is more flexibly intelligent than that of other animals because we have more instincts than they do, not fewer. We tend to be blind to the existence of these instincts, however, precisely because they work so well – because they process information so effortlessly and automatically. They structure our thought so powerfully, he argued, that it can be difficult to imagine how things could be otherwise. As a result, we take "normal" behavior for granted. We do not realize that "normal" behavior needs to be explained at all. This "instinct blindness" makes the study of psychology difficult. To get past this problem, James suggested that we try to make the "natural seem strange." "It takes...a mind debauched by learning to carry the process of making the natural seem strange, so far as to ask for the why of any instinctive human act."

Many psychologists avoid the study of natural competencies, thinking that there is nothing there to be explained. As a result, social psychologists are disappointed unless they find a phenomenon "that would surprise their grandmothers," and cognitive psychologists spend more time studying how we solve problems we are bad at, like learning math or playing chess, than ones we are good at. But our natural competencies – our abilities to see, to speak, to find someone beautiful, to reciprocate a favor, to fear disease, to fall in love, to initiate an attack, to experience moral outrage, to navigate a landscape, and myriad others – are possible only because there is a vast and heterogeneous array of complex computational machinery supporting and regulating these activities. This machinery works so well that we don't even realize that it exists. We all suffer from instinct blindness. As a result, psychologists have neglected to study some of the most interesting

machinery in the human mind.
*Source: Evolutionary Psychology: A Primer, Leda Cosmides & John Tooby, Co-Directors Center for Evolutionary Psychology, University of California, Santa Barbara*

# Kolbe Y index, Detail: p. 187

A sample copy of the results of the Kolbe Y index and the youth questionnaire can be found online at www.kolbe.com.

Designed for youth with a fifth grade vocabulary, the questions for completing the index revolve around school and home environments as opposed to the workplace. Unlike the Kolbe A, the results of the Kolbe Y index do not recommend career paths or identify jobs done successfully by other people with similar results. Kolbe Corp does not include that information, because they do not want to pigeon-hole kids. Its philosophy is that kids need to discover who they are and what will make them successful. Often the solution is as simple as redefining a task so that they can be successful by doing it their way, even if their way is different from how others might do it.

Since pressures of the teenage years, particularly the push to conform, frequently lead to results indicating a young person is going through a period of transition, the greatest amount of care needs to be exercised in the interpretation. Transition shows up when a person gives contradictory answers to similar questions, indicating that she has lost sight of her own natural talents or is suppressing them in an attempt to conform to someone else's standards.

Findings show that young people try to reflect (or deflect) how they believe others want them to act, rather than being true to themselves. It was Kolbe's hope in writing the "Transition" result that what was said about their responses would help kids think about the opportunity they are losing to explore their natural abilities in a non-threatening way.

While parents can read the questions to their children and explain a few words that may not be fully understood, care must be taken not to make any suggestions regarding the answer, or to influence choices in any way. For a child's privacy, and in accordance with federal regulations, Kolbe asks that parents use only their own email address and not provide any information which would cause unintended, direct communication with a child younger than 13.

The most important support parents can provide their children as they go through the self-discovery process is to provide optional ways for getting things done. While children need to be responsible for accomplishing certain goals at home and at school, the key is for them to have the freedom to accomplish tasks through their own methods. School can be a very Fact Finder/Follow Thru world and if the child doesn't fit that pattern, she may find that environment confining – even depressing. If her parents expect her to do something the way they would do it, the process could be detrimental. She needs to find her own way of accomplishing – which is how she will build self-esteem and confidence.
*Source: The Writings of Kathy Kolbe*

# Comparison Studies of Kolbe Index to Cognitive and Affective Assessments, Detail: p. 188

## A. Theoretical Positioning

The Kolbe Index evolved from Kathy Kolbe's observation that quite often, humans' actions and behavior do not go hand in hand with either their different abilities or their perceived desires. For centuries three facets of the human mind have been postulated involving knowledge, desire and volition. Kolbe's research on the conative dimension of the mind includes a review of the historical works of philosophers, psychologists, sociologists, and anthropologists, from Plato and Aristotle to the present. In this review she found that the predominant thinking regarding the three dimensions of the mind had never been fully disputed. During the early 20th century, however, the focus was on the cognitive dimension and normative testing such as the new IQ measurements. When it became clear that cognitive norms were influenced by cultural biases, a dual focus developed that included numerous attempts to assess affective behaviors. Generally fueled by Jungian archetypes, tests of social style or preferences often reported results that implied action-orientations without explicit indication of the conative dimension. The Kolbe Index reflects the interaction between humans and their environment which was central to the work of Dewey, Jung and other theorists, but further explores the conative dimension.

John Dewey's work was premised on the belief that all learning involves a response of the individual to environmental factors. He described the process of developing coping skills based upon the individual's inherent skills in an environmental context as "instrumentation," suggesting that individuals can develop tools that allow them to use their abilities in different experiential settings. Dewey's work is a foundation for the Kolbe A index in its identification of thinking and doing as complementary processes and of the significance of instrumental application of abilities in concrete behavioral settings.

Carl Jung, who, like Dewey, focused on the interaction of the individual with the environment, premised his theory of human development upon the idea that individuals have persistent preferences for certain types of human/environmental interaction. Jung's theories suggest that much of the apparent randomness in human behavior is actually a reflection of these persistent individual preferences. Jung identifies four basic functions or ways in which these personal preferences are evidenced: sensing, thinking, feeling, and intuiting. According to Jung, personal types are developed through a process of individuation in which, as individuals mature, they come to recognize a dominant or primary function and an auxiliary function as primary ways of interacting with the environment, while maintaining a respect and understanding of their less dominant functions. Jung also identified two attitudinal continua which, he believed, were overlays or filters for the individual's environmental response. The continua are extroversion – a focus on objects or other individuals, and introversion, an internal reflective focus.

Jung's work is an important foundation for the Kolbe index in its recognition of the following ideas: The first is the existence of persistent patterns or types of behavior that influence environ-mental interaction. The second is the recognition of an individual's dominance of a single pattern. The third is the recognition that behavioral responses can be used to measure dominance of the patterns. And finally, that there are overlays in behavior that may be represented as a continuum between two polar positions, and that these may in turn determine how individuals employ their cognitive or emotional responses in a specific setting.

The Kolbe theory recognizes that individuals have persistent predispositions for conducive interactions with the world. These predispositions can be measured through behavioral manifestations that can be reflected on a continuum. Like Isabel Myers and others who have extended Jung's theories, the Kolbe instrument does not measure the underlying functions identified by Jung, but rather focuses on the overlays that predispose an individual to apply the function in a particular way. For example, Myers added a "judgment-perception" preference to Jung's extroversion and introversion continua. She believes that individuals filter their functional responses through a filter that organizes responses in order in terms of a tendency to impose convergent or divergent order upon the environment. Kolbe's research led her to conclude that there was no proven reliable assessment of the conative dimension, which at the time was generally ignored. So she set out to measure and predict the outward manifestation of human instinct.

Through the use of observational studies, behavioral patterns were detected in a wide range of settings mentioned above. From these, Kolbe postulated four different continua that reflect individuals predispositions to: 1) probe, 2) organize, 3) improvise, and 4) construct. She further postulated that these patterns, like the extroversion, introversion, and judgment/perception continua, were patterns that remained constant over time and influenced the manner in which individuals use their functional preferences. Testing confirmed the stability of the measures and their relative independence from the continua employed by Myers and others. Further testing established correlation between predispositions and job performance, and also demonstrated that the measures were independent of race, gender, or other confounding criteria.

Each pattern or creative instinct triggers observable behavior or modes of action through which an individual performs. These four continua or modes each have an operational definition for the "insistence" zone, the primary function:

An initiating Fact Finder will most likely succeed at tasks which require an individual to:

| probe | allocate | define | calculate |
|---|---|---|---|
| research | deliberate | prove | inquire |
| formalize | prioritize | specify | evaluate |

An initiating Follow Thru will most likely succeed at tasks which require an individual to:

| structure | prepare | arrange | plan |
|---|---|---|---|
| consolidate | discipline | integrate | budget |
| translate | coordinate | schedule | chart |

An initiating Quick Start will most likely succeed at tasks which require an individual to:

| invent | devise | risk | improvise |
|--------|--------|------|-----------|
| brainstorm | challenge | play hunches | promote |
| originate | contrive | reform | intuit |

An initiating Implementor will most likely succeed at tasks which require an individual to:

| form | craft | build | fix |
|------|-------|-------|-----|
| mold | shape | render | repair |
| demonstrate | put together | construct | practice |

## B. Construction of the Index

Based upon these constructs, 200 items were developed as a part of the first instrument. A decade of research began with item analyses of those 200 questions. The test instrument was refined through the use of criterion-group analysis and correlation studies through which any extraneous variables, such as cognitive or affective variables, were eliminated.

The instrument was first given to groups of subjects with known estimates of intelligence. Those items which discriminated between individuals of varying intellectual levels were deleted from the instrument. The remaining items were given to subjects who had also completed the Wonderlic Personnel Test, which tests on cognitive abilities. All items which distinguished between subjects based on high and low scores on the Wonderlic were also removed in order to reduce bias based on cognitive differences.

In continuing studies, further items were eliminated when, for subjects who had also taken traditional personality instruments, endorsement of those items revealed significant correlation with items defining affective patterns. One of the personality instruments used was the Myers-Briggs Type Indicator, whose results a 1991 National Research Council report concluded have no verifiable relationship to performance.

At this point, 50 of the original 200 items remained. These 50 items were then given to 200 subjects, who were asked to complete the index in such a way as to attempt to present themselves in a socially desirable manner. Those items which proved to be part of a "socially desirable response set" were then deleted. Of the 44 items in the pool of possible questions, 36 were finally selected to comprise the current version of the Kolbe index. These were found to be sufficient in order to maintain the accuracy of the instrument while reducing the effects of boredom and moderating other sources of measurement errors. By including items which relate to both normal and emotionally stressful circumstances, as well as affective and cognitive influences, the choices are counterbalanced.

*Source: The Writings of Kathy Kolbe and the Research Files of Kolbe Corp*

## List of Creative Dyslexics, Detail: p. 190

Terry Bradshaw, retired Quarterback of Pittsburgh Steelers
Charles Schwab, founder of Charles Schwab Online Brokerage Company
Woodrow Wilson, former President of the United States
Nelson Rockefeller, former Governor of New York and Vice President of USA
Tom Cruise, movie star with several awards for Best Actor
Albert Einstein, most renowned physicist of the 20th Century
Henry Ford, inventor, manufacturer, and automobile pioneer
Alexander Graham Bell, inventor of the telephone
Leonardo da Vinci, Italian painter, sculptor, scientist, musician and architect
Walt Disney, cartoonist and pioneer motion picture animator
Harry Belafonte, famed motion picture actor
Jay Leno, comedian and late night talk show host
Quentin Tarantino, movie director
Bruce Jenner, Olympic Decathlon gold medallist
General George Patton, famed World War II tank commander
Winston Churchill, war time Prime Minister of Great Britain
Hans Christian Andersen, Danish author of children's books
*Source: www.dyslexiahelp.com/FamousDyslexics*

# Index

# SHARING THE MAGIC OF YOUR 'MO'
## Kathy's Special Offers

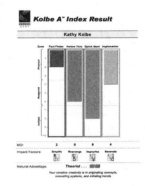

*Powered by Instinct is* **more than a book –
it is a purpose.**

My purpose is to help you discover your hidden strengths and find the joy of acting freely upon them. This book is the tip of the iceberg. There's so much more that I've developed to help you on the exhilarating journey to fulfilling your destiny.

Because I appreciate your commitment to making your best efforts - and helping others do the same - I want to provide you with Special Offers for **Kolbe Wisdom products and services.**

I will personally select those Kolbe Wisdom products that will change monthly and will be made available to you at a considerable savings.  As an advocate of being Powered by Instinct you can use the following special code – **PBI2004B** – at **www.poweredbyinstinct.com/special.**

It's important that we work together to improve our schools, communities, parenting, business practices and interpersonal relationships. Your experiences as you become more Powered by Instinct will help me develop additional resources to accomplish these goals.  I encourage you to share these with me by emailing **editor@poweredbyinstinct.com.** I'll be answering questions through an on-line discussion - which you can join or eavesdrop on as you have with me and Ev!

I look forward to hearing from you.

*Kathy Kolbe*

Kathy Kolbe

P.S. **Please don't forget to help our schools by passing this book along to teachers.**

We make giving Powered by Instinct an easy and affordable gift - that will literally last a lifetime (especially when packaged with a Kolbe index). You can take advantage of this opportunity to make it available to your extended family, co-workers, clients, and others who will benefit from acting on the 5 Rules by calling Pat at 602. 840. 9770.

# Do You Know Your MO?

## Discover how to make your *best* efforts.

**Kolbe A index: to validate your instinctive abilities.**
The Kolbe A index measures what you WILL or WON'T do. This quick and easy, 36-question assessment tool gives you greater understanding of your own natural instincts.

You'll answer questions according to how you would naturally act. You simply choose one most and one least likely option for every item. It's that simple. Then pay for your Kolbe A index results on Kolbe's highly secure website, and you'll receive a report online almost instantly.

**Kolbe R index: to enhance relationships.**
What do you really look for in a relationship? Do you want your date to plan the evening from start to finish or do you like to "fly by the seat of your pants?" Do you wonder why you are impatient when your Uncle insists on the same Thanksgiving dinner every year?... The Kolbe R index, a 36-question instrument, will reveal the instinctive being you are looking for... in a friend, a spouse, a family member, a co-worker...instantly!

**Kolbe Y index: to bring out the best in our youth.**
Kids are often those who can benefit the most from understanding their natural talents.  The Kolbe Y index is specially designed for kids with a fifth grade reading level through high school. Knowing the results helps parents have a better understanding of their role in nurturing their child's natural talents. Kids learn what their Natural Advantage is and how using it will help them achieve more with less stress.

**Think-ercise! Books and Activities: to strengthen kids' mental muscles.**
If you enjoyed the Think-ercises in *Powered by Instinct*, visit the *Powered by Instinct* website to learn about Think-ercises for kids.  Kathy Kolbe's been writing and publishing Think-ercises for decades, and every one is designed to inspire creative thinking.

## Visit www.kolbe.com or link from www.poweredbyinstinct.com

- Kathy Kolbe lectures, seminars, and executive coaching

- *Powered by Instinct* special interest seminars

- Kolbe Wisdom 3-day Certification programs

Call: 800 642 2822 for information on these opportunities

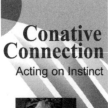